THE NATIONAL TRUST BOOK OF

FORGOTTEN
HOUSEHOLD
CRAFTS

THE NATIONAL TRUST BOOK OF

FORGOTTEN HOUSEHOLD CRAFTS

JOHN SEYMOUR

Dorling Kindersley · London

The National Trust and Crafts

As a charity for the conservation of places of historic interest, the National Trust looks after a wealth of buildings housing fine examples of forgotten household crafts.

There are dairies and butteries which show the amount of work involved in processing milk before the advent of modern machinery, and herb gardens where household medicines were grown. Apiaries, breweries and home farms added to the contents of larders, and ice houses preserved food long before refrigerators were invented. Wells and laundries bear witness to the labour of washing by hand, and kitchens full of gleaming brass implements record the skills involved in preparing meals without present-day, labour-saving devices.

Most Trust houses have examples of hand-sewn bed linen, chair covers or patchwork quilts testifying to many hours of patient needlework, and there are a number of costume collections showing how fine sewing and embroidery were applied to personal adornment.

The author wishes to thank Angela Ashe for her invaluable help in researching material for this volume.

Art Editor Alex Arthur
Project Editor Jane Laing
Editor Heather Dewhurst

Senior Editor David Lamb
Editorial Director Jackie Douglas
Art Director Roger Bristow

Major illustrations by Eric Thomas

First published in Great Britain in 1987 by
Dorling Kindersley Limited, London
in association with the National Trust

British Library Cataloguing in Publication Data

Seymour, John, *1914–*
 The National Trust book of
 forgotten household crafts
 1. Home economics—Great Britain—
 History
 I. Title
 640'.941   TX57

ISBN 0–86318–174–0

Typeset by MS Filmsetting Ltd,
Frome, Somerset
Reproduced in Singapore
Printed and bound in Italy by Lego

CONTENTS

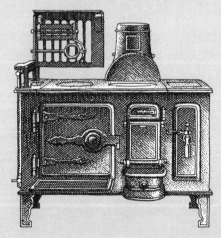

DAIRY CRAFTS 69

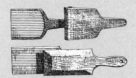

LAUNDRY CRAFTS 85

AROUND THE HOME 103

TEXTILE CRAFTS 143

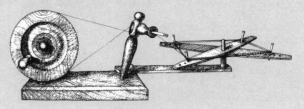

DECORATIVE CRAFTS 175

INDEX 188

INTRODUCTION

"I'm only a housewife, I'm afraid." How often do we hear this shocking admission. I'm afraid when I hear it I feel very angry indeed. Only a housewife: only a practitioner of one of the two most noble professions (the other one is that of a farmer); only the mistress of a huge battery of high and varied skills and custodian of civilization itself. Only a typist, perhaps! Only a company director, or a nuclear physicist; only a barrister; only Prime Minister! When a woman says she is a housewife she should say it with the utmost pride, for there is nothing higher on this planet to which she could aspire.

INTERIOR DECORATING
Whitewash was ritually
applied to ceilings every
spring as part of the
spring cleaning. Wall
stencilling and papering
was not carried out as
frequently. However, when
a room was repapered
the new paper was pasted
directly on top of the old,
as such strong paste was
used that it was virtually
impossible to scrape off the
last layer! (See Painting &
Papering, p.176.)

It may be argued that the profession of the housewife has been downgraded in recent decades; that people nowadays eat meals that do not need any preparation or cooking; that houses today are not built and fitted out for comfort, beauty, or even elegance, but for "easy working" and nothing else. There are indeed such dwellings (I will not call them homes) and bleak and cheerless places they are, too. It is sad that so many people have to live in them, but then they do have the anodyne of the telly. Glued to that flickering screen they can ignore their own dull surroundings: we can all live in Dallas. But real homes and real housewives do still exist and this book has been written in praise of them both. It describes the art of housewifery through the ages, but it is not just a museum-on-paper. Many of the activities may be seldom practised nowadays—some of them are sadly dead and gone—but many of them are living activities and several of the skills that seemed to be dying are now being revived, for many people have passed right through the pimply-adolescent stage of post-industrial civilization. They have tired of the take-away way of living and the machine-for-living way of living. They have found that art galleries, theatres, public libraries, shopping precincts, public houses and even bingo halls, though good facilities in themselves, are no substitute for a real home. They have tried living in the dwelling in which the television is the most important feature of any room and rejected it, turning anew to the true altar of the hearth.

And therefore I believe that this book, the work of many hands, both male and female, will be of great use. It records the past, and that in itself can be quite a useful thing, but it has been written also to inspire and instruct us for the future. For, I am convinced that the future does not lie in the direction of fish fingers, and telly snacks, and Formica and other plastic rubbish. It lies in the recreation of real homes.

Why should a man write about such a very feminine subject? Of course, if a woman had written it, the book would have been very different—it would have been a look from the inside rather than from the outside, but, by looking from the outside, I have been able to see both the broad principles and the familiar detail, and, possibly, I have been able to praise more abundantly the housewife's art than a practitioner might have done. For this writer stands in awe of the real housewife: an accomplished housewife must be far more knowledgeable than the average so-called professional man or woman and much of the knowledge, as she will tell you, is difficult to achieve.

When we think of civilization we tend to think of people like Michelangelo, Shakespeare, Beethoven and Einstein. Well, all praise to such people, their works have enriched our homes, but of what use would their endeavours have been without the basis of a civilized home; of what comfort would their works be to us if our homes were brutish and boring, if we lived, like Nebuchadnezzar, like the beasts but without the beasts' natural grace and dignity? Everything that people do outside the home—on the farm, in the forest, in the factory and counting-house, down the mine or out at sea—is done to provide the essentials of a seemly and comely human existence: to sustain and embellish the home. If the home itself is allowed to go to pot then what is the use of it all? Whatever an honest man is doing, always somewhere in the back of his mind is the thought of his home.

Our age has produced more rubbishy substitutes for home than any other: the beastly burger bars and fried-chicken mess-ups, and fast-food this and take-away that (the places where both plastic chairs and tables are fastened to the floor so that the customers have to perch like parrots to eat their food). What kind of domestic culture do we call this? These things save work? I was talking to an old lady in the Golden Valley of Herefordshire many years ago and she gave me an account of a week's work when she was a child: washing on Monday, selling eggs and butter at the market on Tuesday, baking on Wednesday, and so on. "Wasn't it all a lot of work?" I asked her. "Yes," she said. "But nobody had ever told us there was anything wrong with work." She was one of the happiest old ladies I have ever met and as fit as a trout at eighty.

Wash Day

Before the advent of the washing machine, the weekly wash was an awesome task, which took up the whole day, usually Monday. Most of the linen had to be pounded with a peg dolly in the wash tub, then rinsed and passed through the mangle, before hanging out to dry; more delicate pieces had to be rubbed gently by hand with soap; and many articles had to be starched. (See Washing Linen, p.90.)

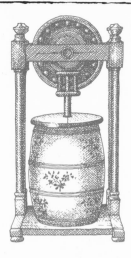

And what do people do with all the time they "save" by not having to look after their homes properly? Do they spend all that time improving themselves or their environment? They do not, for life without the firm base of a good home is unsatisfactory and unpleasing.

So such people seize on any cheap thrill that comes along to allay the boredom. They besot themselves with the telly; they fly to the Costa Brava, where they find the same sorts of fast-food bar that they left behind. They lead lives which, in any other age since the Palaeolithic, would have been looked upon as barbarous.

So it is fitting that we should look at the homes of former ages, which were not barbarous, to see if we can learn from what we find. We will find, of course, that some labour-saving devices have come along which have freed men and women to do rewarding things. The vacuum cleaner has eliminated fleas, God bless it. Electricity, properly and moderately used, enables us to run and embellish our homes better. But we must not delude ourselves; labour-saving devices can never of themselves create a home. This is the work of human hands. And working to create a home is only drudgery if we think of it as such. It saddens me to see mothers carrying far too heavy a load of housework while thousands of young girls fritter their lives away. But it delights me, as it must delight everyone, to enter a home that is a real home, where the children are joyful and secure and show every sign of growing up to be proper home makers themselves.

In the great ages of the world the home was held sacred and so it must be again or we have no future on this earth. I feel sure that Beecher and Stowe, the authors of *The American Woman's Home*, published in 1867, would have agreed with me. They declared in the introduction to their excellent volume that they wished "to elevate both the honor and the remuneration of all the employments that sustain the many difficult and sacred duties of the family state, and thus to render each department of woman's true profession as much desired and respected as are the most honored professions of men." *Homo sapiens?* What a ludicrous and arrogant title we men have given ourselves and those that we evidently feel are our appendages! "Woman the home maker'' would be a better title. And, not to leave him out altogether, ''man the husbandman''. These are the people we must become or, I am convinced, there is no future for either of us.

Why do I assume that it is only women who can really understand the mysteries of the home? There is a strong move in the Western world today to pretend that there is no difference between women and men at all. I once lived in a farm community in which this view was the prevailing one. The women were out in the fields ill treating the tractor, with which they had absolutely no affinity, while the men struggled on in the kitchen and living quarters, making a mess. Our pet pig, Esmeralda, reared on the bottle and accustomed to grunting about under the dining-room table at meal times, eventually stopped coming inside the door. I had no doubt whatever that the pig, like myself, was simply disgusted with the state of the place: she had higher standards. Without the firm base of a comfortable and well-ordered household the whole farm suffered: soil, crops, animals and people alike. The community collapsed.

Under the worst of conditions, having to trudge miles to fetch fuel or water, having to cope with idle or drunken husbands, having to rear large families with no help or support, housewives everywhere have managed somehow to continue the struggle. It is nonsense to think that men could, equally well, have done this work! Men are strong and clever, very creative in fact, but they are just not imbued with the driving instinct that makes a good woman ready to sacrifice everything for her home. I have seen places of abode run by men only. I have never seen a home.

I can even now hear the howls of rage at what I have written. Most will start with the words: ''This male chauvinist wants to chain women to the kitchen sink!'' Of course, everybody in the house, if tall enough to reach it, should take a turn at the kitchen sink. Going, we hope, are the houses in which the man, on his arrival from work, gobbles up a meal, belches, and slumps in front of the telly with a six-pack of lager beside him. Such a man does not deserve a happy home, and certainly he won't be getting one.

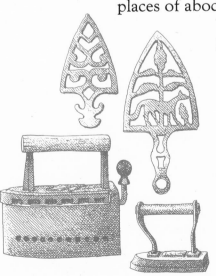

QUILTING BEES

In the nineteenth century quilts were often given as presents to women about to be married. This custom was practised mostly in America, where groups of women would gather together enthusiastically to make beautiful decorative friendship quilts: their quilting parties came to be known as quilting bees. (See Quilting & Patchwork, p.170.)

Vive la difference! What was wrong with the Victorian age was not that it did not recognize the difference between men and women but that people of both sexes believed that one sex was superior to the other. Men are different from women just as apples are different from oranges and the qualities of both put together make the greatest human power for good there is; not the power to "conquer the earth" as the brutish, male-dominated thinking of the Victorian age had it, but the power to nurture and husband the earth peacefully, so as to turn it into something very akin to our conception of paradise.

This book celebrates the home makers and the home. It recognizes and records some of the diligence, high skills, and love that has gone, over the ages, into creating and nurturing the true basis of all civilization. This book is the creation of a team of people, at least half of them women, but I would like to dedicate my small part of it, most gratefully and humbly, to the priestesses who serve the high altar of the hearth.

KITCHEN CRAFTS

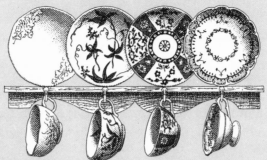

Fifty years ago George Orwell was struck by the
"physical degeneracy" of the people about him.
"Where are the monstrous men with chests like barrels
and moustaches like the wings of eagles, who strode across
my childhood gaze?" he demanded. Where are they indeed?
I remember them, too, but it does not surprise me that
they are not much in evidence today. For such men were
not fed on fish fingers, ready-to-eat this and packeted that.
They were reared on good beef, pork and mutton, fine
fresh vegetables, fresh fruit, good bread and beer, and their
food was properly prepared and cooked for them by
skilled women. Undoubtedly there is much labour in the
preparation of meals from fresh ingredients. To shell a
bushel of peas, for example, takes a long while and you can
do nothing else at the same time. But those of us who are
privileged to live in a home where the ancient skills of preparing
and cooking food are still carried out often wonder,
as we contemplate another culinary delight, if the time saved
by the "modern" housewife is really worth it. For, my God,
what a world of difference there is in taste between the
heated-up instant meal and the meal that is carefully
prepared and cooked from fresh ingredients.

PREPARING FOOD

THE GREAT, IMMOVABLE, WELL-scrubbed table of the old-fashioned kitchen, built of heavy slabs of beech or other white wood and supported by extremely solid legs, aptly symbolizes the stability of country-house life before the unsettling days of the Second World War.

I remember huge joints of beef being prepared on that table. You never saw the boned, rolled-up pieces of meat so common today—the joint was always on the bone—and there was such a thing as mutton (as opposed to lamb) in those days, and mutton joints could be noble things.

SAVOURY PUDDINGS

The country people of the east of England, in Essex and Suffolk, always had pudding with their roast beef. Similar to Yorkshire pudding, it was eaten as a dish on its own before the meat in some cottages and always with plenty of "dish gravy" poured over it. Serving the meat last ensured that there was enough for all as everyone was too full by then to eat much. Preparing such a pudding meant there would be a big, glazed, earthenware mixing bowl on that great white table, scoops of flour from the bin, and tins of baking powder. There would be plenty of scrubbing and clearing up afterwards, too.

Another common activity that took place on the kitchen table was the grating of suet. Beef suet is the hard fat that lines the abdominal cavity of the ox. It was often used in pastry, which was far more prevalent in those days—there was nearly always a pastry-encased game pie in the larder to be eaten cold by anybody who came into the house hungry. It was also used to make that marvellous stuff, suet pudding. The grated suet was rubbed into the flour and a little water added to make the dough. The dough was then pressed inside a white china pudding basin, lining it completely. A mixture of meat and onions was placed in the middle and a cap of dough on top. Finally, the whole lot, bowl and all, was wrapped in a pudding cloth and lowered into a big saucepan of boiling water. The resulting meat "pudden" was the staple food of those who performed hard, manual work out of doors, whatever the weather. Sailors, fishermen, wildfowlers and farm labourers, who all

THE VICTORIAN KITCHEN
The kitchen was always a hive of activity—the very heart of the home. If the family was a large one there was an enormous amount of work involved in preparing the main meal of the day, and all offers of help were gratefully accepted.

SUGAR NIPPERS
After refining and clarifying, sugar was poured into conical moulds to set. Metal sugar cutters or "nippers"— small, hand ones, or larger ones mounted on wood— were used to break up the sugar loaves. Grippers could be used to hold the sugar while cutting it.

SCALES

For centuries the most common type of scale has been made on the even-arm balance principle. A pin is inserted through the centre of the beam and a dish is hung from it on one side for the ingredients to be weighed and a plate on the other for the weights to be piled. Steelyards worked on the uneven-arm balance principle and allowed heavy goods to be weighed. Hanging spring-balance machines with a dial to indicate the weight have been in use since Leonardo da Vinci invented them, although the free-standing type was not in common use until this century.

expended great amounts of energy in the winter time, relied on it to keep them going. I have often had the pleasure of sharing a beautiful suet pudding in the fo'c'sle (the forward cabin) of an Essex fishing boat.

DESSERTS

Honey was used by many as a sweetener until the supply of sugar increased and the price dropped towards the end of the eighteenth century. The sugar was still black with molasses when bought and the housewife had to embark on the long process of refining and clarifying it before she could cut it up into lumps for table use or pound it for cooking. This involved adding beaten egg white and water to the sugar and boiling and reboiling it, continually skimming the scum off the surface. When the sugar seemed clear she would strain and then boil it once more. Four pounds of unrefined sugar usually

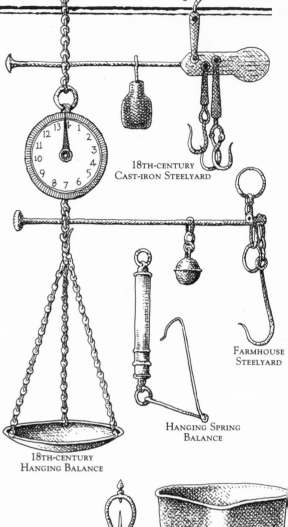

18TH-CENTURY CAST-IRON STEELYARD

FARMHOUSE STEELYARD

HANGING SPRING BALANCE

18TH-CENTURY HANGING BALANCE

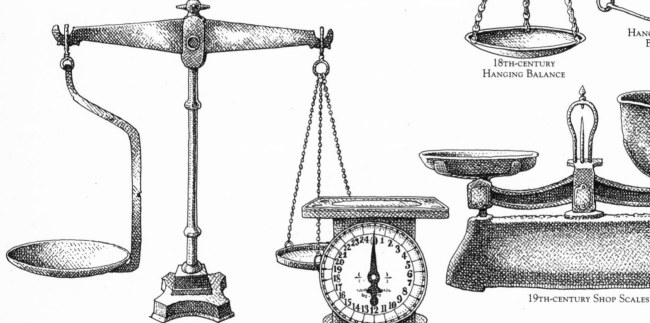

CAST-IRON AND COPPER BALANCE

TABLE SPRING BALANCE

19TH-CENTURY SHOP SCALES

WEIGHTS AND MEASURES

Iron weights were fitted with iron lifting rings to slide on to steelyards, while bell and stacking weights were made for the beam and shop scales. Measuring cups were used to measure more than just liquids—potatoes were often measured by the gallon, nuts by the quart and butter by the pint.

BRASS BELL AND STACKING WEIGHTS

EXTENDED ENGLISH MEASURE

IRISH BALUSTER MEASURES

18TH-CENTURY BALUSTER MEASURE

18TH-CENTURY WOODEN MEASURE

made about a pound of clarified sugar. Fine sugar was added to breadcrumbs, flour, minced dates, currants, pepper, shredded suet, eggs and warm milk to make the delicious "Cambridge" or "college" pudding. A slab of butter was placed in the centre and the pudding wrapped in a pudding cloth and thrown into a pot of boiling water.

Cream was the main ingredient of many desserts: whitepot was a mixture of cream thickened with eggs; cabbage cream was simply a mixture of cream, sugar and rose-water; trifle was the same with the addition of ginger; and fool was a rich, creamy custard. Meringues arrived from France in the middle of the eighteenth century. They were shaped with a cool, wet spoon until that ingeniously simple tool, the piping bag, arrived in the nineteenth century.

CHOPPING, POUNDING AND PULPING

The cook had to do all cutting and chopping by hand until the end of the nineteenth century and by the middle of the eighteenth century there was a large number of implements made specially for use in the kitchen, from simple knives, choppers and scissors to mechanical cutting devices, such as marmalade cutters and hand-operated food choppers and mixers. She could choose from a large array of tinplate graters, from the tiny, flat, portable graters with a lid, suitable for grating nutmeg into the hot evening drink, to the large, rounded graters for grating breadcrumbs.

Dried herbs and spices were pounded in metal mortars, for, as every housewife knew, they penetrated wooden mortars, spoiling the individual flavours. Alabaster and marble mortars were used for pounding sugar, and traditionally the potato masher and the sugar crusher were shaped like a club.

She would crush and press fruit and vegetables to extract the juice for cooking. Probably, she would have had a lemon squeezer made of hard wood and containing a dip in which to place the fruit. By the nineteenth century they were more sophisticated: a pottery cone was inset into the dip of one piece of wood and a perforated dish into the other; the two pieces of wood were hinged together, so they needed only to be closed to squeeze the juice out of the fruit inside, making the job that much less messy! Sieves, colanders, strainers and funnels were in common use from early times, but potato peelers and raisin stoners were not widely available until the late nineteenth century.

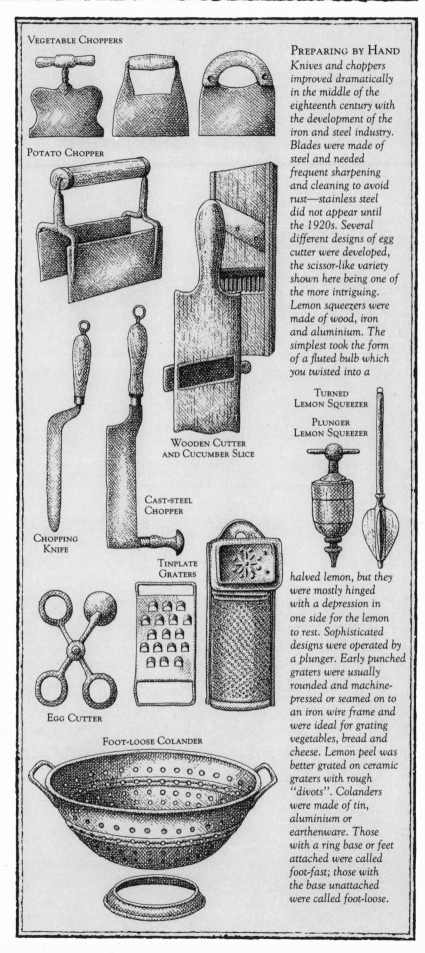

VEGETABLE CHOPPERS

POTATO CHOPPER

CHOPPING KNIFE

WOODEN CUTTER AND CUCUMBER SLICE

CAST-STEEL CHOPPER

EGG CUTTER

TINPLATE GRATERS

FOOT-LOOSE COLANDER

TURNED LEMON SQUEEZER

PLUNGER LEMON SQUEEZER

PREPARING BY HAND

Knives and choppers improved dramatically in the middle of the eighteenth century with the development of the iron and steel industry. Blades were made of steel and needed frequent sharpening and cleaning to avoid rust—stainless steel did not appear until the 1920s. Several different designs of egg cutter were developed, the scissor-like variety shown here being one of the more intriguing. Lemon squeezers were made of wood, iron and aluminium. The simplest took the form of a fluted bulb which you twisted into a halved lemon, but they were mostly hinged with a depression in one side for the lemon to rest. Sophisticated designs were operated by a plunger. Early punched graters were usually rounded and machine-pressed or seamed on to an iron wire frame and were ideal for grating vegetables, bread and cheese. Lemon peel was better grated on ceramic graters with rough "divots". Colanders were made of tin, aluminium or earthenware. Those with a ring base or feet attached were called foot-fast; those with the base unattached were called foot-loose.

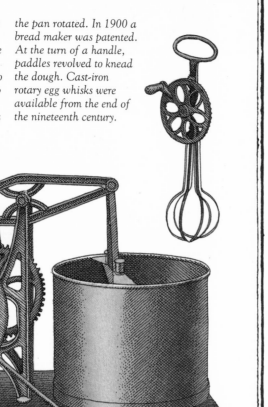

MECHANICAL DEVICES
Hand-operated chopping and mixing machines were available after 1850. As you turned the handle, two chopping blades moved up and down within a cylindrical tinplate pan as the pan rotated. In 1900 a bread maker was patented. At the turn of a handle, paddles revolved to knead the dough. Cast-iron rotary egg whisks were available from the end of the nineteenth century.

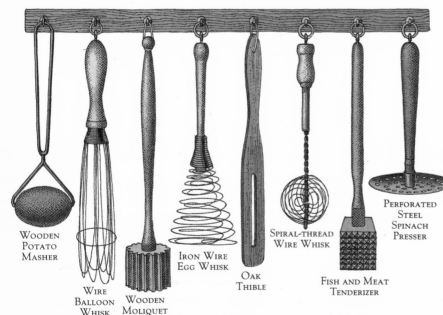

WOODEN
POTATO
MASHER

WIRE
BALLOON
WHISK

WOODEN
MOLIQUET

IRON WIRE
EGG WHISK

OAK
THIBLE

SPIRAL-THREAD
WIRE WHISK

FISH AND MEAT
TENDERIZER

PERFORATED
STEEL
SPINACH
PRESSER

HANGING TOOLS
Milk and eggs were beaten with cocoa using a moliquet to make a frothing chocolate drink. It was also used to beat egg whites for puddings and cakes until a variety of iron wire whisks were marketed in the mid-eighteenth century. Preserved fish and meat had to be soaked and pounded with a wooden hammer-like utensil called a meat tenderizer before cooking. Vegetables were mashed or pressed with either a wooden, pestle-like implement or a perforated metal disc. The metal type gave a finer mash but the wooden presser could also be used for pounding meat.

Mincemeat was never bought ready-made from the butcher's when I was a child and every kitchen I ever saw then had a mincing machine in it. Spinach was forced through a horsehair sieve with a wooden "mushroom" to emerge a kind of green porridge, which I, personally, found revolting. There were no electric food mixers; in fact, in the house in which I was brought up, there was no electricity at all.

BEATING

Until the late seventeenth century the only way of whisking eggs was in a bowl with a bunch of birch or willow twigs bound into a small brush. At this time copper bowls began to be made in quantity and housewives discovered that if the bowl was held over the heat a much thicker stiffness was obtained with eggs beaten in a copper bowl than those beaten in an earthenware bowl. Because copper conducts heat so well copper pans became popular despite their cost.

I don't remember the days before the American egg whisk—a cunning steel device with two interlocking beaters that rotate in opposite directions when the handle is turned—that, apparently, crossed the Atlantic in 1873. I remember my mother's fury at finding the cook making mayonnaise with one. Barbarous! Mayonnaise, she said, should be made by beating the oil and vinegar into the egg with a fork, stirring clockwise all the time (to reverse the turning would, everyone was assured, be fatal) and slowly dribbling in the oil. That matriarch of the English Edwardian kitchen, Mrs Beeton, however, recommends a wooden spoon for the beating. But it was done with a fork in Maryland, where my mother was born, and therefore, to her way of thinking, it *must* be the right way.

CAKE MIXES

As a small boy I nipped into the kitchen many a time to beg to be allowed to scrape the recently prepared raw cake mix from the sides of the mixing bowl. Sometimes this privilege was granted unconditionally; sometimes the granting was preceded by a lecture on how indigestible the stuff was (I never seemed to have any trouble digesting it); sometimes, if the cook was a grumpy one, a blank refusal might be encountered, in which case speed and cunning had to be employed. It always seemed to me that the finished cake was not a patch on the lovely uncooked batter.

PASTRY MAKING

A crude, indigestible oil-and-flour paste mixed in earthenware, stoneware or wooden bowls and rolled with a straight-sided stoneware flagon made the first pie shells or "coffins". Butter and lard gradually replaced oil in the paste, and the most buttery "short" pastry was eaten by itself.

The cook was making delicate flaky, or puff, pastry by the middle of the seventeenth century. Butter and eggs were mixed with fine flour and the resulting paste divided into pieces. The rolling pin now came into its own. Each piece was buttered, refolded and rolled five or six times to make decent puff pastry. By the eighteenth century wooden pie moulds were available in a large range of sizes, and "hoops" or "traps" (wooden or metal bands) supported the tarts and pies in the oven while they baked. Rowel-wheeled jiggers of various sizes and thicknesses were used for cutting rolled-out pastry for tarts, or the edge of an unbaked pie crust, making an attractive, wavy edge. Tinplate pastry cutters and jiggers and flat baking sheets were in use by the end of the eighteenth century.

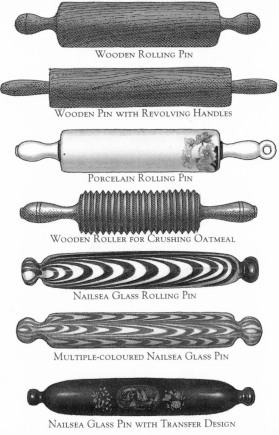

WOODEN ROLLING PIN

WOODEN PIN WITH REVOLVING HANDLES

PORCELAIN ROLLING PIN

WOODEN ROLLER FOR CRUSHING OATMEAL

NAILSEA GLASS ROLLING PIN

MULTIPLE-COLOURED NAILSEA GLASS PIN

NAILSEA GLASS PIN WITH TRANSFER DESIGN

ROLLING AND CRUSHING

The young woman above is using one of the flat wooden rolling pins found in many nineteenth-century households. They were usually made of sycamore, which does not colour or flavour food. Some were ridged to crush oatmeal and salt. Although more expensive, porcelain rolling pins were also common. They could be filled with water to provide extra weight and keep the pastry cool whilst rolling. Nailsea glass rolling pins were very popular. Hot, molten glass was rolled in coloured enamel chips, reheated and then reblown to create marvellous coloured patterns. Made near English ports, they were often given as "love tokens" by departing mariners. Many held salt and were hung by the fire so that the salt kept dry.

OPEN-HEARTH COOKING

DURING SEVERAL YEARS OF LIVING IN the bush of southern and central Africa I ate very little food that was not cooked on an open fire, outside on the ground. Meat (usually antelope) was thrown on the fire, turned once or twice in the hot flames with a stick to seal it and then pulled to rest in the glowing embers, turning it once so that both sides were cooked. Meat cooked in this way, with the addition of a little salt, was delicious beyond any telling of it: the most elaborate preparations of the finest chef in the world couldn't come near it. Sweet potatoes and cobs of maize were also cooked like this, and corms and bulbs dug up in the veld with a sharpened stick or oryx horn were also simply thrown into the hot ashes to cook.

The only cooking utensil in common use in those parts was the three-legged iron pot; it had to be three-legged because any object with four legs will not sit comfortably on uneven ground. The metal trivets or pot stands used in the eighteenth and nineteenth centuries for open-hearth cooking had only three legs for the same reason. In the pot was cooked the ubiquitous mealie-pap or ugali—a stiff porridge made by boiling ground maize in water. Porridge is perhaps a misnomer, for it was nearly as solid as bread and was eaten, usually after dipping it in gravy, with the fingers, and sometimes in alternate bites with grilled meat.

INDOOR FIRES

I mention these practices to give an idea of the very simplest cookery of all. In dry weather the cooking was always done out of doors, but during heavy rain it was transferred to an open fire on the beaten earth

RAISED BRICK HEARTH
The development of the raised, brick-topped hearth in the seventeenth century reduced the danger of cooking in long, spreading dresses, as the fire was made in the centre of the wide brick top. The wood was stored underneath.

SCOTTISH COTTAGE HEARTH (right)
Coal took a long while to reach the Scottish Highlands but peat was widely available as fuel. An iron fender contains this peat fire over which an iron cauldron is suspended by a pot-chain and hook.

IRON CAULDRON
An entire meal for the whole family could be cooked in one large iron pot or cauldron, and the hot water supplied for washing at the same time. For example, bacon was wrapped in linen and placed at the bottom of the cauldron beneath a pierced wooden board. Earthenware jars filled with fowls and meat stood on the board, while puddings and beans wrapped in linen were suspended in the water.

AMERICAN FIREPLACE (right)
The cauldron is suspended above the fire from an adjustable chimney crane, while the kettle, complete with lazy-back (see p.29), hangs from a ratchet-hanger or trammel.

inside a grass and mud hut. There was no chimney, of course, and when you walked into the hut the smoke would appear intolerable. However, if you sat down immediately, as politeness required that you should, most of the smoke passed above your head, where it did an excellent job of keeping all the flies and mosquitoes away.

In an Anglo-Saxon farmhouse a wood or peat fire was built in the middle of the floor. Sometimes a small hole was cut in the thatch especially to allow the smoke out, but more usually the smoke had to find its own way out. You could still find chimneyless houses in remote parts of the British Isles as late as the nineteenth century; one is preserved at the Folk Museum at Saint Fagan's in Wales.

THE CHIMNEY

The widespread introduction of the chimney in the fourteenth century made cooking a much more pleasurable business, for it was then possible to keep an eye on the cooking without being choked by the smoke. The

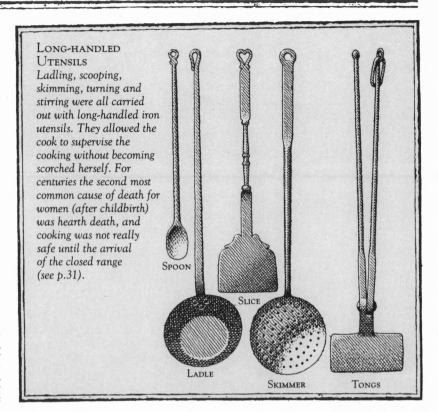

LONG-HANDLED UTENSILS
Ladling, scooping, skimming, turning and stirring were all carried out with long-handled iron utensils. They allowed the cook to supervise the cooking without becoming scorched herself. For centuries the second most common cause of death for women (after childbirth) was hearth death, and cooking was not really safe until the arrival of the closed range (see p.31).

SPOON

SLICE

LADLE

SKIMMER

TONGS

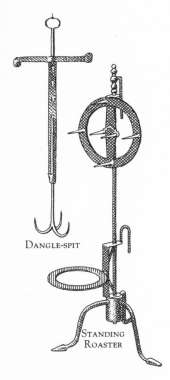

DANGLE-SPIT

STANDING ROASTER

hearth was gradually moved from the centre of the room to the side, where the fire was built on the ground or on a slab of stone. Wood was the most commonly used fuel until the nineteenth century, although peat, or turf, was also used in some areas, and in Ireland it was more often used than wood.

The more prosperous country houses in turf-burning parts of Ireland had (and some still have) a machine called a "fanner" to encourage the fire. This is a centrifugal wind pump, operated by a handle and mounted to one side of the open hearth. A pipe leads from it, passing under the floorboards to emerge through a hole in the hearth floor. The housewife has merely to give a few turns of the handle to transform the smouldering turf fire into a hot blaze. Most of these little machines were made in Pierce's famous foundry in Wexford. By the seventeenth century firewood was in short supply and coal gradually began to take its place. Now coal needs a draught from underneath to burn well, so by the late seventeenth century the iron fire-basket was in use, raising the coal well above the hearth.

ROASTING METHODS

Instead of roasting your meat on a horizontal spit, as shown in the main illustration, you could use a standing roaster. You simply fixed the joint of meat to the spikes of the iron or steel roaster and positioned it before the flames. A circular stand lower on the main shaft of the implement held the dripping bowl. Dangle-spits were commonly used in open-hearth cooking over small fires and, like standing roasters, became more common as the coal-fire grate took over from the open wood fires. You hung the meat to be roasted over the fire or in front of the narrow grate opening and caused the spit to rotate. Weights were added to the arms of the dangle-spit to add impetus to the turning and the more sophisticated versions were turned by means of a clockwork device called a bottle jack. Whatever the type of spit used, meat roasted before an open fire always tasted wonderful!

BOILING

Boiling was always the most common method of cooking and large pots or cauldrons stood in the fire or were suspended over it first by means of a wooden stick or rope, or later an iron chain or rod, fixed to a wooden or iron crossbar. From the middle of the eighteenth century the housewife could raise or lower the pot by adding or removing pot hooks. A more sophisticated device called a chimney or kettle crane was invented in the eighteenth century, enabling the cook to alter the angle and position of the pot. I lived in a house with an open hearth for many years and we had a beautiful and most elaborate crane. You could swing it out into the room, so that you could stir the contents of the pot out of the smoke.

A whole meal could be boiled in the one iron pot if the ingredients were put in at different stages and kept separate while cooking. Our Welsh neighbours tended to boil all their meat. Their main dish was cawl—a mutton, bacon and leek soup. For some reason nobody but a Welsh lady can cook this to perfection. We had a large iron boiler with a lid and a tap, which we kept either suspended from the crane or perched on a shelf by the side of the fire. Provided that you remembered to top it up from time to time it gave constant hot water.

Chimney Cranes

The first chimney crane to be invented was the single-movement crane. A horizontal bar extended from a vertical iron post, hinged to the side of the fireplace. The pot was hung on this bar, which could swing through an angle of ninety degrees, allowing easy access by the cook to the cooking vessel and making it possible to vary the amount of heat allowed to reach the pot. From this simple crane were developed the two-movement and the three-movement crane with which it was also possible to raise and lower the level of the pots and move them along the bar.

Roasting

Spit roasting was a common method of cooking meat on the open hearth. Usually the meat was skewered by a spit, which was then placed horizontally before the fire, supported by wrought-iron fire-dogs, or, if the fire was a coal one, the grate bars. Meat was also roasted by suspending it over the fire by means of a hook hanging from a crossbar in the chimney. In our house we roasted chickens, ducks, geese and, occasionally, for a great feast, a small pig or sheep on a spit. You had to turn the spit by hand and I used to look upon this as my job. It was also necessary to baste the meat frequently with dripping and a dish was placed under the spit to catch it. I used to judge the length of time that a fowl or joint would take to roast by the number of bottles of wine I could consume during the operation; thus, a goose was a four-bottle bird.

Until the eighteenth century spits were often turned by animals, especially small dogs. The poor dog would be made to tread a small wooden wheel attached to the spit until the joint was done "to a turn". However, this arrangement was not found to be terribly practical as the dog was never anywhere to be seen if it suspected there was to be roast for dinner.

By the eighteenth century two sorts of mechanical device were available to turn the spit: the wind-up jack and the smoke jack. The first was powered by a weight on a rope or chain. You operated it by winding up the weight and letting it descend, pulling against gear wheels that turned the spit. The smoke jack consisted of a fan situated above the fire inside the chimney. The rising hot air and smoke caused the fan to rotate, activating the rods and gearing that turned the spit below. By the nineteenth century there were many new designs to suit the smaller coal fire-baskets. Many were operated by clockwork: the bottle jack was one such. The joint was suspended vertically underneath it and was turned first one way and then the other, giving an even roasting.

The first roasting screens appeared in the eighteenth century. They were placed in front of the roasting joint to reflect the radiant heat on to the meat and shield it from the draughts that blew across the floor and up the chimney. The Victorians manufactured beautiful tinplate screens raised on legs and arched across the top, so that they enclosed the front of the fire-box and chimney. They had doors in the back so that you could baste the meat. Hasteners or Dutch ovens (see p.32) were developed from these.

Grilling and Toasting

Meat and fish could also be grilled on a grid-iron—a long-handled framework of iron bars—and there was a wide variety of toasters for bread, cheese and slices of meat. Standing toasters with prongs set at different levels were commonly used and there were the traditional hand-held toasting forks.

Flat loaves of bread and oatcakes were baked on a suspended circular baking sheet known as a griddle or girdle or sometimes a bakestone (see p.35). Bread was usually baked in a dome-shaped oven built into the wall to one side of the hearth but could also be baked by placing it in a portable lidded container and burying the lot in the hot ashes of the open fire. This was especially common in peat-burning areas (see p.35).

SINGLE-MOVEMENT CHIMNEY CRANE

THREE-MOVEMENT CHIMNEY CRANE

STANDING THREE-MOVEMENT CHIMNEY CRANE

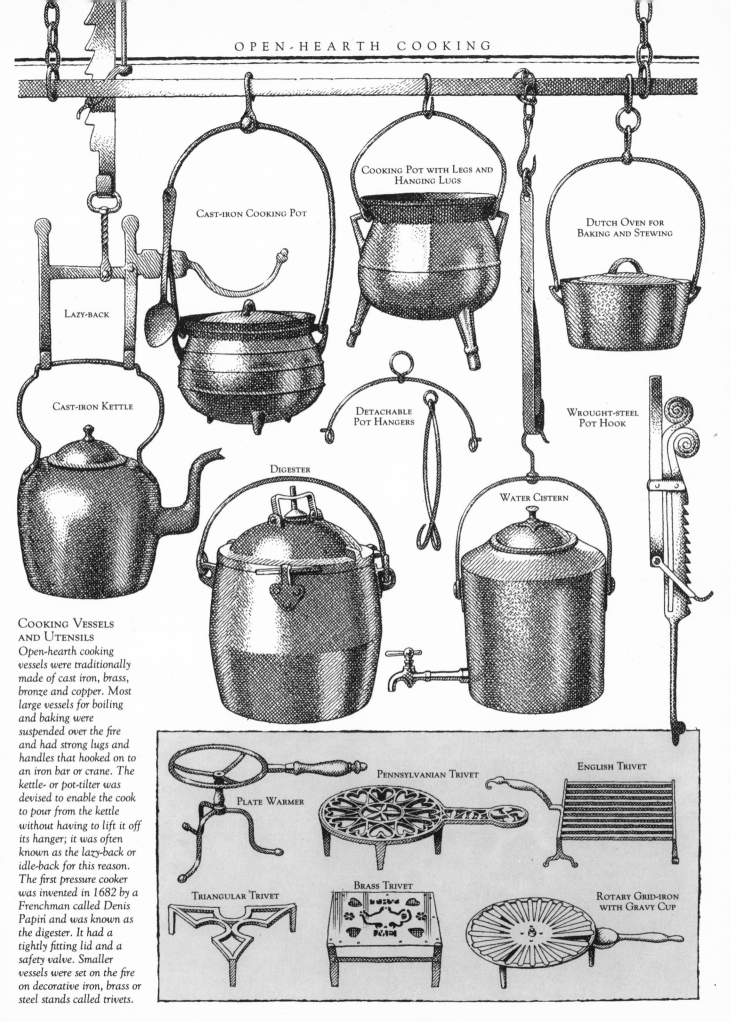

LAZY-BACK

CAST-IRON COOKING POT

COOKING POT WITH LEGS AND HANGING LUGS

DUTCH OVEN FOR BAKING AND STEWING

CAST-IRON KETTLE

DETACHABLE POT HANGERS

DIGESTER

WROUGHT-STEEL POT HOOK

WATER CISTERN

PLATE WARMER

PENNSYLVANIAN TRIVET

ENGLISH TRIVET

TRIANGULAR TRIVET

BRASS TRIVET

ROTARY GRID-IRON WITH GRAVY CUP

COOKING VESSELS AND UTENSILS

Open-hearth cooking vessels were traditionally made of cast iron, brass, bronze and copper. Most large vessels for boiling and baking were suspended over the fire and had strong lugs and handles that hooked on to an iron bar or crane. The kettle- or pot-tilter was devised to enable the cook to pour from the kettle without having to lift it off its hanger; it was often known as the lazy-back or idle-back for this reason. The first pressure cooker was invented in 1682 by a Frenchman called Denis Papin and was known as the digester. It had a tightly fitting lid and a safety valve. Smaller vessels were set on the fire on decorative iron, brass or steel stands called trivets.

COOKING AT A RANGE

HE GREAT KITCHEN RANGE WAS A product of the coal and iron age of the eighteenth and nineteenth centuries. In the middle of the eighteenth century a way of making good quality iron using charred coal (coke) was discovered, and ironmasters no longer had to use dwindling supplies of charcoal to make poor quality, brittle cast iron. Immediately, iron became abundant and good enough for large castings to be made and sold cheaply throughout the British Isles. At the same time, a cheap, plentiful supply of coal meant that coal gradually took over from wood as the most popular domestic fuel, and lead to the development of grates.

OPEN-RANGE COOKING
The first open ranges consisted simply of a cast-iron "perpetual" oven (one with its own grate and flues) built into the fireplace to one side of the open grate. By 1815 ranges were available not only with an oven but also a boiler, both heated by a central grate. In many designs the boiler was L-shaped, extending along the back of the grate.

Free-standing iron grates were being made in the eighteenth century (see p.26) and these were soon developed to fit into the fireplace, where they were flanked by iron plates or hobs on which pans and kettles could stand. The open range was born.

THE OPEN RANGE

In 1780 Thomas Robinson designed the first open kitchen range. At the centre of the range was a hob grate. To one side of the metal hob was an iron oven with a hinged door and on the other an iron tank for hot water. Fitted to the top bar of the fire grate was a hinged trivet which would swing forward for a pan or kettle to stand on.

One of the main disadvantages of this range was that food cooked in the oven tended to be burnt on one side (the side nearest the fire) and undercooked on the other. Fortunately, modifications were soon made to the design, and passages for the circulation of warm air round the oven were introduced, improving the evenness of the cooking dramatically. Other disadvantages of the open range were that it made the kitchen unbearably hot and burned vast amounts of coal. Dampers were introduced to control oven and fire heat but these ranges were never efficient and the fire-box could still become hot enough to melt the fire-bars!

THE CLOSED RANGE

By the 1840s the enclosed kitchen range or kitchener became widely available. A metal hot-plate covered the fire-box and was fitted with rings for pans and kettles to rest on. Movable panels covered the front of the grate so that you could still roast meat in front of the fire if you wished, or warm the kitchen after cooking. Later versions featured a metal door and eventually the fire was completely encased in iron. Ovens were placed on both sides of the fire-box in some designs or a boiler might stand on one side and an oven on the other. An arrangement of flues and dampers controlled the temperature of the oven and boiler to some degree and the systems were gradually improved.

The arrival of the closed range spelt the end of the soot-blackened pots. No longer hung over the open fire from pot hooks and kettle cranes, pots were placed on the iron plate that formed the top of the stove, where

OPEN PEAT-BURNING RANGE

OPEN COAL-BURNING RANGE WITH OVEN AND BOILER

THE CLOSED RANGE

EORGE BODLEY PATENTED THE CLOSED RANGE in 1802. Similar to Robinson's open range (see p.30), he reduced the size of the open-range grate and covered it with a cast-iron hot-plate. A fire brick was inserted between the grate and the oven to reduce the heat on that side and flues were incorporated on the other side, so that the heat could circulate round the oven. In the 1820s William Flavel began making closed ranges, which he called "patent kitcheners". The name stuck and closed ranges became generally known as kitcheners. The closed range was much more economical than the open range, as the heat was contained within the (smaller) grate instead of being allowed to disappear up the chimney. Pots and kettles stood on the clean hot-plates, so they were not blackened and trivets and chimney cranes were no longer needed. Roasting in front of the fire, using a hastener (see p.32) was only possible with those kitcheners where the fire was open at the front and the grate adjustable at the bottom, so that the size of the fire could be increased. With the completely enclosed ranges special ovens were provided that allowed sufficient air to circulate for roasting.

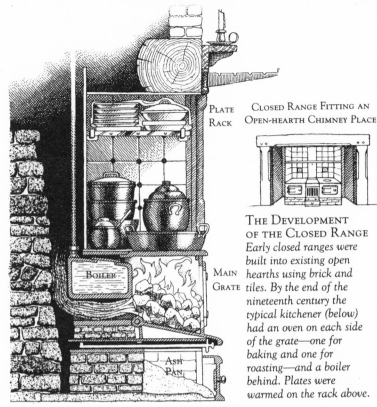

PLATE RACK

CLOSED RANGE FITTING AN OPEN-HEARTH CHIMNEY PLACE

BOILER

MAIN GRATE

ASH PAN

THE DEVELOPMENT OF THE CLOSED RANGE
Early closed ranges were built into existing open hearths using brick and tiles. By the end of the nineteenth century the typical kitchener (below) had an oven on each side of the grate—one for baking and one for roasting—and a boiler behind. Plates were warmed on the rack above.

they could become red hot if the cook wanted. Later, circular holes were cut in the hot-plate. These were usually plugged by iron plates, but, for a quick boil, one of these plates could be removed and a pot or kettle placed directly over the flames.

MAINTAINING THE CLOSED RANGE

The kitchener made the kitchen a cleaner place. No longer did great dollops of soot flop down the chimney and burst into the room; no longer could the pot or the kettle call the other black. But the soot was still there all right, up the chimney, and the chimney had to be swept even more than before. The complicated system of flues and dampers that channelled the heat around the range also had to be kept clean. This was the poor cook's job, unless she had a kitchen maid to do it for her. I well remember the cooks we had in my childhood home—large, motherly women, with strong, usually bare, arms, sometimes a trifle short-tempered but kindly underneath. Cooks were always called *Mrs* something even though they were never married. The other maids, who were always smaller in bulk, were called by their Christian names, *tout simple*, no matter how old they were.

The open fire could be kept in, often for weeks at a time, by throwing on huge logs last thing at night, but the kitchener went out at night. So, before the cook could so much as make an early morning cup of tea, she had to clean the thing, black-lead it, polish it, and then re-light it. Once the range was lit the kitchen was soon transformed from a cold, cheerless place to the cosiest room in the house.

THE GAS COOKER

Three factors contributed to the end of the great kitchen range within 150 years, at most, of its inception. The first was the widespread introduction of gas. To begin with the gas was coal gas, produced by a diversity of private companies and distributed throughout the towns and cities in the 1880s. The gas stove had a number of advantages over the coal range. The temperature could be regulated to a much finer degree simply by adjusting a tap, and the temperature could be maintained for as long as was required. It was smaller than a range, for it was designed simply to cook food, not boil water and heat rooms, too, and could therefore be installed in smaller kitchens at much less expense. Gas cookers were far

ROASTING IN A HASTENER

After the dangle-spit, the standing roaster (see p.26) and the roasting screen came the hastener, sometimes known as the Dutch oven (not to be confused with the true Dutch oven, see p.34). Designed to stand in front of the coal-grate fire, hasteners were crafted out of sheet tin and shaped to increase the heat in which the joint cooked. The meat was hooked on a dangle-spit, which was turned by means of a bottle jack. Dutch ovens had doors in the back so the cook could baste the meat while it was roasting.

INTO THE TWENTIETH CENTURY

The gas cooker became more common in the 1850s when cast-iron black boxes with four legs, containing an oven, a grill and a hot-plate with burners were marketed. Gas cooking didn't become popular, however, until the introduction of the prepayment slot machine in the 1890s, which for the first time made gas affordable for those on lower incomes. The more expensive combination gas and coal ranges were available by the end of the nineteenth century.

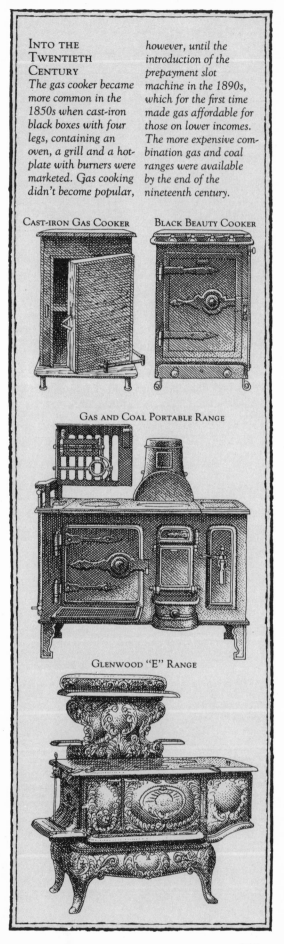

CAST-IRON GAS COOKER

BLACK BEAUTY COOKER

GAS AND COAL PORTABLE RANGE

GLENWOOD "E" RANGE

cleaner than the guzzling coal monsters that preceded them and the cook could lie in for a bit since there was no early morning lighting up to do—the gas cooker could be lit in a moment. However, it was still made of cast iron, and still required black-leading and polishing.

Efficient, properly ventilated gas ovens were available by 1900. The ovens were well insulated with shelf runners, grills and removable enamelled fittings. Thermostats were not included until 1923 when, for the first time ever, food could be cooked at a specific temperature, making cooking a much more precise art.

THE ELECTRIC COOKER

The second factor was the advent of electricity. Electric cookers were first designed in the 1890s but they took some time to catch on because of the slow spread of electricity supplies throughout the country and the high initial cost of both electricity and electric cookers. By the late 1920s electric cookers were cheaper, featured longer-lasting, more efficient heating elements, enamel finishes and automatic temperature controls, and electric cooking finally began to compete with gas.

AGA COOKERS

The third factor was the arrival from Sweden during the late 1920s of the highly efficient, fully enclosed Aga stove still in use today. The Esse arrived later and worked on exactly the same principle.

The original Aga oven operated on solid fuel but was clean and economical to run. The coal was held inside a cast-iron fuel-box enclosed in an insulated jacket. The fire was strictly regulated by restricting the amount of air allowed to it. The heat was stored in a mass of cast steel—the Aga weighs nearly a ton—and conducted to the hot-plates and ovens at precisely the right temperatures.

These stoves were, and still are, extremely efficient. You can carry out different types of cooking at once, the hot-plates are always ready for instant boiling, the hot oven and cool oven (or ovens) always at their working temperatures, and the fuel consumption is a small fraction of that of the ranges.

The great kitchen ranges—those magnificent shiny monsters—have now nearly all gone for scrap. They were too hungry and they belched forth too much heat, which went where it was not wanted and spoilt the temper of the cook.

CAST-IRON SAUCEPAN

CAST-IRON FISH OR HAM KETTLE

COPPER SAUCEPAN

BRASS KETTLE

COPPER TEA-KETTLE

METAL FOOD WARMER

COOKING VESSELS
Now that cooking vessels stood on hot-plates they needed to be flat-bottomed and equipped with handles that could be held. Saucepans or stewpans appeared in the first half of the eighteenth century when they were made in sets of varying sizes. Fish was boiled in a pan called a kettle with an inside container or strainer. Tea-kettles proliferated as tea drinking became increasingly popular (see p.53). By the beginning of the twentieth century pans of food could be reheated in tin containers filled with hot water.

BAKING

T IS EASY TO SEE HOW LEAVENED bread was invented. The people who first ground wheat or barley between two stones, wet the meal and roasted it near a fire must soon have discovered that if they left the moistened dough overnight in warm weather, it would rise. Although they would not have realized it at the time, this was due to the action of wild yeast. The yeast organism—a microscopic fungus—eats sugar and excretes carbon dioxide, and it is the carbon dioxide that as it expands causes myriad holes to form in the dough, making it rise.

I have used wild yeast many times in Africa, where the tame stuff was not for sale. You make a sweet, sloppy dough and leave it exposed to the air for a day or two. When it begins to froth you add it to the main dough and knead and bake it. Making yeast bread is a time-consuming and skilful business. You must first knead the dough thoroughly with your hands, then allow it to prove, or rest for a few hours until it has risen. You then knock it down, kneading it thoroughly once again, before placing it in baking tins and allowing it to rise once more. Finally, you must transport it to the oven without bumping it if it is to bake well.

OVENS IMPROVISED AND PURPOSE-BUILT

We made ovens in termites' nests, which might have been designed for the purpose. We dug a cavity in the side of the nest, ran an air vent from it to the top of the nest and lit a big fire in the chamber, keeping it roaring for about three hours. We then let the fire go out and popped the dough in the hot ashes, which retained sufficient heat to bake the bread perfectly.

The early brick and stone ovens worked on exactly the same principle. They were usually let into the wall to one side of the fireplace and had a wooden door. Small

BAKING IN A POT OVEN

In peat-burning areas bread and pies were often baked in a pot oven. The dough was placed directly on the heated and cleared hearth and covered with an iron pot, which was then surrounded by burning peat. Oval or round cast-iron portable ovens, often known as Dutch ovens, worked on the same principle. These were stood among the hot ashes of the open fire and burning peat or hot embers placed on the lid to speed up the cooking.

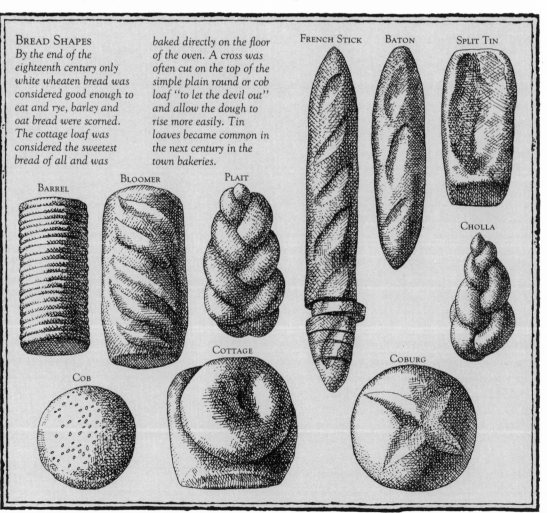

BREAD SHAPES
By the end of the eighteenth century only white wheaten bread was considered good enough to eat and rye, barley and oat bread were scorned. The cottage loaf was considered the sweetest bread of all and was baked directly on the floor of the oven. A cross was often cut on the top of the simple plain round or cob loaf "to let the devil out" and allow the dough to rise more easily. Tin loaves became common in the next century in the town bakeries.

BARREL

BLOOMER

PLAIT

FRENCH STICK

BATON

SPLIT TIN

CHOLLA

COB

COTTAGE

COBURG

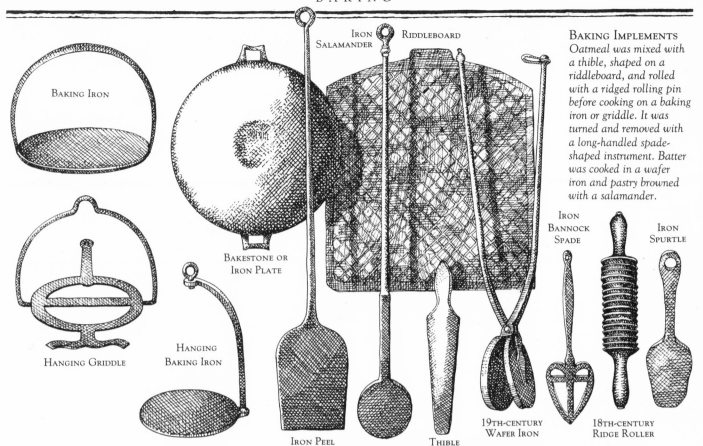

BAKING IRON

BAKESTONE OR
IRON PLATE

HANGING GRIDDLE

HANGING
BAKING IRON

IRON
SALAMANDER

RIDDLEBOARD

IRON PEEL

THIBLE

19TH-CENTURY
WAFER IRON

IRON
BANNOCK
SPADE

IRON
SPURTLE

18TH-CENTURY
RIDGE ROLLER

BAKING IMPLEMENTS

Oatmeal was mixed with a thible, shaped on a riddleboard, and rolled with a ridged rolling pin before cooking on a baking iron or griddle. It was turned and removed with a long-handled spade-shaped instrument. Batter was cooked in a wafer iron and pastry browned with a salamander.

pieces of wood, such as hedge trimmings, were generally used for fuel, together with a few faggots (compressed sticks). The ash was brushed out and the floor of the oven wiped clean before placing the bread inside. By the middle of the nineteenth century, ovens with cast-iron doors and two chambers were common. The fire was kept burning during baking in a chamber beneath the baking chamber. Solid-fuel ovens also worked on this principle but were usually part of the kitchen range and had damper-controlled flues to help distribute the heat evenly.

BAKING ON THE FIRE

You could also bake bread (as the Irish, Scottish Highlanders and Welsh country people very often still do) by placing the dough in a lidded iron or pottery container and burying it in the hot ashes of the open fire. Peat-burning areas commonly baked bread in this way. Of course, it takes good judgement and experience to know how hot the ashes should be and when to take the bread out of the pot.

Oatcakes, flat bread and pies were all cooked over the fire on a bakestone, griddle or baking iron. In Wales they baked bara planc, the Welsh version of griddle cake, on a circular iron baking sheet and cooked and crisped batter in a waffle iron.

COMMUNAL OVENS

Communal ovens were often built into the thickness of an outside wall and bakehouses were still popular when I was young. I remember staying at a fisherman's cottage in the summer holidays, where the small kitchen contained a simple coal range with no oven. It was my delight once a week on baking day to run down to the bakehouse, carrying an array of uncooked bread, pies and cakes. There I would hand over our creations, together with a few pennies, and the baker would open the great cast-iron door of the oven, revealing a glowing chamber, and place them inside beside those of half the village. When they were perfectly done, he would pull them out again for me with a long-handled wooden paddle called a peel.

STORING FOOD

EFORE YOU COULD BUY ASPARAGUS grown in Mexico in Soho in December, and strawberries flown from Spain in March, and before the advent of freezers, storing and preserving food was a matter of supreme importance.

STORING MEAT AND FISH

At school we were told that in former times most of the cattle had to be killed in the autumn and salted down because there wasn't enough winter fodder to feed them on. We were not told that the reason there was not enough winter fodder was that it was customary to remove all the fences after the harvest so that everybody's cattle could graze on everybody's land. As it paid no individual farmer to grow winter fodder crops, none were grown, and the cattle had to be slaughtered in the autumn.

It was certainly not a good idea to slaughter a bullock during the summer months as the meat would deteriorate rapidly in the heat, and fly-proof, well-ventilated buildings were not very often available. A city butcher could do it only because he was able to sell the meat within a day or two of slaughtering. The practice of corning beef—lightly salting it in brine—extended the period that he could store the meat by a week or two.

There was no refrigerator, of course, but by the nineteenth century nearly all houses had a spacious, walk-in larder or pantry. Fish and vegetables were laid directly on its cool stone or marble shelves and covered with muslin, while meat and game were hung in the larder or in a meat safe.

STORING DRY AND DAIRY FOODS

Grain—the edible dried seed of plants—was the foodstuff that made civilization possible. Small grain—wheat, barley, oats and rye—would keep perfectly well stored in the rick or stack, provided that you kept the rat and mouse population in reasonable check and covered the rick with a good coat of thatch. Held securely in the straw, the grain would gradually dry out naturally and would keep quite well for years. When the farmer wanted to sell or use some he simply threshed out a rick, or part of a rick. The housewife stored grains in wooden bins, which she stood above floor level to keep them out of the reach of greedy mice.

When I was a boy, every cottager I knew had a bin in his outhouse. This was a large wooden box (big enough for a man to hide in) with a sloping roof, lined with sheet zinc. It was used to store the barley meal for the cottager's pig. There might be another to hold bran, which would also be food for the pig or for the rabbits. In the larder there would be a flour bin of some sort—often a four- or five-gallon earthenware crock, which was sometimes glazed on the inside only, and often not glazed at all. This crock would have a wooden plug that fitted the hole in the top exactly. There might be another, smaller, crock for dried peas and another for broad beans. Peas pudding was a common dish among country people and broad beans, or fava beans as they are known in America, were a good, high-protein standby.

Eggs, cheese and butter all need to be kept in a cool place and so were all stored in the larder. Between them, the larder and the kitchen housed a great variety of wooden, earthenware, glass, and stoneware containers for the dry goods that the good wife needed, or thought she needed. These included salt, sugar, pepper and a few spices such as cloves, cinnamon and ginger (country food was not heavily spiced). Herbs were stored in paper bags, while sugar and flour kept best in wooden tubs. There would also always be some earthenware or glass jars containing pickled onions or shallots and other pickles. Fruit was often kept in nets and apples were usually dried, cored and strung to the ceiling, or laid on shelves in a cool, dry loft.

CARRYING FOOD

Always somewhere in the kitchen, usually at the end of a shelf, you would find a little pile of calico bags. These were used for collecting the shopping. They were taken to the grocer's or the village shop and filled with the goods the housewife needed—flour, sugar, lentils, rice, or whatever. This marvellous system eliminated all need for the messy and environmentally damaging "packaging" that litters our countryside today. There were no horrible plastic bags and there was no "rubbish mountain". In fact, there was practically no rubbish. Tinned food was only just creeping in and most country

MEAT SAFES
Meat was generally hung before cooking to ripen its flavour. In wealthier households it was stored in a large meat safe which was suspended from the ceiling. In this way it was kept out of reach of vermin and its muslin covering prevented the flies from landing on it.

people never saw it. You might find the odd tin of Tate and Lyle's golden syrup (with that fascinating picture of the apparently dead lion with bees buzzing round it), the very occasional tin of sardines from Portugal, and sometimes a bottle of Bovril.

STORING LIQUIDS

The flood of tasteless fizzy water (known today as "mineral water") had not yet started: most country women brewed their own wines and farm workers took a bottle of home-made wine with them to the fields to drink with their morning "snap". I've been given many a swig from such a bottle, the proffering of which was always preceded by a ritual wipe over the top of the neck with an earthy hand. Before glass bottles were widely available at the end of the seventeenth century, housewives would fill wooden, barrel-like containers with hot or cold drink, depending on the time of year. Wood was ideal because it did not conduct heat but bottles and jugs made of tough ox hide were also widely used. When I was young small stoneware ginger beer bottles might appear at fêtes or special occasions (see p.40); they had screw tops with threaded stoneware "corks" in rubber washers. Lemonade was sometimes sold in glass bottles with glass marbles inside the neck, held firmly against a rubber ring at the top by the pressure within the bottle. I remember smashing the bottles to get at the marbles.

THE LARDER
Many different types of container were used in the larder for storing all sorts of food. Stoneware or earthenware jars were used for storing vinegar and pickled foods, while jams, jellies and salted food were stored in salt-glazed earthenware jars. Bread was kept in large crocks or bins, and tin jars were used for storing tea and biscuits.

OVAL-SHAPED
WALL SALT

19TH-CENTURY
PINE WALL SALT

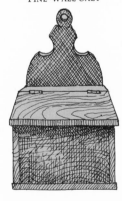

WALL SALTS
Salt was often stored in a container known as a wall salt. It was hung on the kitchen wall in a position convenient for the cook to take spoonfuls to add to the cooking pot.

BRICKCLAY
STORAGE JAR

EARTHENWARE
STORAGE JAR

STONEWARE
STORAGE JARS

19TH-CENTURY
BREAD CROCK

BREAD BIN

PEWTER FLOUR
CONTAINER

SALT-GLAZED
STORAGE JAR

19TH-CENTURY
GLAZED JAR

19TH-CENTURY
DECORATED
STARCH JAR

BLACK JAPANNED
TIN TEA CONTAINER

TIN SUGAR JAR

TIN BISCUIT
BARREL

SALTING & PICKLING

WHEN I WAS YOUNG THE SALTING trough was found in every country household of any standard. In the east of England it was likely to be made of wood, although I have also seen lead and stoneware troughs. I once had a stoneware ham bath the size and shape of a large ham. This was used for sweet pickling: curing a ham in a brine that included salt, sugar and various spices. Every country lady had her own favourite recipe.

In Wales, and every other slate country, salting troughs were hewn out of slate. Twenty years ago every Welsh farmhouse, large or small, had slate troughs set up on stone buttresses in the dairy and larder. In the dairy the trough was used for skimming the cream off the milk (see p.73) and in the larder it was used for salting pig meat. In some houses the same trough was used for both purposes: skimming milk in the summer, salting pig meat in the winter.

Dry pickling took three weeks to three months to complete, depending on whether you were salting thin joints or massive hams. In either case the meat had to be frequently turned and rubbed in the salt.

Meat from larger animals was cured in wet pickle. Before I had a deep freeze I pickled the greater part of many a sheep in brine. The meat was completely immersed in a brine with enough salt in it to float a potato or an egg, and placed in a cool larder. After curing, the meat was generally soaked for twelve to twenty-four hours to extract some of the salt and then boiled. Such meat, generally beef or mutton, was used to victual ships until very recently.

Hand-salted meat tastes better and is more reliable: the meat is cut into pieces and rubbed carefully with dry salt a couple of days before being put into the brine. The initial dry salting extracts some of the moisture so that the brine is not diluted.

A sensible precaution, if you are going to keep the meat many months, is to draw away the brine from time to time. Either add water to it and augment its salinity by boiling in some more salt, then let it cool and return it to the meat or, if you can afford to waste the salt, throw it away and pour in some freshly made brine. A handful of peppercorns, or even a few chillies, thrown into the cask can do only good.

PICKLE JARS
Pickles were preserved in vinegar in sealed pickle jars. Glass pickle jars were preferred as glass is not porous and does not admit air, which would spoil the pickles.

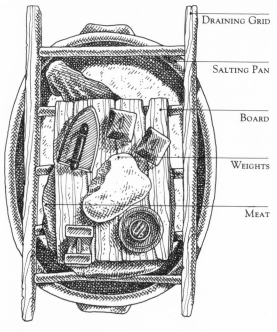

DRAINING GRID

SALTING PAN

BOARD

WEIGHTS

MEAT

DRY PICKLING (above)
The meat was compressed by placing a board laden with weights on top. In this way the juice was forced out and the salt could penetrate the meat more quickly.

PICKLING FISH (left)
Fish was baked in good vinegar and then rolled up and preserved in a vinegar-and-onion pickle in a sealed jar.

SALTING A WET PICKLE
Before pickling, meat was rubbed with dry salt and left to drain over a trough of brine for several days, more salt being rubbed into it each day. It was then immersed in the brine and left to soak in a cool place for a few weeks. As the pickle became diluted with the meat juices more salt was added to the solution.

BRINE

DRY SALT

MEAT

TROUGH

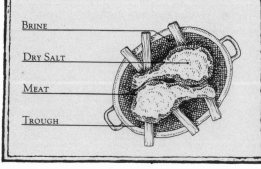

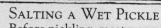

DRYING & SMOKING

NYONE WHO HAS VISITED THE COAST of Belgium will have seen dabs or flounders nailed to the walls of fishermen's sheds to dry. After placing them for an hour or two in brine they are left in the sun and cool sea breeze to dehydrate and are then eaten raw.

DRYING IN THE WIND
We caught an occasional skate or ray when fishing in the South Atlantic. We would head and gut them so that just the "wings" remained joined together, and hang them in the rigging without further ado. They would keep like that for weeks and improved with age. We also caught some sea birds on baited fish hooks, which we skinned and gutted and hung in the same manner.

DRYING AND PRESERVING IN THE SMOKE
Smoke helps keep away the flies and preserve meat, and I have sat over many a fire in central Africa, watching strips of buck or buffalo meat drying in the smoke.

If you peer up a great chimney in a farmhouse or mansion kitchen in Europe you will probably see the remains of horizontal rods or perches fixed across the width of it. Bacon and ham were hung from these, or in a separate smoke-house.

Two methods of smoking have evolved: cold smoking and cook smoking. With cold smoking the fire is damped down and built so that no heat but a lot of smoke encircles the meat, allowing the pyroligneous acid in the smoke to preserve it, but leaving the meat uncooked. Bacon, kippers, bloaters and haddock should be cold smoked. Salmon, eels, buckling, and mackerel are generally cook smoked, that is they are subjected to enough heat to cook them as well as smoke them and are ready to eat immediately. I have also cook smoked both ducks and geese and they are quite delicious.

HICKORY SMOKE
Traditionally the North Americans are great smokers and my Maryland cousins are always talking to me about the supremacy of hickory smoke. Certainly they smoked fish of many kinds and some American housewives still have plenty of recipes for bacon and ham, generally smoked in some kind of outdoor smoking house.

COMMUNITY DRYING
Fruit was dried to last families throughout the winter. Sometimes, after a bumper harvest, the whole community was involved in the work of preparing the fruit for drying.

SMOKING
Meat was most commonly smoked by hanging it in the chimney but some people used a smoke-house or an inverted barrel in which the bung hole served as a smoke vent. Inside, the meat was hung from hooks and smoked over a sawdust fire. The home-smoker was similar but used smoke from a wood-burning stove.

CHIMNEY SMOKING

SMOKE-HOUSE

HOME-SMOKER

FRUIT DRIER

DRYING IN THE HOME
The fruit to be dried was stacked on the wire-mesh racks of the drier. This was then positioned over the kitchen stove and the heat that rose from it would dry the fruit most effectively and speedily.

BOTTLING & CANNING

F YOU HEAT ANY KIND OF FOOD stuff sufficiently to destroy the bacteria and mould organisms and then, while it is in this sterile state, seal it completely, it will keep indefinitely. When the tins of "bully-beef" left by Scott of the Antarctic's party back in 1912 were opened when rediscovered years later, the beef was found to be in perfect condition.

POTTING MEAT

From the days of Elizabeth I in England, and no doubt before then in Spain, extensive sea voyaging stimulated the search for effective methods of preserving foodstuffs. Salt meat was considered good enough for the poor sailors who had to do the gruelling work of sailing the ships but when gentlemen began to go to sea, and even more so, gentle-women, then salt tack was not considered good enough and the art of potting meat and poultry was perfected. The meat was cooked and the fat used to cover it. The bladder of a pig or sheep or ox was wetted and then stretched over the top of the pot and tied down. As it dried it shrunk, making a very tight seal and preserving the meat.

THE FIRST BOTTLED FOOD

A Frenchman named Nicholas Appert pioneered the art of bottling. He was making a bid for the prize of 12,000 francs offered by Napoleon to the person who could find a way of preserving food for his army which, as every schoolboy knows, marched on its stomach. Appert placed the food in glass jars and cooked it by immersing the loosely

CANS AND JARS
After tin cans had proved their value in war time, they became part of daily life and revolutionized the storage and preservation of food. Apart from their improved design, cans have changed very little since then. The tradition of preserving fruit in jars continued and several types of sealer were used to seal the jar tightly.

THE CAN OPENER
The first canned foods carried the helpful instruction that a chisel and hammer were the best tools for opening them! Sixty years later, in 1875, the first can opener was invented. It was made of cast iron and steel and at one end was a carved bull's head, especially apt as it was sold with every can of bully-beef. There followed a wave of imaginative can openers.

BULL'S HEAD CAN OPENER

19TH-CENTURY CAN OPENER

CAP-LIFTER AND CAN OPENER

SARDINE TIN OPENER

LARGE-JAWED CAN OPENER

CAN OF PROCESSED PEAS

CAN OF OYSTER SOUP

EMERGENCY WAR RATIONS

CAN OF ROASTED VEAL

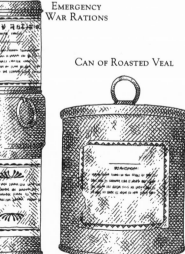

JAR OPENERS AND SEALERS

FRUIT JAR FILLER

IRON FRUIT LIFTER

LID TIGHTENER

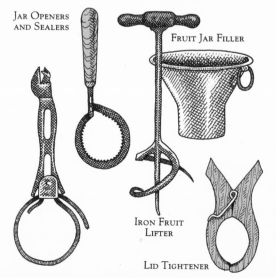

FRUIT PRESERVE JAR

corked jars in boiling water. He then pressed home the corks and sealed the jars.

The famous Kilner jar was long used in England for preserving fruit and is still manufactured. All good country house-wives "put up" tomatoes, plums, goose-berries and other soft fruit in Kilner jars in times of surplus and a few shelf loads of such produce is a great standby: we use Kilner jars to this day. The ubiquity of the deep freeze, however, has meant that the art of bottling is now practically lost. This is sad, as tomatoes, plums, strawberries and other soft and mushy fruit taste infinitely better bottled than frozen.

THE FIRST TIN CANISTERS

An Englishman named Peter Durand took out a patent in 1810 for tinned iron or steel cans and by 1814 a firm named Donkin and Hall was supplying tinned meat to the Royal Navy. At first the process was improperly understood. Sometimes temperatures were not high enough to destroy all the bacteria and sometimes the tins were too large and the heat was not able to penetrate to the centre of the contents. Tins would blow up and sometimes people would be poisoned.

It was not until Louis Pasteur discovered the facts about bacteria, and how to kill them, in the 1860s that canning, as it was called in America, or tinning, as it was known in England, became a safe and re-liable process. By 1840, the Australians were sending tinned meat to England and, soon after, the United States and the Argen-tine went into the production of canned beef in a big way. Upton Sinclair's novel *The Jungle* contains a vivid and pretty horrifying description of large-scale beef canning in Chicago in the early twentieth century.

In the late nineteenth century cheap tin-ned cans became available. Made of tinned steel plate, the cans were boiled with their contents already inside them. Then the tops were clamped on to make an airtight seal and they were boiled again. Using this method, the contents were sterilized completely and would remain sterile until the tin was opened, however many years later.

The famous wedge-shaped can of bully-beef kept the Allied armies fed during the First World War and the British armies in the Second. I lived on it for months at a time in the Second and can honestly say that I never got *really* tired of it. You soon learned the rationale behind the wedge-shaped can. You opened it by unwinding a special strip near the middle of it with a little key that came with it. You ate *half* the contents (no man was ever known to eat more) for lunch, then fitted the top half of the can to the bottom half and put it away until supper time when you ate the second half. Occa-sionally, misguided people would make attempts to cook the stuff. The result was disgusting in the extreme.

HOME CANNING

During both wars the Homcan was a com-monly used device. I managed to get hold of one in Suffolk after the Second World War and canned many a sheep with it. You bought the Homcan tins from the Women's Institute (they got them from the Metal Box Company) and sealed them with the Homcan machine. Meat and fruit could be canned at home simply and safely using this method. However, green vegetables were not sufficiently acid for safe home canning and would, likely as not, be "off" by the time you opened the tin.

THE MARBLE STOPPER
Corking was but one way of sealing bottles. An alternative method was to seal the bottle with a glass or marble stopper. These were used most frequently in fizzy drink bottles. The pressure inside the bottle wedged the marble stopper tightly against the rubber ring in the bottle neck, thus sealing it.

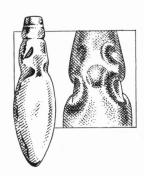

BOTTLES IN THE HOME
A wide assortment of bottles was produced. A lot were specifically used for storing drinks, from gin to ginger beer, while other bottles, usually narrower and ridged so you could tell them straight away, were used for keeping medicines and poisons.

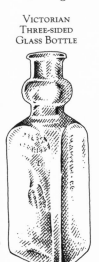    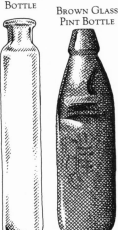

VICTORIAN THREE-SIDED GLASS BOTTLE — BROWN GLASS BOTTLE — STONEWARE GIN BOTTLE — CHAMPAGNE-TOP STONEWARE BOTTLE — MOULDED GLASS MEDICINE BOTTLE — MEDICINE BOTTLE — BROWN GLASS PINT BOTTLE

PRESERVES & CONFECTIONERY

OST FRUITS AND VEGETABLES CAN be preserved using one of the following five methods: salting, immersing in alcohol, pickling in vinegar, drying or sugaring.

Salting is inappropriate for fruit, although absolutely the perfect way to preserve runner beans. If you cover any fruit in brandy, or any other strong spirit for that matter, you will preserve it indefinitely. By soaking fruit or vegetables in vinegar you make pickle; by boiling them in vinegar you make chutney. Small fruits, such as grapes and blackcurrants, will keep for a long time if they are dried quickly enough. Plums dried in this manner become prunes. Drying fruit is common in hot, dry areas, such as the lands bordering the Mediterranean and southern California. Figs and dates can be preserved by drying and pressing.

SUGARING

The art of preserving fruit in sugar or syrup is a very old tradition in northern Europe. No doubt before cane sugar arrived from the Near East, honey was used. Before preserving in syrup, fruit must be boiled or blanched in water. In this way the skin of the fruit is softened sufficiently for the syrup to permeate it. Two parts of white sugar should be dissolved in one part of water to make the syrup. The old cooks always knew the exact strength of the sugar solution needed for any purpose. Today few householders bother to

PREPARING FRUIT
Before fruit could be dried or preserved in syrup it usually had to be peeled and stoned. There was a large number of paring devices available, ranging from a simple hand-held parer to the extremely complicated "Bonanza" fruit parer, which was not, in fact, very effective as it only worked with fruit that was "standard-sized".

MARMALADE
CUTTER

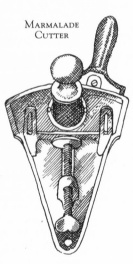

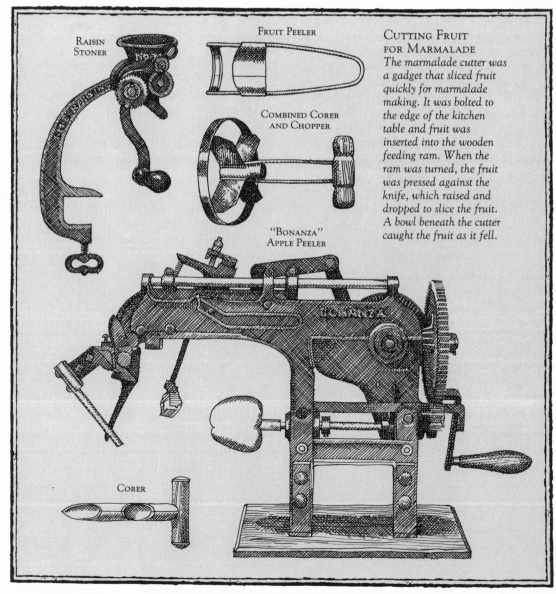

RAISIN
STONER

FRUIT PEELER

COMBINED CORER
AND CHOPPER

"BONANZA"
APPLE PEELER

CORER

CUTTING FRUIT FOR MARMALADE
The marmalade cutter was a gadget that sliced fruit quickly for marmalade making. It was bolted to the edge of the kitchen table and fruit was inserted into the wooden feeding ram. When the ram was turned, the fruit was pressed against the knife, which raised and dropped to slice the fruit. A bowl beneath the cutter caught the fruit as it fell.

make syrup: they buy candied or crystallized fruit, or fruit in syrup directly from the confectioners. In any case, nowadays we can buy fresh fruit at any time of the year, rendering fruit preservation less important.

MAKING MARMALADE

Marmalade is said to have been invented especially for Catherine of Aragon. When that unfortunate lady married Henry VIII, and had to leave her glorious sunny land and come to live in gloomy England, she found that she craved oranges. These could not be shipped to England in their natural form without deteriorating so much that they were inedible on arrival. So it was necessary to discover a method of preserving them on their long journey. It was not long before marmalade was born.

MAKING JAM AND JELLY

Jamming and jellying are both methods of preserving fruit. To make jam you simply boil the fruit with plenty of sugar until much of the moisture has boiled away. Until comparatively recently most households consumed a colossal amount of jam: they ate jam tarts and jam-filled roly-poly puddings, and bread and butter spread with copious amounts of jam made up a considerable part of the diet of both rich and poor. After all, after the settlement of the West Indies sugar became extremely cheap and, in the countryside at least, fruit was there for the picking and usually was.

To make jelly you simply boil the fruit, strain it through a fine strainer, preferably one made of muslin, mix the solution with sugar, and boil it again until it jellies. The mixture jellies because of the action of pectin, usually present in the fruit. If pectin is not present in sufficient quantity the fruit will not jelly, no matter how much you boil it or how often you spoon some of it out, taste it, and pour a dribble on to a cold plate. If your fruit will not jelly you must either add pectin, bought at a shop (surely a base expedient), or give up and brew the stuff into wine, perhaps not a bad idea in itself.

Nowadays, with the realization that sugar is really quite bad for you, jam and fruit jellies are not made or consumed in such vast amounts, which is probably just as well. Of course, jelly does not have to be sweet or contain fruit. Jelly made with a type of gelatin known as isinglass was being used as a basis for sweet and savoury dishes from the sixteenth century.

CHOCOLATE AND CANDY MOULDS

METAL CHOCOLATE MOULD

COPPER JELLY MOULD

VICTORIAN COPPER JELLY MOULD

PRINCE OF WALES FEATHERS JELLY MOULD

POTTERY JELLY MOULD

GLAZED EARTHENWARE JELLY MOULD

METAL EASTER EGG MOULD

COPPER "TIMBALE" MOULD

CONFECTIONERY MOULD

CLASSIC COPPER JELLY MOULD

JELLY AND CANDY MOULDS
The housewife took great pride in presenting attractive desserts at the table, and there was a wide choice of decorative moulds to use for jellies, puddings and sweets. Jelly moulds were often made into elaborate castle shapes, while candy and confectionery moulds popularly came in the shapes of birds, animals and flowers. Moulds were also made in two halves, which were held together with straps while the confectionery set inside—the chocolate Easter egg is an obvious example.

CHILLING FOOD

MOVING ICE BLOCKS
Hoisting tongs were used to haul ice blocks on board ship and up steep slopes. They gripped the blocks securely as they were dragged or lifted.

HOISTING TONGS

 WENT TO SCHOOL IN SWITZERLAND and every winter we used to move up into the mountains to a ski resort called Villar sur Bex. The Palace Hotel, even at that late date, which must have been about 1927 or 1928, had its own natural ice plant. They had a large wooden frame at the back of the hotel on to which a man would play water from a hose every morning. The water would freeze almost instantly into the most wonderful shapes and, as the winter went on, the whole thing began to look like the creation of one of the architects of Kubla Khan's stately pleasure dome at Xanadu. In the spring men would wade in with sledge hammers and smash it all up (an operation in which I longed to assist) and then sled it all to the great cellar under the hotel, which doubled as an ice house. This store of ice would always last the hotel until the freezing cold winter came round again.

STORING AND TRANSPORTING ICE

From Tudor times on, the ice house was a common adjunct to most big country houses. The climate of northern Europe was colder then and only in Dickens' time was the snow-bound winter becoming more of a nostalgic memory than an actuality. In any event the ice houses that were built up and down the country could be stocked each winter with ice cut from the nearest pond, canal or river. As the nineteenth century wore on, and the British winter was no longer severe enough to provide enough ice to stock the ice houses, sailing ships, which had sailed to the Baltic with freights of coal, would return loaded with ice.

It was not as easy as one might suppose to obtain the ice needed to load the ships. Special ice picks were used to cut holes through the ice and saws were inserted into these holes and the ice sawn out in huge chunks. Irons designed for the purpose were

ICE HOUSES

There were conflicting views over the siting of an ice house. Some held that it should be constructed above ground in the shade of trees, and perhaps made into a garden feature. Others believed that an underground pit made the coolest ice house, but an important requirement for this type of ice house was that there should be good drainage. In either case, the ice house was lined with straw to keep the ice cold and to keep out the heat. Ice was inserted in the underground pit through an opening at the top and was accessible through an underground passage. Water was allowed to drain off whilst the ice was kept in the pit by the siting of a cartwheel directly over the drain.

GARDEN ICE HOUSE

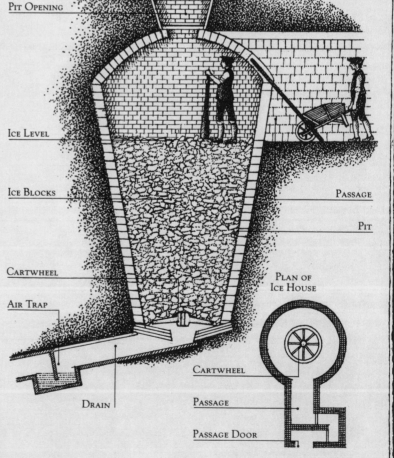

PIT OPENING

ICE LEVEL

ICE BLOCKS

CARTWHEEL

AIR TRAP

DRAIN

PASSAGE

PIT

PLAN OF ICE HOUSE

CARTWHEEL

PASSAGE

PASSAGE DOOR

inserted under a chunk and the whole thing—weighing perhaps tons—was levered up on to the uncut ice and dragged by horse to the waiting ship. Once there it would be slung up by tackles and dumped into the hold. In the United States ice was cut on various lakes in the north and transported to the warmer parts of the country and abroad. Ports in Britain housed great insulated ice warehouses by the 1830s to store the imported ice before it was distributed.

THE ICE BOX

Before the coming of refrigerators and, eventually, deep freezes, the ice box was in common use in households throughout the United States and, eventually, England. To begin with these were simply wooden boxes lined with zinc or slate and insulated most commonly with charcoal, ash or felt. Ice was delivered daily and the housewife placed it in the inner casing. She then put the fish or other food to be preserved on top of the ice. By the second half of the nineteenth century ice boxes were built into the top half of a chest or cupboard and the food placed in the bottom half. The cooler air from the ice box descended on to the food as the air warmed by the food rose to melt the ice. It was a very effective cooling system.

In Africa, we wild colonial boys used to build makeshift ice boxes called "charcoal coolers". We built the boxes out of galvanized steel sheet and constructed a wire-netting covering over them. We stuffed charcoal between the two and contrived a shallow water tray on top with small holes in the bottom of it. The water dripped from the tray down on to the charcoal and evaporated, taking the heat out of the box. Provided the air was dry enough the thing worked marvellously.

The ancient Greeks also understood this principle and kept drinking water in porous pottery containers. As the water nearest the edge of the vessel evaporated, the water remaining inside gradually cooled. Everyone who has soldiered in the desert will know the chargal, or canvas water-bag. You hung it on the mirror bracket of a lorry and the water always kept cool—much cooler than the desert air.

THE FIRST "FRIDGES"

The first refrigerators were wooden cabinets insulated with zinc and porcelain. Blocks of ice were kept in the top compartment, and the cold air from this cooled the food stored below, while the warm air from the food rose, gradually melting the ice.

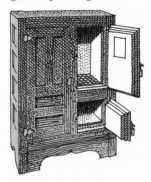

MAKING ICE IN THE HOME

Before refrigerators were common, ice-making machines could be found in many homes. The Raplin ice-maker was one of the many machines available. It froze water at the turn of a handle, making a block of ice in about twenty minutes. Once made, the ice block was put in the ice box where it kept perishable foods fresh.

THE RAPLIN ICE-MAKER

DOMESTIC PICKS AND SCOOPS

Ice picks were used to chip demarcation lines in a large block of ice so that smaller blocks could be sawn off. Ice scoops were used for shovelling up crushed ice.

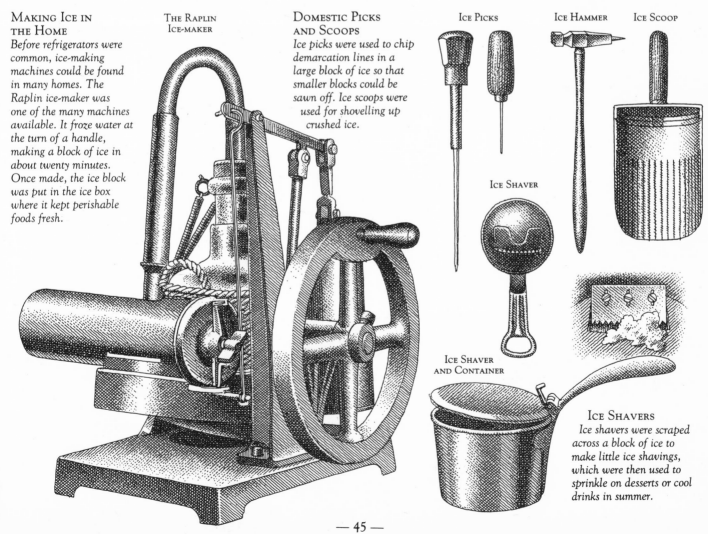

ICE PICKS

ICE HAMMER

ICE SCOOP

ICE SHAVER

ICE SHAVER AND CONTAINER

ICE SHAVERS

Ice shavers were scraped across a block of ice to make little ice shavings, which were then used to sprinkle on desserts or cool drinks in summer.

CLEANING & MAINTENANCE

I N SMALL FARMS AND COTTAGES *everything* was done in the kitchen, which very often doubled as the living room, too. Sometimes, in fact, it was the only downstairs room and keeping it clean was a major task. Slightly larger houses would also have a parlour—a freezing cold, often damp room, used only for formal occasions, such as funeral parties.

In large farmhouses and the country houses of even moderately prosperous families the kitchen was reserved for cooking only. Washing up and cleaning were done in a small adjoining room called the scullery and food was stored in the larder. Even crockery and cutlery were very often not kept in the kitchen itself, as any room with a fire in it tends to be rather dusty.

It was the fire that created the most cleaning problems. With an open fire soot is apt to fall down the chimney and all over the floor, and the wind is almost certain to blow smoke into the room. It was extremely difficult to maintain a high standard of cleanliness in these circumstances but, with the introduction of the enclosed stove in the early nineteenth century, smoke ceased to be such a problem.

SWEEPING THE FLOOR
Up until the nineteenth century most kitchen floors were made of beaten earth. Such a floor was usually swept with a besom broom until it became as hard and as smooth as concrete, but it could not be scrubbed with water in the way that a tiled

THE RANGE
The kitchen range involved a great deal of work for the housewife: each morning the fire-box had to be cleaned, the ashes removed, the flues swept, and the oven scraped, washed and dried. Then the whole iron case had to be black-leaded and the brass fittings polished vigorously till they shone.

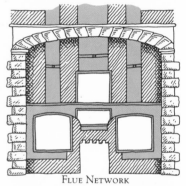

FLUE NETWORK

CLEANING THE FLUES
Warm air from the range fire was directed along a network of flues, or passages, to heat the ovens of the range. Soot was continually deposited in the flues and, to prevent them from becoming clogged, they had to be cleaned daily. Special long-handled flue brushes were used for this dirty but essential job.

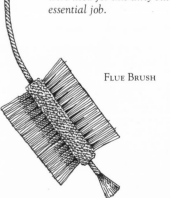

FLUE BRUSH

floor, for example, can be scrubbed. Although those with stone floors were not spared the weekly scrub, the sort of aseptic cleanliness that has become almost an obsession today was not possible.

I am not old enough to remember the regular visits of the sand man, although my mother used to tell me that the sand man visited me every night and sprinkled sand in my eyes to make me go to sleep. In earlier days most kitchen and dairy floors were sanded and so, often, were halls and stairs. Once a week perhaps the sand would be swept out, together with any dirt that had collected, and clean sand sprinkled on.

LEAVING THE KETTLE BLACK
For most of the history of civilization cooking was performed over an open fire (see pp.24–29) and it was this practice that gave rise to the saying about the pot calling the kettle black. For, anything that is hung over

an open fire becomes black very quickly, just as the hands of anyone supervising the cooking over an open fire tend to become black. It was pointless trying to remove the black from the pots and kettles as, within minutes of putting them back into use, they would be black again. However, many women would still scour them regularly with handfuls of sand.

The changeover to coal-burning grates in most of Britain during the eighteenth and nineteenth centuries increased rather than decreased the amount of kitchen cleaning, as coal is a far dirtier fuel than wood and carting coal about the house resulted in a constant stream of dirt and dust, which had to be removed immediately it fell or it would be trodden everywhere. Pots continued to be suspended above the fire or placed on hobs or trivets directly on top of the fire (see p.30), so they were still black.

MOPPING AND SCRUBBING
Stone and tile floors were mopped frequently using long-handled string or rag mops. Mopping was quite a skill—the floor had to be left clean yet almost dry! Wooden floors were always scrubbed on hands and knees, using flat scrubbing brushes, soapy water and lots of elbow grease. Strapped on knee-pads, or kneelers, were often worn for this gruelling task.

WEARING PATTENS
Pattens are wooden clogs or sandals with a raised wooden platform. Housewives wore them, with or without shoes, to keep their feet dry when they were mopping and swilling the floor.

LIFTS FOR SWILLING
Lifts were solid squares of pottery or stone that were set underneath the legs of dressers and chests to raise them off the floor. Then, when the floor was swilled and mopped, the furniture was kept dry.

"Basket" Slop Pail · Slop Pail and Lid · Tin Pail · Double Wing Stove Brush · Bass Sink Brush · Scrubbing Brush · Bent Oval Stove Brush · Ipper Hearth Brush · String Mop · Kneeler · Reeded Hearth Brush · Rag Mop

Keeping the Range Clean

The introduction of the enclosed, coal-burning range or kitchener (see p.31) meant that pots, frying pans, and kettles were no longer blackened by the smoke and could therefore be kept burnished and polished.

The smoke was led into the chimney by stove pipes, so it was impossible for soot to fall down and burst out into the room. Chimneys ceased to smoke very much, if at all, and the ashes were confined. But, if anything, there was even more cleaning to be done, for the great iron ranges sooted up very quickly and their numerous flues had to be swept out frequently. Wide-angled stove brushes were made especially for this purpose. I well remember the servants in the houses in which I spent my childhood spending much time black-leading the kitchen range with special little black-lead brushes with turned handles. This prevented it from rusting and made it shine; cooks took great pride in their gleaming ranges.

Shortage of Water

The difficulty of obtaining water (see p.86) made cleaning a problem for both city and country people. My old friend Mrs Light of Brockweir in Gloucestershire, a small-holder's wife, told me she used to bath the children every night and then wash the kitchen floor with the dirty water. Washing-up water was often used for the same purpose. In spite of such difficulties the great kitchen table was always kept scrubbed (as white as snow, the cook would boast) and, with the advent of tiles, the floor, too, was frequently scrubbed. In addition, stone hearths were whitened at least once a week with hearth stone.

Butlers and Footmen

Before the advent of stainless steel at the beginning of the twentieth century, cutlery had to be scrupulously cleaned and especially scrupulously dried or it would quickly corrode. Many larger households had knife cleaners which were operated by turning a handle. In great houses cleaning the silver generally fell to the butler or footman.

But most of the work was done by the cook and, as a reward for all her labour, she reigned over a glorious queendom. The gleaming black iron stove, with its hot coal fire visible behind its bars, was the focus of the house and, as a child, I far preferred the kitchen to any other room. The company there was better, too.

KNIFE CLEANER

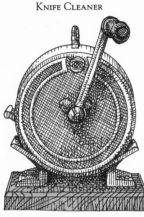

Cleaning Knives
Knives were cleaned by rubbing them to and fro on a long, flat board called a knife board, sprinkled with brick dust. They were then wiped clean. A knife-cleaning machine could clean up to ten knives at once. Knives were slotted into the holes around the rim and cleaned, at the turn of the handle, by a rotating brush covered with emery powder.

THE KITCHEN DRESSER

THE BEAUTIFUL OAK DRESSERS THAT FETCH such a high price in antique shops nowadays, only made their appearance in any great number in the eighteenth century with the advent of cheap china. Before that a few small shelves fixed on brackets to the walls and generally covered with American oil cloth, or paper with scalloped edges, sufficed for the few plates and utensils people owned. Saucepans and other pots were hung on nails fixed to the wall and cups, jugs and tumblers were placed in one small cupboard, sometimes glass-fronted, let into the thick stone wall. I know many old people, both in Ireland and Wales, who continue to manage perfectly happily with similar simple arrangements.

The first dresser consisted of a flat board fixed to the kitchen wall at waist height. Food was prepared or "dressed" on this hanging table. Soon shelves were fixed above the board and by the end of the seventeenth century cupboards were also constructed underneath. It was but a small step to joining the three elements together in one piece of furniture. The back of the dresser, which was often as tall as the room, was boarded and the shelves were set apart at different widths to suit different-sized crockery.

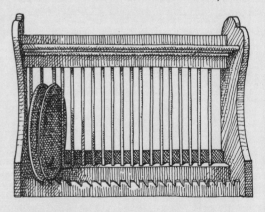

Racks for Storage
Before drawers and cupboards were commonly used, kitchen utensils were stored in open wooden racks. Plates and cutlery had separate racks, which stood on table tops or were hung on a convenient wall for easy access.

WASHING UP

THE HOUSEWIFE WOULD OFTEN clean her greasy dishes by rubbing ashes on them, for if you rub wood ash on greasy plates you make soap. To shift more stubborn dirt she would use sand or brick dust, which was once transported round the towns and villages by old men driving donkeys, and sold to housewives for cleaning dishes.

SINKS WITHOUT TAPS

In the days before the closed range, water was heated in the big black boilers that were either hung over the open fire or sat on hobs by the side of the fire. Provided that the housewife remembered to top them up, she had as constant a supply of hot water as any modern housewife. The only inconvenience was that she had to carry the hot water to the sink; she could not simply turn on a tap.

Kitchen or scullery sinks tended to be made of wood, or slate, if you lived in slate country. When the big commercial potteries started up, glazed stoneware sinks became commonplace. I remember many a cottage in which the sink drained into a bucket and the housewife had to empty the slops by flinging them outside the door whenever the bucket was full. Sometimes lead piping carried the dirty water through the wall and simply dumped it in the yard.

NOT SO LABOUR-INTENSIVE

Although there was a large amount of labour involved in washing up, it should be remembered that in days of old there was very little to wash up! I saw houses in the west of Ireland in the early 1950s that contained practically no crockery at all. There would be a huge black kettle hanging over the fire, an equally big and black pot, chiefly for cooking potatoes, and a few wooden bowls. When cooked, the potatoes were placed in a shallow basket and perched on top of the cooking pot; the family would sit about it on three-legged stools and eat with their fingers from the common stock. And the food, I imagine, tasted none the worse for that.

In Europe cheap china and earthenware infiltrated all classes of society from the late eighteenth century onwards and by Victorian times eating utensils had proliferated to absurd lengths in wealthier households and washing up had become a considerable chore. Happily the tendency now is towards greater simplicity.

WATER AVAILABILITY
Apart from the rain that ran off the cottage roof into the butt below, all water had to be fetched from the nearest well, spring, stream or village pump. By using a wooden yoke supported across the shoulders, the woman of the house could carry two buckets of water at a time.

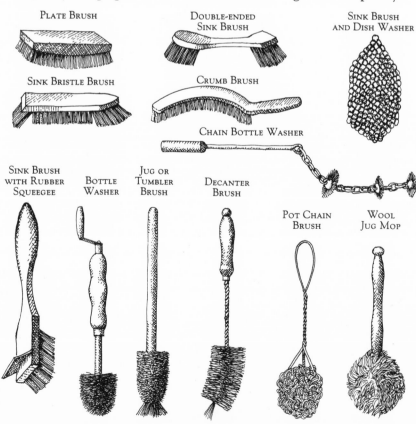

PLATE BRUSH

DOUBLE-ENDED SINK BRUSH

SINK BRUSH AND DISH WASHER

SINK BRISTLE BRUSH

CRUMB BRUSH

CHAIN BOTTLE WASHER

SINK BRUSH WITH RUBBER SQUEEGEE

BOTTLE WASHER

JUG OR TUMBLER BRUSH

DECANTER BRUSH

POT CHAIN BRUSH

WOOL JUG MOP

BRUSHES AND MOPS
There was a huge number of washing-up brushes and mops to choose from. The fan-shaped, stiff-fibred sink brush was very common and was used for scrubbing pots and pans as well as the sink. Short-handled bristle brushes were used for cleaning plates and, occasionally, sinks, while wire brushes called pot chains were used exclusively for cleaning pots. Long-handled wool mops or brushes were used for china and glass. Long, thin bottles were scoured with chain bottle washers: wooden, lead-weighted beads surrounded by bristles were set at intervals down the chain, which was connected to a wooden "stay" or handle, so that it could not drop to the bottom of the bottle, never to be seen again!

THE SINK

The arrival of piped water in the kitchen itself, either through a tap in the wall or a pump, changed the lives—and the kitchens—of people who had been used to carrying it long distances in all weathers. A wide, flat-bottomed stone sink, or "slop stone", was built against the wall under the tap: this was shallow enough to be used as a work-table for boning or chopping meat and poultry, gutting fish and preparing vegetables. The sink was set at a slight angle, taking the water down to a drain hole and into a bucket beneath or, better still, away through a waste pipe. More sophisticated glazed white stone sinks had a built-in overflow. Washing up was never done in the sink itself, but in a bowl or wooden tub standing in the sink. A separate, smaller, basin was kept for the more delicate jobs.

SLOP STONE

SLATE TROUGH AND PUMP

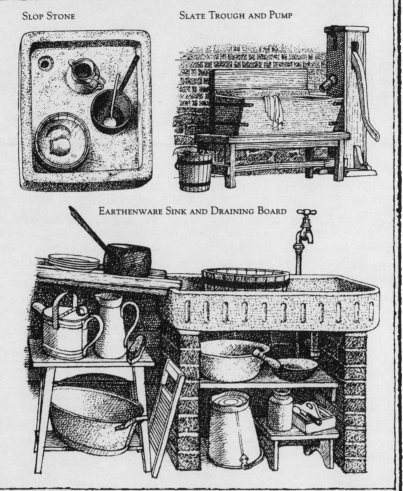

EARTHENWARE SINK AND DRAINING BOARD

SINK BASKET

Manufacturers began to produce special equipment for the sink at the turn of the last century, and an early twentieth-century kitchen might have boasted a perforated iron sink basket like the one below. This stood in the corner of the sink and any waste matter was drained through to catch solid material that might otherwise block the pipes.

ENAMELLED IRON
SINK BASKET

THE DEVELOPMENT OF PLATES

The earliest plate was made of bread. The dough (1) was cooked until it had risen (2), when it was turned over (3) until it had finished baking (4). The bread then had only to be cut in half (5) to make two "plates". Even when the trencher came to be made of solid wood, washing up was no chore: it would simply be wiped clean. The first real plates were made of pewter, which did not stand up well to frequent scouring. The growth of the Staffordshire potteries made cheap china and earthenware available and washing up began in earnest. The Victorian kitchen maid scoured endless dishes, whilst the more delicate china was washed at the dining table.

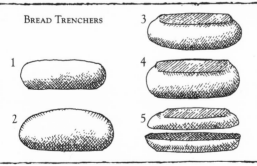

BREAD TRENCHERS

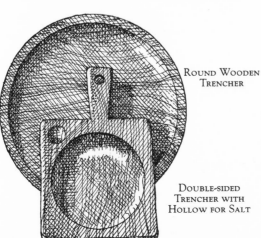

ROUND WOODEN
TRENCHER

DOUBLE-SIDED
TRENCHER WITH
HOLLOW FOR SALT

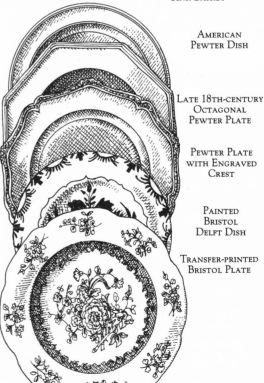

AMERICAN
PEWTER DISH

LATE 18TH-CENTURY
OCTAGONAL
PEWTER PLATE

PEWTER PLATE
WITH ENGRAVED
CREST

PAINTED
BRISTOL
DELFT DISH

TRANSFER-PRINTED
BRISTOL PLATE

PROVIDING WATER

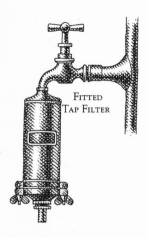

FITTED
TAP FILTER

DRINKING WATER
Unless you happened to live near a spring or fresh water stream, table water had to be boiled or filtered before it was fit to drink. As a result domestic water filters, whether fitted directly to the tap or cistern, or free-standing, became extremely common household items from the middle of the nineteenth century. Filtered water tended to taste flat and servants in well-to-do houses would pour the water from the filter into the table jug from a great height, or throw it back and forth between two jugs to aerate it.

APS WERE UNKNOWN TO MOST country people during my childhood, sixty years ago. Every farmhouse and cottage had a rain butt to store the rain water so prized for washing because it was soft—I seem to remember that cats were always drowning in them. However, the rain butt never provided enough water for the whole household and more had to be fetched, as a routine chore, from a pond or well. Many houses actually contained a well under the floor in the scullery or kitchen and sometimes the inhabitants benefited from the luxury of a pump, in which case the water supply was no problem at all! Generally, though, the well was situated at the bottom of the garden and the water had to be carried into the house. Lucky was the family that lived near a spring, for their water would be clean and fresh to drink.

Occasionally streams and rivers were polluted by untreated sewage and industrial waste, and water from a shallow well could be contaminated by drainage from the scullery or privy. In such cases, drinking water had to be boiled and some country dwellers constructed their own filters. They filled a wooden bucket or barrel with Fuller's earth or sand and poured the doubtful water into it, drawing it from the bottom by means of a small tap as it was needed.

Piped water is still not universal in the countryside and plenty of people still carry water some distance. Many country people declined piped water when it was offered to them because they didn't like the taste of it, most of it being heavily chlorinated. You got used to the bugs in your own horse pond and they did you no harm, they claimed.

WATER IN THE TOWNS
By the mid-nineteenth century water was piped to many towns in England from outlying districts. This did not mean that every house in the town had its own water taps: one tap at the end of the street for communal use was much more usual. Indeed, it was only after the Second World War that indoor water taps became common in the poorer houses in towns—generally one brass tap in the scullery and nothing more.

Although water was supplied by conduits in many towns and cities, mains and household drainage was still appalling and water supply to the poorer districts almost non-existent until the town corporations began to take over responsibility from the private, profit-making water companies in the second half of the nineteenth century. Even then progress was slow and piecemeal, and drawing unpolluted water for drinking in urban areas continued to be a problem. This unhealthy situation gave rise to the development of the domestic filter.

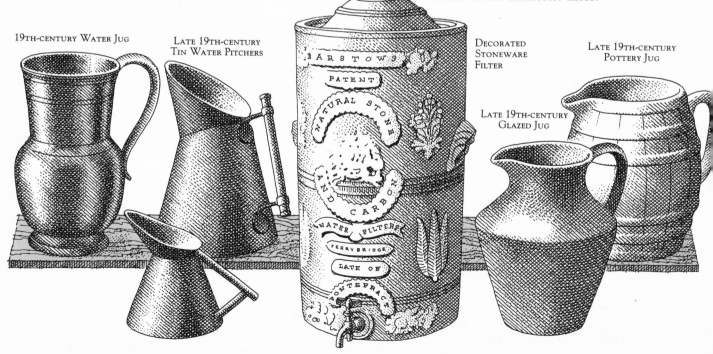

19TH-CENTURY WATER JUG

LATE 19TH-CENTURY
TIN WATER PITCHERS

DECORATED
STONEWARE
FILTER

LATE 19TH-CENTURY
POTTERY JUG

LATE 19TH-CENTURY
GLAZED JUG

TEA MAKING

UST AS AMERICANS COULD NOT really continue to function without coffee, so the inhabitants of the British Isles could scarcely support life without tea. It is also a fact that Americans seem totally unable to master the art of tea making but have no trouble making coffee, while the British fail shamefully at making coffee but produce excellent cups of tea—perhaps it has something to do with the Boston Tea Party.

Tea found its way to Britain in the seventeenth century, when it was probably imported by the Dutch. The British were used to "infusing" herb drinks and soon adopted tea despite its being expensive. By the end of the eighteenth century tea drinking was widespread and all watery hot drinks had become known as tea. Moralists condemned it, saying that it led to idleness and gossip. William Cobbett held the view that "the rattle of the tea tackle" was "the short road to the gaolhouse and the brothel". Today, however, many a charlady manages to get through twenty or thirty cups of the stuff a day and still avoid both institutions.

THE ART OF MAKING PERFECT TEA
The secret of making really good tea lies essentially in the amount of time the water remains on the leaves, although, of course, the water should be freshly drawn and the pot warmed first. According to priests returning from China in the seventeenth century, the tea should stand for "as long as it takes to say three Pater Nosters slowly".

EARLY 19TH-CENTURY DUTCH TEA URN

MAKING AND TAKING TEA
Many of the first teapots were of a shallow, rounded design, to allow room for the leaves to expand. However, the globular-shaped teapot copied from the Chinese design soon became more fashionable. Elegant silver, brass and copper tea-kettles, which could be heated by a spirit stove, became popular for drawing-room use, together with the tea urn. The first china teacups and saucers were made in the mid-eighteenth century and the popularity of tea drinking helped the enormous growth of the ceramic industry.

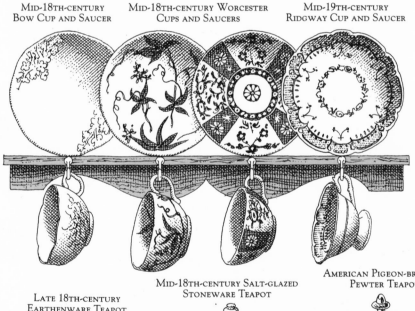

MID-18TH-CENTURY BOW CUP AND SAUCER

MID-18TH-CENTURY WORCESTER CUPS AND SAUCERS

MID-19TH-CENTURY RIDGWAY CUP AND SAUCER

LATE 18TH-CENTURY EARTHENWARE TEAPOT

EARLY 19TH-CENTURY STAFFORDSHIRE EARTHENWARE TEAPOT

MID-18TH-CENTURY SALT-GLAZED STONEWARE TEAPOT

AMERICAN PIGEON-BREASTED PEWTER TEAPOT

EARLY 18TH-CENTURY SILVER TEA-KETTLE AND STAND

STRAINING THE LEAVES

Although some teapots were fitted with spout strainers, most were not and the wire tea strainer abounded. Porcelain strainers were also made but for upper-class drawing-room use only.

WIRE STRAINER

TEA PARTY

Tea parties were genteel, restrained affairs from which children were normally excluded. These three girls show that it was by no means just the grown ups who took tea drinking seriously.

STORING TEA

To protect its delicate flavour, tea should be kept in an airtight tin, where moisture and strong odours cannot get to it. When it first arrived in Britain tea was very expensive and the first tea caddies came equipped with locks, so that the mistress of the house could dole out only as much as was required daily to the servants. Caddies were made of silver, earthenware and wood and some had compartments for different teas.

LUDWIGSBURG TEA CADDY — ENGRAVED TEA CADDY

In the tea-producing areas of Sri Lanka and India a method of brewing tea has been developed that would appal any English tea guzzler. The tea is brewed, mixed with lots of milk and plenty of sugar and then poured from glass to glass (it is drunk from glass or metal tumblers) until it foams like beer. Strangely, in those climates, it tastes rather good drunk like this.

As for the British soldier, he would be a miserable fellow without his tea and would certainly be defeated in every war. In Africa and Burma during the Second World War, tea was commonly made in four-gallon petrol tins heated over a fire built of twigs. A double handful of tea leaves would be dumped into the boiling water, together with a couple of tins of condensed milk and a double handful of sugar. We would then each dip our mess tins into it—drinking tea out of the corner of a rectangular mess tin was an experience all its own. This tea was very refreshing and there was no way that we could have carried on the war without it. Both Nelson and the Duke of Wellington, we are told, would not go to war without their tea and the duke took his famous silver teapot with him everywhere.

The Russians and Persians are also addicted to tea. They make it in graceful samovars, pouring water into a jacket around a cylinder full of burning charcoal. Drinking tea is gradually becoming more popular throughout the rest of Europe, too, but Continental Europeans still do not really know how to make it. Furthermore, they drink it out of glass tumblers and commit other barbarous practices—unfortunately, use of the pernicious tea-bag is widespread in those countries.

THE RITUAL OF TEA DRINKING

The making and drinking of tea bears a ritual quality in some countries—a ritual usually presided over by the female of the species. You will often hear one of a group of tough and macho navvies say to another on requesting that he pour out the tea, "You be mother!" In Japan the tea ritual has been elevated to the status of a religious ceremony and even in Britain it can be quite an art. Anyone who has had the privilege of taking a delicate cup of China tea, together with cucumber sandwiches and toasted teacakes, with an English country vicar's wife out on the lawn will know how different from the brutish swilling of "char" out of chipped enamelled mugs tea drinking can be.

COFFEE MAKING

BYSSINIAN GOATHERDS, WE ARE told, noticed that their charges leapt about in a happy and abandoned manner after eating the berries of a certain small tree and, wishing to share in their felicity, they ate some of the berries themselves. They didn't have to eat many before they became addicted to them. No doubt they tried to soften them by boiling them, and on doing so they found that the flavoured water that remained was what they were after, and the noble art of coffee making was born.

Coffee drinking spread rapidly throughout the east African and Arab world, where it holds first place in the league of beverages to this day. If you make a social or business call in any Arab country, the coffee is inevitably brought out. The Arab coffee pot is an elegant vessel, often with Koranic scripts incised on it, and the cups are very small. The coffee is drunk black and very sweet, and there is always a sediment of finely ground coffee at the bottom of each cupful. On being proffered a second cup it is polite to accept it. However, on the offer of a third, good manners require that you refuse it.

ROASTING AND GRINDING THE BEANS

When I was in southern Africa before the Second World War coffee was very cheap and we used to buy it by the hundredweight sack. We roasted the berries in a frying pan over the open fire, ground them in a small hand mill, and then threw a handful of the ground coffee in a saucepan of boiling water. After the mixture had boiled for a few minutes we would take up a burning stick from the fire and plunge it into the brew. This was supposed to cause the grounds to sink. We would then pour it out to drink. I have never tasted better coffee and would prefer it to filter coffee today.

COFFEE DRINKING

In 1650 the first coffee house was opened in Britain. Coffee houses abounded in the eighteenth century but coffee drinking was gradually superseded by tea drinking as the nation's favourite drink.

It is interesting to note that in England today, where tea is the hot beverage of the masses, there is a certain snobbery about drinking coffee, and in America, where coffee is the universal drink, the opposite is true. Moreover the British are as inept at making coffee as the Americans are at making tea. So difficult and mysterious does this simple process seem to them that they resort to those horrible ersatz mixtures, either in powder or liquid form, which have no right to be called by the name of coffee. Perhaps there should be an exchange of missionaries between the two countries.

IRON COFFEE ROASTER

COFFEE ROASTERS AND MILLS

As coffee became more popular, a wide variety of hand-operated roasters and mills was produced. Pan-like iron roasters were developed for roasting beans over the kitchen range. The roasted beans were then ground in a mill and the ground coffee stored in a drawer.

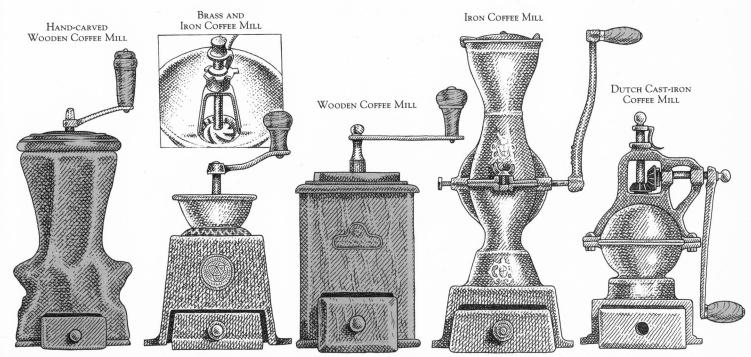

HAND-CARVED WOODEN COFFEE MILL

BRASS AND IRON COFFEE MILL

WOODEN COFFEE MILL

IRON COFFEE MILL

DUTCH CAST-IRON COFFEE MILL

POTS, URNS AND BOILERS

The business of coffee making soon developed its own special rules of etiquette. After the coffee was made, it was kept hot in a coffee pot, from which it was served at table. There was a vast array of pots, urns and boilers for the housewife to choose from. They ranged from plain earthenware or tin pots to the more ornate silver urns mounted on splayed legs over a spirit heater and fitted with brass taps.

GROUND COFFEE

FILTER

HOT WATER

THE REVOLUTIONARY PERCOLATOR

At the beginning of the nineteenth century Count Rumford invented the percolator. Ground coffee was compressed in a container inside the coffee pot, which had a filter at the bottom. Heated water passed through the coffee and the filter and into the space beneath.

TIN COFFEE BOILER

COFFEE URN WITH BRASS TAP

SILVER COFFEE URN

EARTHENWARE COFFEE POT

SPOUT STRAINER

COFFEE INFUSER

TINPLATE COFFEE PERCOLATOR

TIN COFFEE POT

ALE & BEER MAKING

EFORE THE CONTINENTAL HABIT OF hopping ale was introduced in about 1520, the English drank ale not beer. "Turkeys, Heresies, Hops and Beer All came to England in the One Year." Beer is simply ale that has had some of the dried flowers of the hop plant boiled in it. The hop, *Humulus lupulus*, is closely related to the nettle and, incidentally, to the cannabis plant. It has a bitter-tasting flower and once people began to flavour their ale with it they never returned to the old ways. Henry VIII passed laws to prevent hops from entering the country but nobody took any notice of them. I have made ale without hops and it is insipid stuff.

MAKING THE MALT

The main constituent of beer is not hops but barley. The grain of barley is mostly starch, which, though rich in stored energy, is not soluble, and before the beer can be brewed the grain of the barley must be chitted, or caused to germinate. After germinating, the starch can be turned into sugar, which is soluble. It is the sugar that is turned into alcohol by that marvellous living organism, yeast. Traditionally, the maltster germinates the barley grain by wetting it and keeping it warm for about ten days until it spears, chits or shoots, as countrymen say. He then kilns it, turning it on a perforated plate with a fire underneath. It is then cracked in a mill after which it is ready for brewing.

The process of malting takes place today in huge maltings, where the maltose, which is the sugar produced inside the grain, is extracted and sent to the brewery. Beer made from maltose is nothing like as good as that made by the old method of steeping the whole malt. I have made many gallons of both sorts and I know.

Once, many small country mills combined the malting of barley with the grinding of grain. An old neighbour of mine in Wales used to malt the local farmer's barley for them in a little water-driven mill.

BREWING THE BEER

Whenever the malt was made, the beer tended to be made by the individual householder, in the countryside at least. However, the unholy alliance between the big commercial brewers and the nonconformist

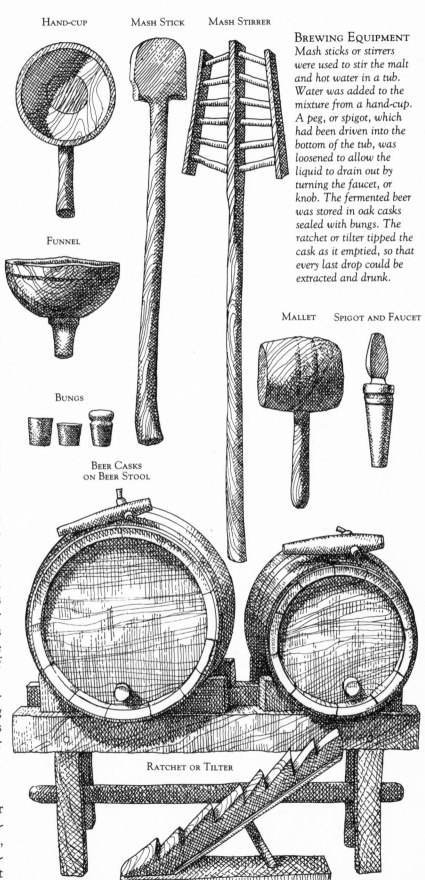

HAND-CUP   MASH STICK   MASH STIRRER

FUNNEL

BUNGS

BREWING EQUIPMENT
Mash sticks or stirrers were used to stir the malt and hot water in a tub. Water was added to the mixture from a hand-cup. A peg, or spigot, which had been driven into the bottom of the tub, was loosened to allow the liquid to drain out by turning the faucet, or knob. The fermented beer was stored in oak casks sealed with bungs. The ratchet or tilter tipped the cask as it emptied, so that every last drop could be extracted and drunk.

MALLET   SPIGOT AND FAUCET

BEER CASKS ON BEER STOOL

RATCHET OR TILTER

churches that grew up in Victorian times caused laws to be passed that restricted home brewing. Despite the laws, it lingered in some places and in the part of west Wales that I farmed for twenty years it continued in unbroken tradition.

The process is simple. The malt—the crushed, sprouted grain—is put into a container, together with water heated to a temperature of 150°F—if it is any hotter, the water will destroy the enzymes that make the beer. The resulting sloppy porridge is called the mash. The mash is left, well wrapped up to keep the heat in, for twelve hours or so and then the liquid in it (the spree or wort) is strained off, put into another container and boiled. A small quantity of hops, generally wrapped in a muslin bag for ease of removal, is added to the boiling spree.

After boiling for say an hour the spree is poured into a container and cooled rapidly. Speed in cooling is important, for if too many wild yeast organisms become established in it they may spoil the flavour of the beer. As soon as it is cool enough for yeast to survive, the yeast is added. The stuff is then left to ferment for several days.

STORING THE BEER

Traditionally all beer-making vessels and storage containers were made of oak and it is not imagination that leads one to think that beer stored in oaken casks has a superior flavour to that stored, say, in stainless steel. However, it is necessary to point out that the oaken casks must be scrupulously clean before the beer is poured into them and the reason brewers and innkeepers tend to favour metal casks is that oaken ones, carelessly cleaned, can cause beer to be undrinkable. But the good farmer's or cottager's wife who brews beer will ensure that the oaken casks are perfectly clean and her beer will be like the nectar of the gods.

REAL ALE

The Real Ale Campaign in Britain saved British beer in the nick of time. The big commercial brewers had gone over to pasteurized, highly chemicalized, top-pressure beer in aluminium or stainless steel casks. This stuff would keep nearly indefinitely and was quite consistent in taste but it took all the *pleasure* out of beer drinking. But now, thank God and the Real Ale enthusiasts, real beer is coming back and gradually the corrupted taste of the English beer drinker is being re-educated.

The pernicious law that prevented home brewing has now been lifted, in the British Isles at least, and brewing is enjoying a strong revival. Hopefully home brewers will gradually be weaned from kit beer, or beer made from malt extract, and graduate to the harder discipline of brewing with true malt.

BARREL SIZES
Strictly speaking a barrel should only be called a barrel if it holds thirty-six gallons. Each of the seven sizes of "barrel" is given a specific name by the cooper, according to its capacity (see below).

BUTT
108 GAL

PUNCHEON
72 GAL

HOGSHEAD
54 GAL

BARREL
36 GAL

KILDERKIN
18 GAL

FIRKIN
9 GAL

PIN
4½ GAL

BREWING AT HOME
Large households often had their own private brewhouses. These took a lot of the physical effort out of home brewing. The equipment was arranged on varying levels to make the brewing process run more efficiently. The copper supplied water along a pipe to the mash tun, which contained malt. The liquid produced from the water and malt (the wort) was in turn pumped back to the copper, where it was boiled with the hops, and then piped to the cooler to cool before the yeast was added and the beer was left to ferment.

BEER TANKARDS

Tankards were popular drinking vessels for beer and cider up to the eighteenth century. They were usually made of pewter or silver and came in varying shapes and styles. The thumb-piece, the knob attached to the hinged lid of the tankard, was often decoratively fashioned.

CYLINDRICAL
ENGRAVED TANKARD

DOUBLE-VOLUTE
THUMB-PIECE

PLUMED
THUMB-PIECE

OPEN CHAIRBACK
THUMB-PIECE

LEAF SPRAY
THUMB-PIECE

BUD
THUMB-PIECE

BIFURCATED
THUMB-PIECE

QUART
TANKARD

BRASS PINT
TANKARD

BRISTOL TULIP-SHAPED
TANKARD

PEWTER-MOUNTED
TANKARD

ALE MULLERS

Ale was heated with spices over hot coals in a muller, or warmer, to make mulled ale. Mullers were sometimes slipper-shaped so that they would not fall over when full.

BEER MULLER
ON HOT COALS

COPPER BOOT
ALE WARMER

TIN BOOT
ALE WARMER

COPPER ALE WARMER

COPPER ALE MULLER
WITH SPIRIT HEATER

BEER MEASURES

In an ale-house, beer was often served in containers known as measures which, as their name suggests, held an exact measure of beer. A popular Irish measure was known as the "harvester" or, sometimes, the "haystack", which came in sizes ranging from half a gill to a gallon capacity. Bottled measures were also available. These were stoppered with bungs and had handles to make them easy to carry.

EARTHENWARE
"HARVESTER" BOTTLE

COPPER ALE MEASURE

IRISH "HAYSTACK"
MEASURE

WINE & CIDER MAKING

RAPES AND APPLES, THOUGH VERY different in most ways, have one thing in common: they both have on their skins the benevolent yeasts that are capable of turning their juice into superb fermented drinks. If you squeeze the juice out of grapes and leave it alone completely you will end up with wine. If you do the same thing with apples you will end up with cider.

WINE MADE FROM GRAPES
Wine is made by peasants and farmers in every country in Europe where the sugar content of the grape is sufficiently high. The process is so simple and the product so delightful and beneficial that it would be amazing if they did not make it.

First the grapes must be crushed or broken. Traditionally this is done with the feet: in this way the grapes are crushed but the pips are left whole. If the pips are broken they might spoil the flavour of the wine. The crushed grapes are then pressed to extract the juice, which is then simply left in a vat and allowed to ferment in its own yeasts. If red wine is being made the skins of the red grapes are left in the must, or grape juice, during the fermentation process. If white wine is required the skins are removed before fermentation.

OTHER SORTS OF WINE
Grapes are not the only fruit from which you can make excellent wine—blackberries and elderberries also make good wine, but for these, as for most of the flower and vegetable wines, you need to add boiling water and yeast. The yeast is thrown into the liquid or placed on slices of dry bread called "toasts", which are then floated on top. The liquid is then left to ferment. Parsnip and

CIDER CHEESE PRESSES
Once the apples had been crushed to a pulp, the juice was extracted using a cheese press. The pulp was wrapped in cloths to make cheeses and then stacked in the press. This had either one central screw or two side screws which supported a heavy block of wood. When the screws were turned by means of a long pole the block of wood was forced down on the stacked cheeses. This pressure squeezed out the juice, which was collected in a vat below.

TREADING THE GRAPES

HAND-OPERATED CIDER PRESS

CRUSHING THE GRAPES
This is the first stage of wine making. Crushing the grapes enables the fermentation process to begin, as the yeast present on the skin of the grapes reacts with the sugar in the fruit. Traditionally it was done by treading the grapes in a barrel with bare feet. In this way the fruit was crushed but the pips were left whole. Broken pips added an unpleasant taste to the wine.

potato wines are old favourites in England and recipes for dandelion wine go back a good few years. Ginger is usually added to dandelion wine to give it extra flavour and lemon and orange rind are often included.

Making Cider

Cider making is still performed on many a Somerset and Devon farm in England. The apples are first crushed—traditionally in a circular granite trough, or chace, around which a huge circular stone is trundled by a blindfolded horse. The crushed apples are then wrapped in strips of coarse hessian cloth to make what are called cheeses, which are laid, separated by square planks, under a press and great pressure exerted upon them. After the juice has been forced out, the cheeses are overhauled by stirring the mush about in the cloths, and then subjected to more pressure to extract even more juice. Finally the spent mush is given to those great waste-disposal units, the pigs.

The juice is then pumped into great tuns, or casks, often as tall as a house, and left there to ferment. Many farmers add sugar or syrup, which is cheating in a way, but modern tastes cannot always cope with the extreme dryness of pure rough cider, called scrumpy by aficionados. When fermentation is in progress the cider is said to be hungry. There are many stories, most one suspects apocryphal, of cider makers throwing legs of beef or other meat into the cider vats to give strength to the brew, and it is said that if a rat, or a cat, or indeed the farmer himself, happens to fall into the vat of fermenting liquor nothing will be left of him (except, one supposes, in the case of the farmer, his buttons).

Adding Spirits

In Normandy the tradition of cider making is well developed but I would not put my neck out and make any comparisons between the virtues of French and English or Welsh cider. The Normans also make calvados by distilling cider (the roughest cider, produced by swilling the crushed mass with water) into a spirit. The west countrymen in England are prevented from practising this beneficial skill for their own use by stupid laws. In apple-growing country in America people make applejack by distilling cider. Some allow the cider to freeze: the water turns to ice before the alcohol and is thrown away to leave an extremely potent brew. Owners of deep freezes please note.

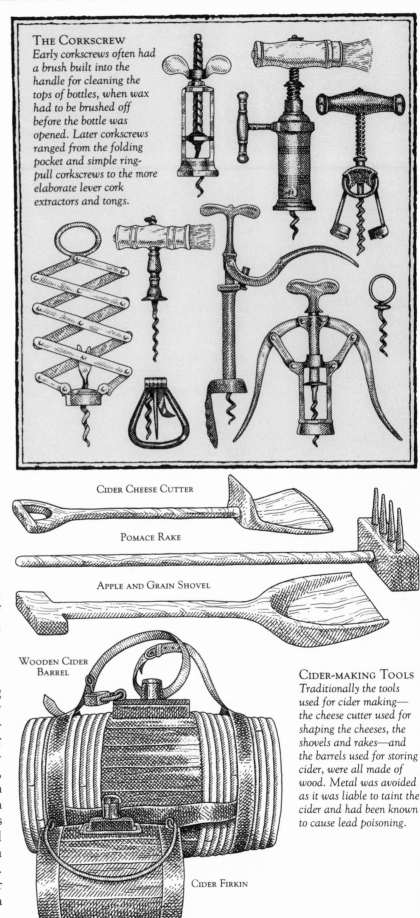

THE CORKSCREW
Early corkscrews often had a brush built into the handle for cleaning the tops of bottles, when wax had to be brushed off before the bottle was opened. Later corkscrews ranged from the folding pocket and simple ring-pull corkscrews to the more elaborate lever cork extractors and tongs.

CIDER CHEESE CUTTER

POMACE RAKE

APPLE AND GRAIN SHOVEL

WOODEN CIDER BARREL

CIDER FIRKIN

CIDER-MAKING TOOLS
Traditionally the tools used for cider making— the cheese cutter used for shaping the cheeses, the shovels and rakes—and the barrels used for storing cider, were all made of wood. Metal was avoided as it was liable to taint the cider and had been known to cause lead poisoning.

HERBS & SPICES

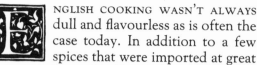

ENGLISH COOKING WASN'T ALWAYS dull and flavourless as is often the case today. In addition to a few spices that were imported at great expense from the East, plenty of native herbs were grown and used liberally in cooking and many herbs that seem pretty exotic to us today—Mediterranean plants like oregano and angelica—were well known to English gardeners in Elizabethan times.

THE VALUE OF HERBS

Herbs have long been valued for their medicinal qualities and in the Middle Ages monks began obtaining those herbs known to have physic properties by the ancient Greeks from orders on the Continent. They planted them in their gardens and acted as physicians to the neighbourhood until the dissolution of the monasteries.

Herbs were grown in the manor house gardens, too, from the Middle Ages. The lady of the manor treated the minor ailments of her family and servants, and sometimes the neighbours, too. She prepared, dried and distilled the herbs for medicinal, culinary and scenting purposes in the still room (see Home Doctoring p.113).

HERB GARDENS

Culinary and medicinal herbs were generally to be found in separate parts of the garden. In the monastery garden, culinary herbs were planted in a series of rectangular beds with paths between them for easy access. They were usually planted near the kitchen along with some vegetables. The physic herb garden was planted near the infirmary.

The herb garden at the manor house was often elaborate and formal arrangements such as chequerboard patterns and wheels were favoured. Patterns of knots based on lacework designs were very fashionable among the rich during the sixteenth and seventeenth centuries: herbs such as thyme, marjoram and lavender outlined the basic pattern and if open knots were created, they were filled with flowers.

Even the poorest cottager had a kitchen herb garden. This was not a formal knot garden but a simple "patch" in which the housewife grew her favourite culinary herbs, together with herbs for making perfumes, ointments and pot-pourris.

KNOT GARDENS

The knot garden was created in the sixteenth century. Different herbs—scented, culinary and medicinal—were planted in such a way that the textures and colours of the foliage overlapped to produce the impression of cords looping over and under one another.

COOKING WITH HERBS AND SPICES

Sage, parsley, fennel, thyme, mint, savory and garlic were popularly grown in the Middle Ages to flavour the main meal of the poor—vegetable broth or pottage—and to make green sauces to accompany fish. The rich required strongly flavoured and scented sauces to disguise the often tainted meat and game that they feasted on. It was fashionable to perfume food during the sixteenth and seventeenth centuries, when sweet herbs, or the bouquet garni, were introduced.

With the opening of trade with the East through the East India Company, spices began to be incorporated into cooking and even to replace herbs. Spices are aromatic berries, buds, bark, fruit, roots or flower stigmas taken from various plants grown in hot countries. Soon spice dealers and grocers were selling a wide range of spices and herbs, both fresh and dried, to housewives in the towns and sadly the herb garden began to disappear until today it can be found in only the most remote rural home. However, there is nothing to prevent you from planting your own herb garden or border. What could be more delightful and useful than a simple herb "patch" with your own favourite culinary and tried and tested medicinal herbs? You might even like to plant a camomile lawn.

BELL GLASSES

Bell glasses were, in effect, miniature greenhouses. About eight inches wide and made from clear glass in the shape of a bell, they were placed over young cuttings and tender plants in the ground in winter to protect them from the cold and frost.

ESSENTIAL TOOLS

Gardening tools have hardly changed. The hoe and fork were used for loosening the soil and removing weeds, and the trowel and onion hoe for digging holes and making planting channels.

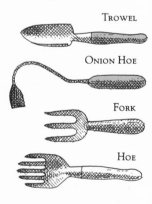

TROWEL

ONION HOE

FORK

HOE

STORAGE AND PREPARATION

Herbs and spices were dried before being stored in one of a variety of containers. The chest-of-drawers spice box had a drawer for every spice. There were also pie-shaped and stacked column boxes. In the latter, spices were kept in separate sections which screwed together to form a column. Some tin boxes were divided into cake sections, leaving the centre space for nutmeg. When the spices were needed, they were pounded in a pestle and mortar. Dried herbs were finely chopped with iron choppers before being used.

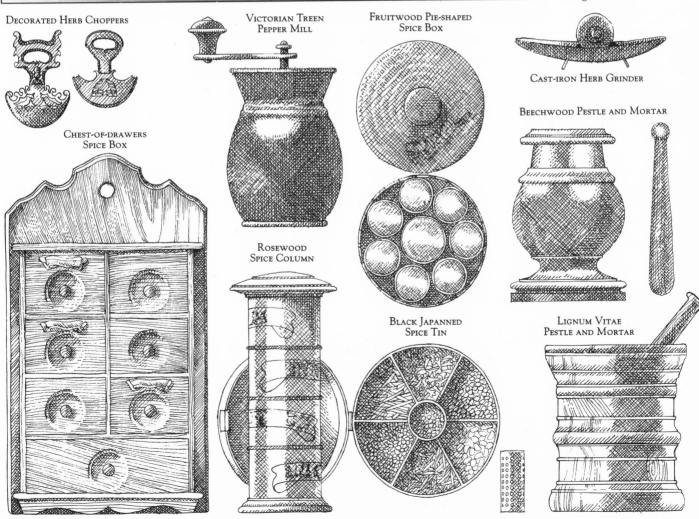

DECORATED HERB CHOPPERS

VICTORIAN TREEN PEPPER MILL

FRUITWOOD PIE-SHAPED SPICE BOX

CAST-IRON HERB GRINDER

CHEST-OF-DRAWERS SPICE BOX

BEECHWOOD PESTLE AND MORTAR

ROSEWOOD SPICE COLUMN

BLACK JAPANNED SPICE TIN

LIGNUM VITAE PESTLE AND MORTAR

KEEPING LIVESTOCK

HE IRISH PEASANTS USED TO CALL the pig "the man who pays the rent", and "a pig in the sty and a pig in the pot!" was an oft-used phrase of my rural neighbours in Wales. Of course, there should have been no rent to pay and the Irishman should have had the pig himself for the sustenance of his family, but that's another story.

Only fifty years ago it would have been considered odd if a country house or cottage did not have a pigsty attached to it. Sties were strongly built of brick or stone because something that all pigs have in common is a predilection for pulling down and totally destroying their housing. Even so, if your pig could get his snout into it somehow, he would, and before you knew where you were the whole thing was in ruins and your pig was roaming free. For pigs do not like to be cooped up and, indeed, always used to be kept out of doors, when they were commonly ringed, like the pig that featured in *The Owl and the Pussycat*, to lessen the amount of havoc that they could create.

In his book, *Cottage Economy*, William Cobbett advised every countryman to keep a cow. In his day many did, but the practice was dying as the "big bull frogs", as he termed the grasping larger farmers, were grabbing all the land, including the old commons, for their own private use.

THE FAMILY HOLDING
A family that could fatten a pig or two a year and also milk a cow was a family that would never know real poverty, for these animals fitted marvellously into the natural ecology of a family holding. The pig consumed all the vegetable and animal wastes that are nowadays carted away at great expense and dumped. It also provided plenty of good manure for the garden, in which cabbages and kale were grown for the cow as well as the humans. The cow provided milk, butter, cheese and buttermilk for the family and whey (full of protein and minerals) for the pig. It also conferred fertility on the land.

Such a family might also have had a few dozen hens, which lived partly on the undigested grain that the cow voided. They helped to keep down the baleful insect population *and* provided chicken meat and eggs. During my childhood, goats were common in country areas, as people with insufficient land to keep a cow could tether goats along the roadside. They were even known as the poor man's cow! If there was a pond or a stream nearby, ducks were an obvious component and, if there was enough grass on the holding, or access to the grassy common, geese were, too. A householder who had all, or even some, of these animals and a good garden didn't need any dole money, even if there had been any!

DOMESTIC LIVESTOCK
Other commonly owned domestic livestock were tame rabbits, which were bred for meat, and ferrets. Traditionally the children looked after the rabbits, coming home with huge armfuls of sheep's parsley, clover, hog weed and other vegetation garnered from the road verges on the way from school. The ferrets were kept for poaching rabbits. A lad with a ferret and a few purse nets could go out at night and return with a rabbit or two for the family. Rabbit pie or stew made a magnificent meal for the whole family, particularly if it had a lump of fat bacon thrown in it. The rabbit hutches and ferret houses were usually made out of old packing cases: doors were hinged on them with strips of leather and a piece of the wood was cut out and replaced by wire netting. I remember many a cottage with these appurtenances sitting at the bottom of the garden.

Keeping pigeons was much more widespread fifty years ago than it is now. Men in the grimmest of industrial conurbations would keep a shed full of racing pigeons, which they railed off to far destinations on weekends, their hearts with them as they winged through the sky on their way home. Country people, too, would keep pigeons, sometimes to eat, sometimes just to look at: pouting pigeons, tumblers, fan-tails and many other ornamental breeds gave delight.

Country people always had a dog and a cat or two as well. The unluckier dogs would spend much of their time chained outside the back door to a kennel or an old wooden barrel turned on its side. Most of them were luckier, though; they were friends of the family and lolled in front of the fire upon a dirty old rag rug, which they saw as theirs by right. As for the cats, they were a law unto themselves, of course.

THE MEAT HOOK
This was an iron hook used for suspending joints of ham in the chimney, where they would be smoked from the fire and thus preserved.

PIGSTIES

In medieval times, pigs roamed in herds, under the charge of a swineherd. During the eighteenth century, they were moved back to the farmyard and changed, through selective breeding, from being hairy and hardy, to being pink and bristly, and vulnerable to cold weather and draughts. Pigs needed some form of housing and shelter, so pigsties were developed.

The first pigsty was a low, loose box, about four feet high, with a ventilation slit or window opening, and a door leading to a small exercise yard. The exercise yard was surrounded by a tall, stout wall and a chute led from the outside of the wall to the trough to prevent the hungry pigs stampeding the person feeding them.

Some pigsties doubled up as hen houses, thus saving space and buildings. The hens were kept above the pigsty in the loft which was accessible for egg collection and feeding, via outdoor stone steps. The Welsh pig pen differed in shape, being round with a conical roof, and built entirely of stone. Large-scale pigsties were known as piggeries and consisted of a series of walled boxes, which looked like a single-storey cow barn. There was a feeding passage and sometimes a manure passage, both under cover.

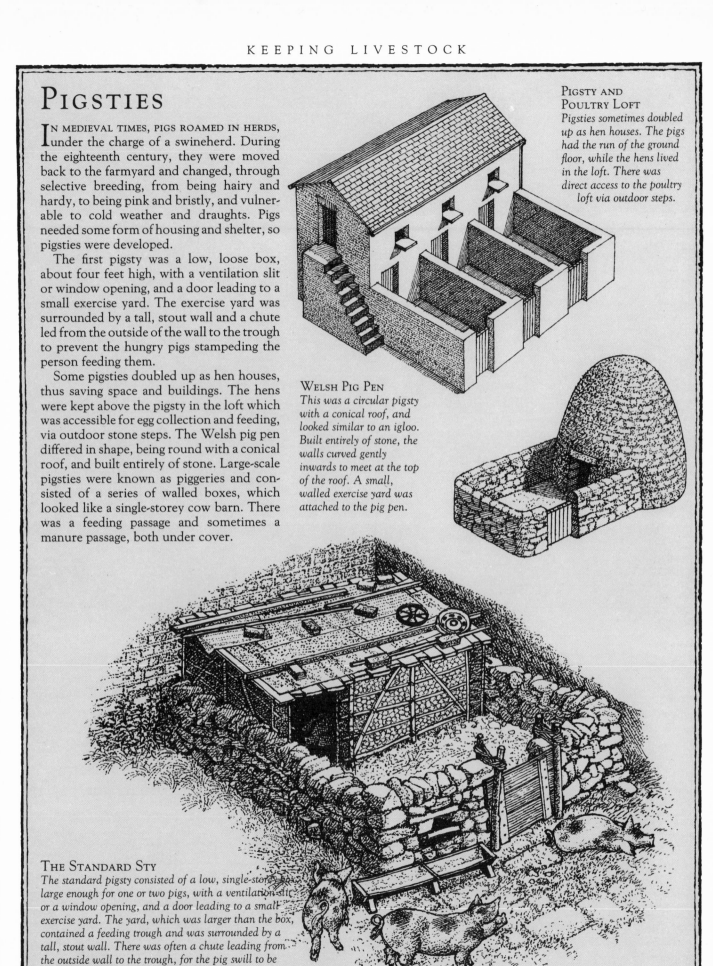

PIGSTY AND POULTRY LOFT
Pigsties sometimes doubled up as hen houses. The pigs had the run of the ground floor, while the hens lived in the loft. There was direct access to the poultry loft via outdoor steps.

WELSH PIG PEN
This was a circular pigsty with a conical roof, and looked similar to an igloo. Built entirely of stone, the walls curved gently inwards to meet at the top of the roof. A small, walled exercise yard was attached to the pig pen.

THE STANDARD STY
The standard pigsty consisted of a low, single-storey box, large enough for one or two pigs, with a ventilation slit or a window opening, and a door leading to a small exercise yard. The yard, which was larger than the box, contained a feeding trough and was surrounded by a tall, stout wall. There was often a chute leading from the outside wall to the trough, for the pig swill to be poured down.

TYPES OF LIVESTOCK

THE COUNTRY PERSON'S LOVE OF ANIMALS was not purely utilitarian. She or he loved a good-looking bird or beast and chose a breed for its looks as much, sometimes, as its usefulness. This explains the popularity of the bantam. These miniature hens and cocks were not really as useful as the full-sized breeds but some of them were as colourful as living jewels. The game breeds, too, were beautiful to look at; the fighting cockerels the epitome of macho virility. Game breeds made fine table birds but were slow to lay eggs. The pigs tended to be rotund fellows—the older breeds like Wessex or Essex Saddlebacks, Tamworth or the delightful Gloucester Old Spots were favourites. Most cottagers bought their pig for fattening as a "weaner", perhaps eight weeks old, straight off the mother, but a few cottagers would keep a sow and provide weaners for other people. Such a pig would be fed for perhaps six months and then fattened on barley meal or boiled potatoes for another three. Most of the meat would be home-cured for bacon and ham, but joints of fresh pork would be liberally distributed round the neighbourhood, as gifts or tokens of appreciation for favours received.

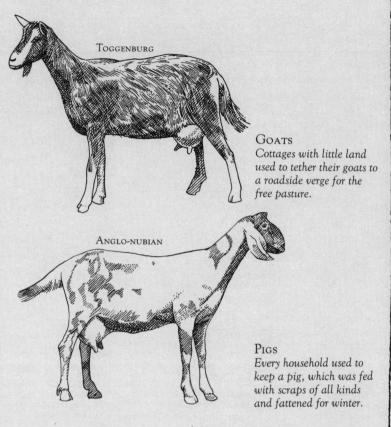

TOGGENBURG

GOATS
Cottages with little land used to tether their goats to a roadside verge for the free pasture.

ANGLO-NUBIAN

PIGS
Every household used to keep a pig, which was fed with scraps of all kinds and fattened for winter.

BERKSHIRE

GLOUCESTER OLD SPOT

TAMWORTH

OLD ENGLISH

BUFF ORPINGTON

WHITE LEGHORN

BRONZE TURKEY

TURKEYS
There was usually one turkey per farmyard, which was fattened up to be eaten on a special occasion, usually of course, Christmas.

RHODE ISLAND RED

LIGHT SUSSEX

ROMAN GOOSE

HENS
Hens were cheap to keep, required less space than other livestock, and provided a regular supply of fresh eggs.

GEESE
Geese were fattened up for roasting, and their soft, downy feathers were often used to stuff eiderdowns and pillows.

KEEPING BEES

T O NON-BEE-KEEPERS THERE IS SOME-thing mysterious about the dedicated keepers of bees. In every decent village there is at least one of them. He is "sent for" whenever a swarm has been found and is expected to be ever ready to remove a wild swarm from somebody's roof. People stand not unnaturally in awe of a person who can work coolly and calmly amid a raging swarm of flying insects which are, after all, quite dangerous. I remember when I was a pupil on a South African farm school seeing one of my fellow students being wheeled away in a wheelbarrow because he had fainted after being heavily attacked by bees. I kept bees later in England and Wales for nearly three decades but left them severely alone unless I was heavily protected. No slap-happy nonchalance for me. If I could have laid my hands on an astronaut's space suit I would not have scorned to wear it.

Hiving a Swarm

If you are an apiarist, the day will come in the summertime when a neighbour will knock on your door and announce that there is a swarm in his garden. What can you do about it? So, you grab an empty bee skep, or a basket, or even an old cardboard box, and follow him to his garden, where a seething bunch of bees as big as a rugger ball hangs in a tree. Your neighbour is terrified of them. You, on the other hand, are not, for you possess the knowledge that they are almost certainly not going to sting you, as they have filled themselves with honey before flying from their old hive to seek a new home. You go up to the swarm, hold the container under it, and give the branch a good shake. The swarm drops with a plomp into the container and you walk away with it nonchalantly. Your neighbour is amazed at your intrepidity. You don't tell him that swarming bees are almost always completely harmless. "Oh, I suppose I just have a way with them," you murmur.

Making and Using Skeps

Before 1851 bees were kept in straw or rush skeps. Any countryman could make a skep. All he needed was some long wheat or rye straw and some split bramble, together with a cow's horn with the point cut off and a

Bee Smoking
When the bee-keeper needed to open the hive, either to inspect the bees or to extract the honeycombs, smoke was puffed into the hive from a smoker to make the bees sluggish and less aggressive. The smoke was produced by the slow-burning fuel contained in the fire-box of the smoker.

BEE SMOKER

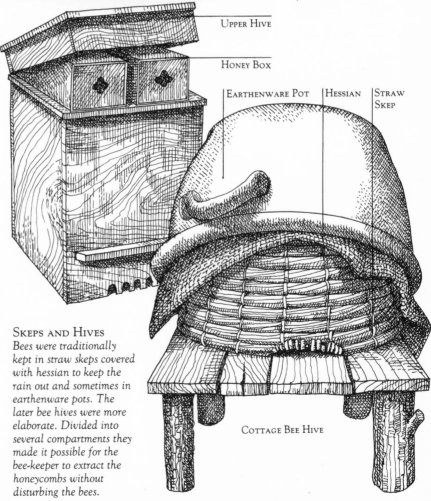

UPPER HIVE

HONEY BOX

EARTHENWARE POT | HESSIAN | STRAW SKEP

Skeps and Hives
Bees were traditionally kept in straw skeps covered with hessian to keep the rain out and sometimes in earthenware pots. The later bee hives were more elaborate. Divided into several compartments they made it possible for the bee-keeper to extract the honeycombs without disturbing the bees.

COTTAGE BEE HIVE

CENTRIFUGAL
MACHINE

DECAPPING A COMB
*When a honeycomb was
brought out of the hive it
was covered with wax. To
extract the honey, the bee-
keeper had to remove the
wax, which was best done
with a sharp, hot knife.*

A BEE STINGER
*The bee stinger was not,
as might be supposed, an
instrument of torture but a
device said to help relieve
rheumatism. A bee was
put inside the glass tube
and the stinger was placed
over the patient's skin.
The base was then slid
open and the plunger
depressed so that the bee
touched the skin and stung
the patient!*

goose or turkey bone. He would feed the straw into the larger, open, end of the horn, pushing it through so that it fitted tightly, and bind it with the bramble as it emerged. In this way he made a straw rope, which he then coiled and sewed together, using the piece of bone as a needle.

The bees hived in a skep built their comb according to their own sweet will. The queen laid an egg in every cell and when the bee-keeper wanted to extract the honey he placed an empty skep on top of the full skep and forced the bees up into it (a whiff of smoke would help them on their way). He then removed the first skep and whipped out the comb, baby bees and all, and squeezed out and strained the honey. The colony thus ousted, and bereft of both brood and honey, might or might not survive. However, in those days there were thousands of skeps about the countryside, huge reserves of nectar for bees, no poison sprays, and new swarms were to be had for the taking all through the summer. There was no shortage of bees then as there is now.

The skeps, not being waterproof, had to be kept out of the rain. This was done by placing hessian or sometimes conical straw hats called hackles on top to protect them. Sometimes the skeps were placed in specially built wooden buildings called bee boles.

HIVES

Modern hives are based on the invention of a Philadelphian named Langstroth, who, in 1851, established the optimum width of the bee space. The bee space is the distance between two vertical surfaces in which bees will build their comb in an orderly manner on both surfaces, and also have enough room to crawl about. The Langstroth hive, and all its imitators, makes it possible to exclude the queen from the area where most of the honey is situated, making it impossible for her to lay eggs in it and easy for the bee-keeper to avoid killing the baby bees when he extracts the honey.

I saw a wonderful bee house in Switzerland. It was essentially a timber shed with Langstroth hives built around the inside. The hives were connected with the outside world through the walls of the shed, but the bees could be inspected and attended to inside the shed by taking off their roofs. This struck me as an eminently sensible arrangement, for the bee-keeper and the bees.

DAIRY CRAFTS

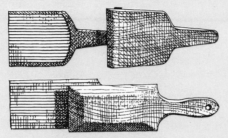

I don't know if you have heard the saying, "Man to the Plough, Wife to the Cow", but on small farms and holdings that was the way it used to be. Not only did the wife milk the cow but she churned some of the milk to make cream and butter and, in times of surplus, she used some to make cheese. Many wives also sold some of the butter and cheese they produced at the local market. So, the possession of a cow meant the possession of a fountain of health for the whole family, something of which Cobbett was well aware. In his marvellous book, *Cottage Economy*, he recommends strongly that the farm worker keep a cow if he possibly can. If he has as little as forty roods of garden, plus access to some common land, he could, in Cobbett's opinion, feed a cow. He might be able to keep little else on the forty roods — and certainly he will not "suffer his ground to be encumbered with apple trees that give only the means of treating his children to fits of the belly ache" — and he might have to farm the land intensively, but, in Cobbett's view, he is bound to consider such disadvantages more than offset by the huge advantage of owning a cow. And I agree with him wholeheartedly.

MILK & MILK TREATMENTS

WAS LUCKY ENOUGH TO BE brought up in a large country house in north Essex, where we kept two cows and employed a cowman. If any one factor has contributed more than any other to a lifetime of good health, I should say it was those cows.

KEEPING DAIRY COWS

The house cow was commonplace among country people in both Europe and North America until the First World War. City people had to be content with milk delivered daily from the town dairies, in which large herds of cows were kept permanently indoors and fed on hay and corn brought in from the countryside. These cows were kept in what were called "flying herds". After one lactation, as soon as their milk yield fell off significantly, they were either sold to the butcher or sent back to the country. It is thought that this intensive method of keeping milk cows encouraged tuberculosis.

This system was already on the way out when I was a child and there were milk churns on every railway station. The milk train imposed a new discipline on the farmer: he had to catch it with a horse-float full of overflowing milk churns every morning, which meant that he had to be up and milking his cows probably by four or five o'clock. Pasteurization had not yet been developed and so the milk had to be absolutely fresh. Milking utensils were sterilized and the milk cooled as soon as it left the cow to combat attack by micro-organisms.

THE MILK ROUND

I remember working on a mixed farm in the Cotswold Hills in 1934. I had to be up at five every morning to milk the cows, run the milk through a cooler and then put it into the clean churns. After breakfast the farmer drove round the nearby town of Northleach delivering the milk. Whenever he went away this job fell to me. A billycan stood outside the doors of our many customers and I would stop the pony at each and ladle two or three pints into the billycan, plus, at the command of my employer, a splash over: he followed the biblical injunction to give "full measure running over".

MILKING A COW
Cows have been milked by hand for centuries. The dairymaid sat on a three-legged stool, enabling her to keep her balance while leaning forward, and the milk collected in a wooden skeel. Milking by hand continued after milking machines were introduced because of their expense.

MILKING ITEMS
When cows were being milked, their legs were often tied with a cowband to stop them from kicking. If they were milked in the fields, the milk was carried back to the farm in a back can. A wooden yoke, carved to fit comfortably around the shoulders, was used to carry pairs of milk pails around the farm. It had adjustable chains that hooked on to the pail handles, which you had to hold firmly to prevent the milk from slopping out. When the milk arrived at the dairy, it was left to cool in wooden tubs before being strained through a strainer set on a wooden brig. It was then emptied into tin churns for delivery by rail and road. Many of the churns bore the name of the farm. The delivery man used a tinplate ladle to pour a precise measure of milk into the housewife's jug.

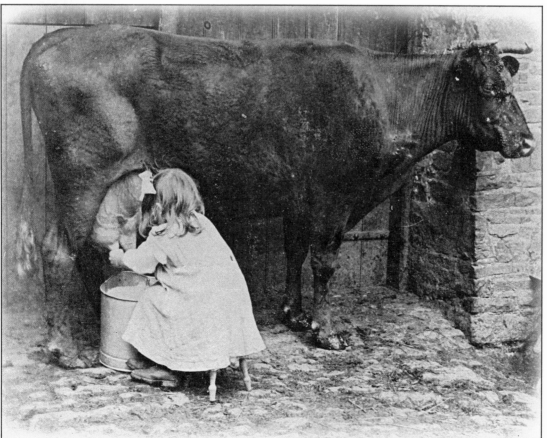

DAIRYMAID'S YOKE

PLAITED COTTON COWBAND

OAK BRIG

OAK SKEEL

OAK MILKING STOOL

VACUUM MILKING MACHINE

BACK CAN

TINPLATE MEASURE

DAIRYMAN'S DELIVERY CAN

SMALL MILK CARRIER

MILK STRAINER

TIN MILK CAN

TWO-HANDLED MILK CHURNS

ONE-HANDLED MILK CHURN

THE DAIRY COW

Not so long ago, many smallholders kept a dual-purpose or dairy cow and a goat. If the cow was kept purely for her milk, she might come from the local farmer to whom she was returned when dry before calving, at which point the goat took over as chief milk provider. Victorian nurses considered goat milk to be good for babies and certainly it was bound to be free of tuberculosis. The Jersey made, and still makes, an excellent house cow. Hardy and affectionate, she is easy to rear and produces the richest milk there is.

Few cows are milked out of doors nowadays, but at one time, in the summer at least, the dairymaids would trip out with their stools and buckets and wooden yokes, milk the tame cows where they stood no doubt knee-deep in grass and buttercups and return to the farm, swinging the heavy buckets full of foaming milk from the yoke chains and trying (or not trying?) to give the slip to the swains who, the poets tell us, were ever trying to waylay them.

RED POLL

This dual-purpose cow produces reliably good milk and beef.

DAIRY SHORTHORN

This dairy shorthorn makes poorish beef, but produces really excellent milk.

AYRSHIRE

This hardy dairy breed from south-west Scotland provides milk rich in butterfat.

BRITISH CANADIAN HOLSTEIN

Primarily a dairy cow, this large, heavy breed, derived from the Dutch Friesian, produces fine beef calves—given the right bull!

JERSEY

GUERNSEY

Jersey and Guernsey cows are exclusively dairy cows and are the only breeds permitted on the Channel Islands from which they originated. Both are small, lean, and easy to rear, and both produce very rich, creamy milk.

MAKING & USING CREAM

REMEMBER THE MAIDS "SETTING" the milk at my childhood home in Essex by putting it, straight from the cow, into wide, shallow white china bowls, covering these with muslin to keep the flies out, and leaving it until the next day. Overnight the cream would rise to the top. And who was to stop a small boy creeping into the dairy when nobody was looking to dip a grubby finger into the thick, yellow cream and lick it off?

SEPARATING THE CREAM FROM THE MILK
The cream was removed from the milk with what was called a fleeter in East Anglia and a skimmer in other parts of England. This was a round, almost flat but slightly dished, perforated disc made of white enamelled metal. It had a handle and the whole thing was perhaps eight inches across. You simply skimmed the thick cream off the set milk with it: the dead white skimmed milk escaped through the holes. I well remember the beautiful way the cream wrinkled as you pushed it to one side: it looked almost solid. But our cows were Jerseys, which yield the richest milk of all.

In the western and northern parts of Britain cream was often separated from the milk by placing the milk in a shallow slate trough (often the same one was used for salting—see p.38), waiting for it to set, and then pulling the plug out. The milk ran away into the under-buck below, leaving the cream clinging to the slate. The cream was then simply scraped off.

People with more than a couple of cows invested in centrifugal separators in those days. These had the advantage that they extracted more cream from the milk, while the milk was still fresh. Indeed the milk was put through the separator straight from the cow; it was not even cooled first.

USING THE CREAM
We didn't have any nonsensical ideas in those days about cream being bad for you. We poured it over fruit and puddings and even made some richer by scalding it. We heated it with spice, sugar and perhaps some orange-flower water, then, when it was cool, stirred in some soft fruit and more sugar, and ate it! We fed the skimmed milk to the calves or pigs.

CREAMY RECIPES
As well as being an accompaniment to fruit pies and puddings, cream was the principal ingredient of a variety of delicious custards, blancmanges and creamy desserts. Chocolate cream was a rich dessert made with thick cream, eggs and melted chocolate, whipped together until light and frothy. Blancmange flavoured with almonds was another favourite. This was made by heating the cream with lemon rind, sugar and crushed almonds and then leaving it to set in an oiled mould. A simple but pleasant custard was made with boiled cream mixed with egg yolks, sugar and rosewater. This mixture was poured over breadcrumbs, sprinkled with sugar and left to set.

DELIVERIES
Cream was delivered together with the milk in what was known as a "dairy pram", a hand-cart with three wheels. The fresh milk was carried in the large churn, whilst the cream was carried in separate cans, hanging on the side of the pram.

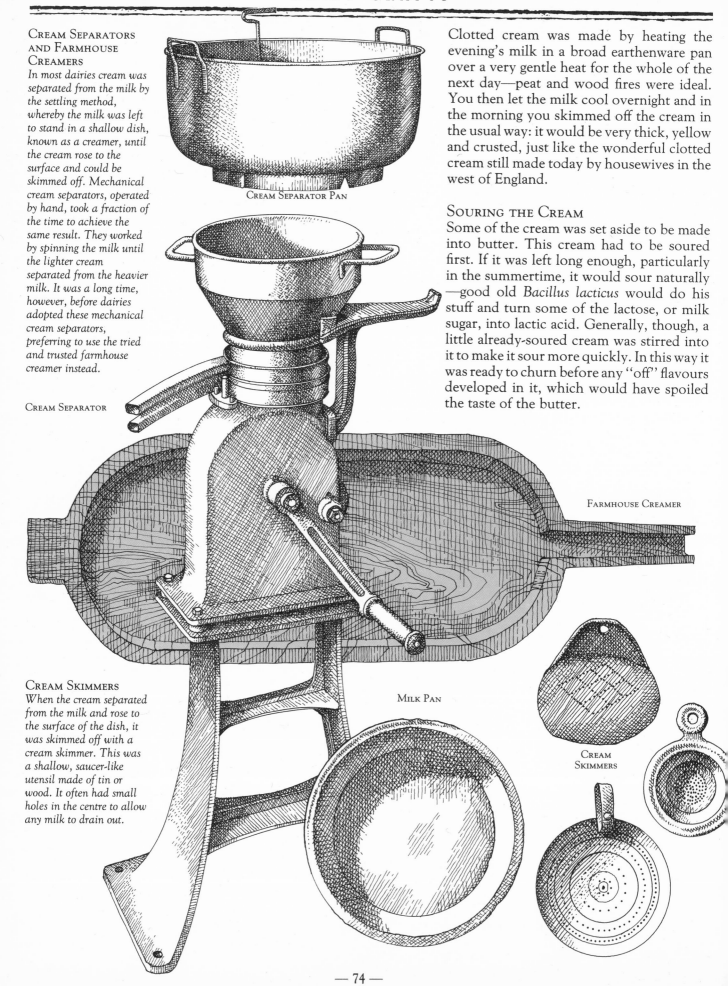

CREAM SEPARATORS AND FARMHOUSE CREAMERS

In most dairies cream was separated from the milk by the settling method, whereby the milk was left to stand in a shallow dish, known as a creamer, until the cream rose to the surface and could be skimmed off. Mechanical cream separators, operated by hand, took a fraction of the time to achieve the same result. They worked by spinning the milk until the lighter cream separated from the heavier milk. It was a long time, however, before dairies adopted these mechanical cream separators, preferring to use the tried and trusted farmhouse creamer instead.

CREAM SEPARATOR PAN

CREAM SEPARATOR

FARMHOUSE CREAMER

MILK PAN

CREAM SKIMMERS

CREAM SKIMMERS

When the cream separated from the milk and rose to the surface of the dish, it was skimmed off with a cream skimmer. This was a shallow, saucer-like utensil made of tin or wood. It often had small holes in the centre to allow any milk to drain out.

Clotted cream was made by heating the evening's milk in a broad earthenware pan over a very gentle heat for the whole of the next day—peat and wood fires were ideal. You then let the milk cool overnight and in the morning you skimmed off the cream in the usual way: it would be very thick, yellow and crusted, just like the wonderful clotted cream still made today by housewives in the west of England.

SOURING THE CREAM

Some of the cream was set aside to be made into butter. This cream had to be soured first. If it was left long enough, particularly in the summertime, it would sour naturally —good old *Bacillus lacticus* would do his stuff and turn some of the lactose, or milk sugar, into lactic acid. Generally, though, a little already-soured cream was stirred into it to make it sour more quickly. In this way it was ready to churn before any "off" flavours developed in it, which would have spoiled the taste of the butter.

BUTTER MAKING

AKING BUTTER IS SIMPLE. SOURED cream (see p.74) is put into a container and shaken until it turns into butter. In Essex we had an over-and-over churn, which I was sometimes allowed to turn. One heard of all kinds of devices for turning churns: water-wheels, horse-engines, even dogs running round in a treadmill, but I never could understand the necessity of these, for if the cream is sour enough and at the right temperature (about 68° Fahrenheit), the butter will "come", as the term is, within a few minutes. So, little exertion is required.

BUTTER CHURNS
The over-and-over churn was undoubtedly the most efficient butter churn and churn-works making them sprang up in small towns throughout the country. Alas, there are no churn-works now and the only churns one can buy are ageing ones, which, no matter how well they have been looked after, will not last for ever.

The plunger churn was an older device used quite recently in Wales, Scotland and Ireland. The operator simply plunged a plunger up and down, thus agitating the cream. It was just as effective as the over-and-over churn but possibly the latter was better for the actual washing of the butter. People with just a cow or two often had a blow churn, which was a glass jar with a small wooden paddle in it turned by gearing and operated by a small handle. I have often seen butter made in very small quantities by beating the soured cream with a fork, whipping it with an egg whisk, or shaking it in a jar or bottle.

WATCHING THE BUTTER "COME"
The over-and-over churn had a small glass window in it, which you peered through to see how the cream was doing. When little grains of butter manifested themselves ("as big as Number Six shot," we were always told), the butter had come. You then opened the end of the churn, flung some cold water in it, and went on churning for a few minutes. The liquid was then carefully poured out: this was the precious buttermilk; what remained was the butter. The generations of mankind that do not know this marvellous drink are deprived indeed.

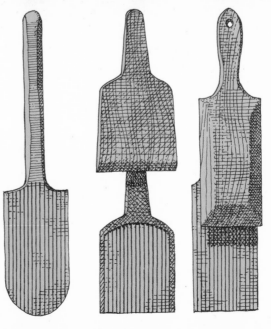

BUTTER HANDS
Butter hands or pats were small wooden bats with deeply grooved blades. They were held one in each hand and were used to divide and shape the butter into square or rectangular blocks. The pat and slap of the butter hands against the butter was a commonly heard sound in the dairy.

EQUIPMENT

THE MOST ESSENTIAL ITEM OF EQUIPMENT needed to make butter was the butter churn. An early sort of churn was the plunger churn, a cylindrical, upright churn fitted with an agitator—a broom handle with a perforated wooden disc fixed to the bottom. The operator plunged the agitator up and down until the cream turned into butter. Hanging churns that worked on a rocking principle were also popular in the eighteenth century. Smaller box churns were developed made of wood to begin with and later of glass and earthenware. These were fitted with slatted paddles connected to a central spindle: the paddles were moved up and down by turning a handle outside the box or jar. Barrel churns were mounted on sturdy stands and turned end over end by means of a handle. After the butter had "come" the excess water had to be squeezed out. The butter worker was excellent for this part of the operation. Wooden scoops were needed to dig out the butter from the butter worker, after which it was formed into blocks, rolls or rounds, or pressed into storage dishes. If it was for sale it was weighed on wooden butter scales.

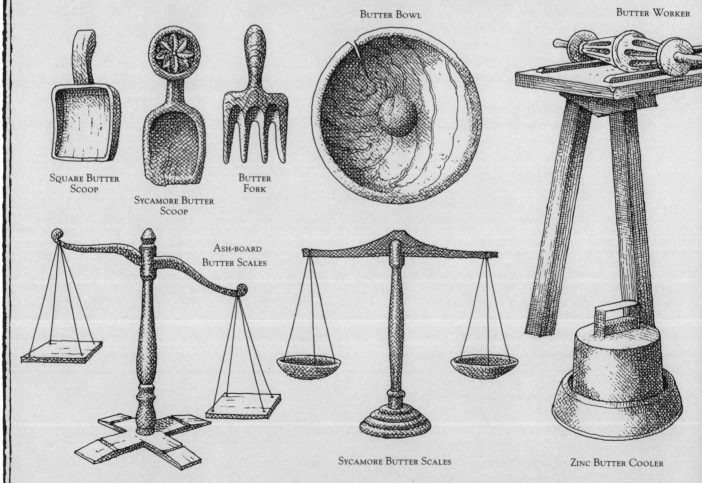

SQUARE BUTTER SCOOP

SYCAMORE BUTTER SCOOP

BUTTER FORK

BUTTER BOWL

BUTTER WORKER

ASH-BOARD BUTTER SCALES

SYCAMORE BUTTER SCALES

ZINC BUTTER COOLER

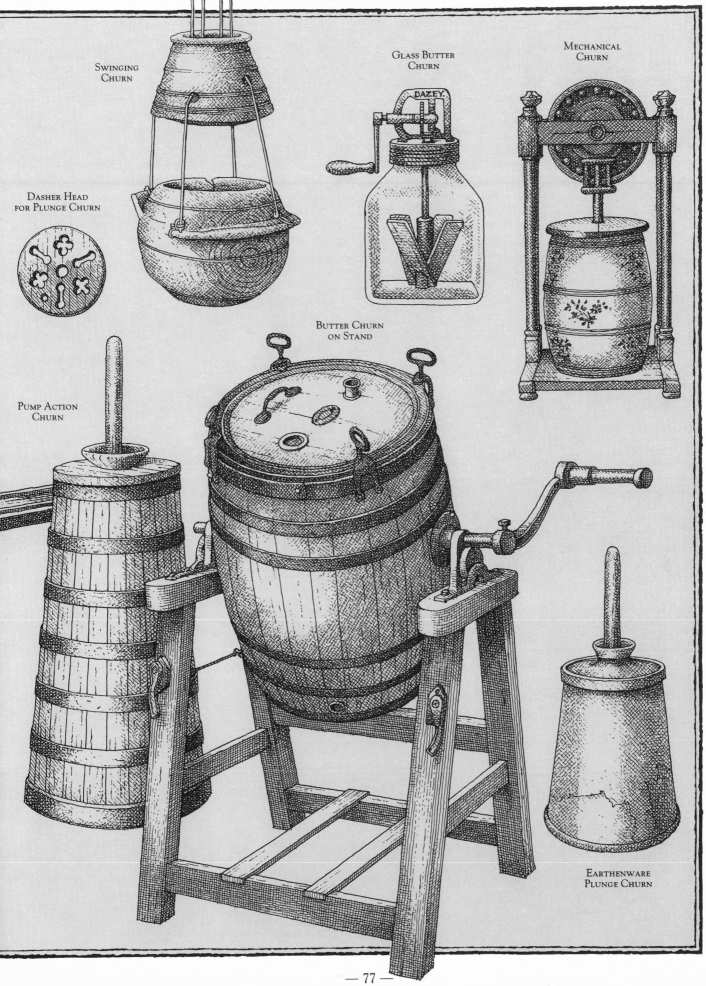

SWINGING
CHURN

GLASS BUTTER
CHURN

MECHANICAL
CHURN

DASHER HEAD
FOR PLUNGE CHURN

BUTTER CHURN
ON STAND

PUMP ACTION
CHURN

EARTHENWARE
PLUNGE CHURN

How people can talk of "progress", in any but a perjorative sense, in a world where fizzy coloured sugar-waters have come in and buttermilk has gone out I cannot for the life of me understand.

WASHING THE BUTTER

After the rescuing of the buttermilk came the washing of the butter. Clean, cold water was poured into the churn in large quantities, the churn turned and the water tipped out.

Now the butter worker came into play. Ours was a shallow wooden trough, kept scrubbed clean, with a wooden fluted roller that rolled up and down the trough when you turned the handle. Copious water was played on the butter while the butter was squeezed by the roller, for it was essential to wash the butter absolutely clean, or it would not keep and "off" flavours would develop in it.

STORING THE BUTTER

Once you were sure there was no buttermilk left in the butter, the butter was salted and worked some more. Afterwards it could be stored in an earthenware crock. The butter was flung into the crock in handfuls to drive out the air and water. When it was full, the butter was rammed hard with a mushroom-shaped wooden tool. All the water and air had to be expelled, otherwise the butter would go rancid. The butter had to be very salty for storing but you could always wash the salt out again before eating it. Well salted butter properly stored would keep indefinitely and taste just as good as fresh.

BUTTER PRINTS
Butter was stamped with decorative designs to make it look more attractive at the table or at the market if it was to be sold. Three types of butter print were used for this purpose: roller markers, flat prints and two-piece moulds.

PRINT MOTIFS
The charming motifs carved on the butter prints were often of flowers, birds or animals. They were usually decorated with a simple repeating pattern around the edge.

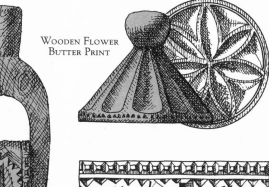

WOODEN FLOWER BUTTER PRINT

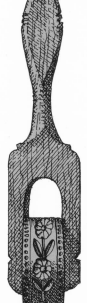

LEAF AND FLOWER ROLLER MARKER

LEAF ROLLER MARKERS

LEAF PRINTS

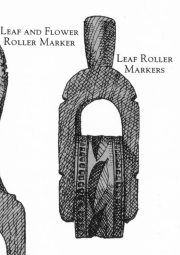

LEAVES AND FLOWERS PRINT

TWO-PIECE SWAN MOULD

COW BUTTER PRINT

OVAL BUTTER PRINT

Sensible people milked their cows in the summer, when grass was plentiful, and stored the milk in the form of butter and cheese for the winter, when one cow might be kept in milk but not fed too highly, just enough to provide milk for the tea and any small children. The present practice of steaming cows up to high winter yields with imported protein was not done.

DECORATING THE BUTTER

Before the sad triumph of industrial agriculture, farmers' wives used to market their own butter, many of them driving into the nearest town market once a week. They would also sell eggs and, in some cases, cheese. Often, too, they would sell fruit and vegetables, such as field mushrooms and blackberries, and any other produce they had available. The money raised from such produce was the farm wife's perk and she could spend it in any way she liked.

It was therefore desirable for the farmer's wife to mark her butter with her own trademark, and there were many rollers and stamps made by village craftsmen for this purpose. The night before market she would pat the butter into brick shapes with butter pats or scotch hands. Then she would add the finishing touches with a ribbed roller or perhaps a specially crafted butter stamp.

Direct selling of butter has now been outlawed and instead of being able to buy fresh butter, prettily decorated and prepared with loving care by a housewife with her reputation at stake, we now have to be content with factory-made grease wrapped in nasty plastic paper. I remember the maids in my mother's house taking great pride in "patting-up" the butter in different pretty shapes with scotch hands to send it up to the table, generally with a sprig of fresh parsley on it. It is a shame that this tradition has almost disappeared.

BUTTER BY THE YARD

It was not uncommon for butter to be sold by the pint in some areas of Britain and in one or two places in East Anglia it was the practice to sell butter by the yard. In fact, in Cambridge the butter sellers, generally men, were once famous. They took the long tube of butter, which looked rather like a long, narrow French loaf of bread, and measured it with a ring gauge. Why they sold the butter in this way is not really known. Perhaps it was easier for the housemaids, or wives, or college butlers, to cut it up into the butter pats which used to be served.

FLOWER BUTTER PRINT

EAGLE BUTTER PRINT

THISTLE BUTTER PRINT

SHEEP BUTTER PRINT

PRIMROSE BUTTER PRINT

CHEESE MAKING

I F YOU LEAVE MILK ALONE IN THE summer it will curdle. That is, it will separate into curds and whey, which will taste slightly sour. No doubt this was the stuff that Miss Muffet was consuming before she had that disturbing encounter with the spider. You can also cause fresh milk to curdle by adding rennet, which is present in a calf's belly to help it digest its mother's milk.

If you take curds and whey, however curdled, and put them in a muslin bag and hang the bag up, the whey will drain out, and the curds will turn into soft cheese. If you then press the soft cheese, expelling more liquid, it will become hard cheese. The value of cheese making is enormous. It enables us to preserve milk, a high protein, very nutritious food, obtained from the cow in summer when the grass is plentiful, until the winter, when we need the energy more and grass is rather thin on the ground. This process is known in all the countries of Christendom and cheese has been made in them for centuries.

Cheese making is not practised in eastern countries, nor in Africa or other parts of the tropical world, as the temperatures are too

CHEESE-MAKING TOOLS
To encourage the milk to curdle with the rennet, the liquid was stirred with a curd agitator. When the curds formed, they were chopped with one of a variety of knives, whippers and cutters, before being wrapped in muslin. The wrapped curds were then placed on a strainer, or in a cheese vat, mould or press with holes in the bottom, so that the whey could drain out. The finished cheese was cut with a fine wire slicer and served on a cheese board.

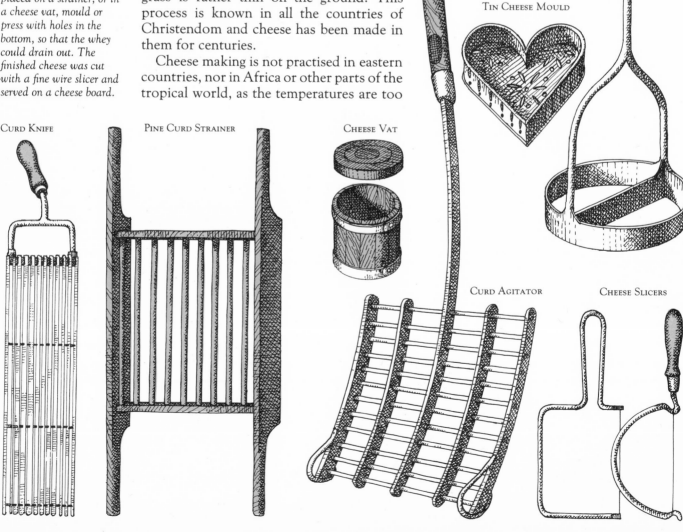

CURD CUTTER

TIN CHEESE MOULD

CURD KNIFE

PINE CURD STRAINER

CHEESE VAT

CURD AGITATOR

CHEESE SLICERS

high. The peoples in those countries do not preserve milk except in so far as the Indians turn butter into ghee, which is storable even in their hot climate.

A Disciplined Approach

Cheese making requires a severely disciplined approach. It is easy enough to turn milk into cheese, but not very easy to turn it into *eatable* cheese. For cheese making is a biological process and the living organisms that accomplish it for us must be very carefully controlled. Otherwise you will have to throw the result to the pigs and even *they* have been defeated by some efforts. In the nineteenth century Suffolk cheese had a terrible reputation and would, we are told, defy the teeth of a starving swine. The stuff was made from skimmed milk, though, as all the whole milk went to London to be sold at a high price on the liquid market. The cheese was just a by-product of the butter.

Cheese is now mostly made out of pasteurized milk in huge factories. The whole process is industrial and there is no individual skill required by the workers: temperatures, acidity, the type of bacteria present: every factor is controlled precisely. The result is that the cheese is completely consistent but consistently dull. Thank God farm-made cheese is coming back on the market. This is (or should be) made of unpasteurized milk; either subjected to the naturally occurring micro-organisms of the dairy in which it is made, or inoculated with strains of bacteria carefully bred, and allowed to ripen properly. All the best cheese in the world is made like this.

Hard Cheeses

To make hard cheese the farmer and his wife would pour the evening milk into a vat and then the next day mix in an equal amount of the morning's milk. By then the cream of the night before's milk would have risen and this was sometimes skimmed off and used for making butter. Half evening and half morning milk was the traditional recipe for Cheddar and most hard cheese. Sometimes a ripener (a culture of bacteria) was also added. Then, when the milk reached exactly the right temperature, rennet was added. After this came the skilful process of stroking the top of the milk as it curdled to "keep the cream down".

The milk was left to curdle, after which the curds were cut into cubes. Those making cheese on a small scale would use a kitchen

knife but larger producers would use a pair of curd knives (one with blades laid horizontally, the other with blades laid vertically), or later what was called in England an "American curd knife", which was simply two curd knives joined together. The cutting had to be done very gently so as not to destroy the very delicate curd.

The curd was then left to pitch, as the expression was, in the whey; that is, it was just left. The longer it was left, the more acidic it became and the timing of the pitching was extremely important. In larger farms an instrument known as an acidimeter was used to measure the acidity. Many a farm wife, however, measured the acidity using the hot iron test. They touched a piece of curd with a hot iron and drew it away. If the curd broke away from the iron when the string of cheese drawn out from it was under half an inch long it was not acid enough and needed to be left a little longer. If the string was longer than half an inch the curd had been left too long and was too acid: it would have to be given to the pigs as it would never make good cheese.

When exactly the right level of acidity was reached the whey was drained off. It had many uses besides feeding the pigs. Paint was made from it and it was used for washing floors. Thirsty farmers drank it if they had nothing better.

STRAINING THE CURDS
After the milk had curdled, separating into curds and whey, it was poured into a trough lined with muslin. The muslin strained the curds to be used for making cheese, allowing the unwanted whey to pass through.

WOODEN-SCREW PRESS

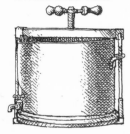

SPRING-LOADED TINPLATE PRESS

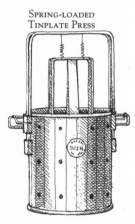

CHEESE PRESSES
There were many gadgets invented for pressing cheese. The curds were packed in a metal or wooden container with holes in the side or bottom, called a chessit. Weights were used to exert pressure on the cheese inside and these were operated by a lever. The cheese was pressed for at least a day until the whey had drained out through the holes and the cheese had become solid. Spring and screw thread presses replaced lever presses late in the nineteenth century.

As for the curd, this was subjected to a variety of treatments, according to the kind of cheese that was to be made. It would be milled (broken up into pieces the size of a walnut), either by hand or by inserting it into a curd mill, a simple instrument with two spiked rollers. Then, if true hard cheese was required, it would be wrapped in a cheese-cloth and placed in a chessit, or vat, made of wood or metal with holes pierced in the base to allow the cheese to drain. Finally it was put in the cheese press, where it was turned after about an hour. There were many kinds of cheese press and some could exert a pressure of a couple of tons.

After pressing, the cheese was taken out of the press and put away for ripening. Choice of storage room was most important: the temperature had to be an even 65 to 70° Fahrenheit, the ventilation good, the humidity just right and the deleterious cheese-mite non-existent. The cheese had to be turned every day for many weeks and scrupulous hygiene had to be observed.

The bigger the cheese, especially with true hard cheese such as Cheddar, the longer it would keep and the better tasting it would become. The Dutch make a great distinction between "niewe kaas", or new cheese, and "oud kaas", or old cheese. The latter is much more expensive and has a fine bite to it, delightful to the taste of your true cheese lover. It is noteworthy that all the best Dutch farm-made cheese is sold to France, whereas all the Dutch cheese sold to England (or very nearly all) is factory made. This tells us a lot about the gastronomic tastes of the French and English.

OTHER CHEESES
Cheeses such as Roquefort (which is made from sheep's milk) and Stilton (which is made from cow's milk) are not true hard cheeses, for they are not pressed. They are inoculated with a mould to turn them blue or green and cannot be stored indefinitely but must be eaten when they are ripe.

Then, of course, there is the great tribe of soft cheeses, or semi-soft cheeses: Brie, Camembert and, in France, at least 100 others, all made locally by farmer cheese makers, all quite distinctive from one another, and nearly all delicious.

General de Gaulle once asked how he could be expected to govern a country with so many different kinds of cheese. Fortunately, you can't, and that is why the French are such a happy race.

MAKING ICE CREAM

ICE CREAM IS SAID TO HAVE BEEN invented by Catherine de Medici. It was made by placing a tin or pewter container inside another container, which was filled with a mixture of ice and salt. Cream was then poured into the inner container and sugar and flavouring, such as fruit juice, liqueur, or even jam, added. The mixture was then stirred continuously with a spaddle or revolving paddle, generally made of copper, and, at the same time, the inner pot was turned by a handle. By keeping the mixture constantly on the move, the ingredients would not separate before congealing and no lumps would form. As the cream was churned it also froze slowly to make ice cream.

ICED PUDDING

To make iced pudding, the housewife stirred together milk, sugar, eggs and sometimes almond paste over a medium heat until it thickened. She took the mixture off the heat and allowed it to cool naturally before placing it in the ice-cream freezer to freeze in the usual way. Iced pudding was delicious with fruit compote.

SORBETS

Sorbets were invented in Persia. Snow was brought down into the roasting hot streets of Tehran from the Elburz Mountains, where the eternal snows sit. In Tehran it was flavoured and coloured with fruit juice before being presented to the Shah and his court: they ate it to cool their throats.

ICE-CREAM MOULDS

Once the ice cream or iced pudding was frozen, the housewife would usually place it in a pewter or lead mould. The filled moulds would be kept on ice until the family was ready for dessert. Moulds came in a huge range of designs and many were hinged to make it easier to extract the ice cream without spoiling the pattern.

ICE-CREAM APPLIANCES
Ice-cream makers came in different styles and sizes, but they all worked by turning a handle which turned an inner metal drum in the ice-filled pail. When the ice cream was made it was left to set in decorative moulds and was served using a scoop, or disher. Most scoops had a blade that released the ice cream cleanly from the sides of the scoop.

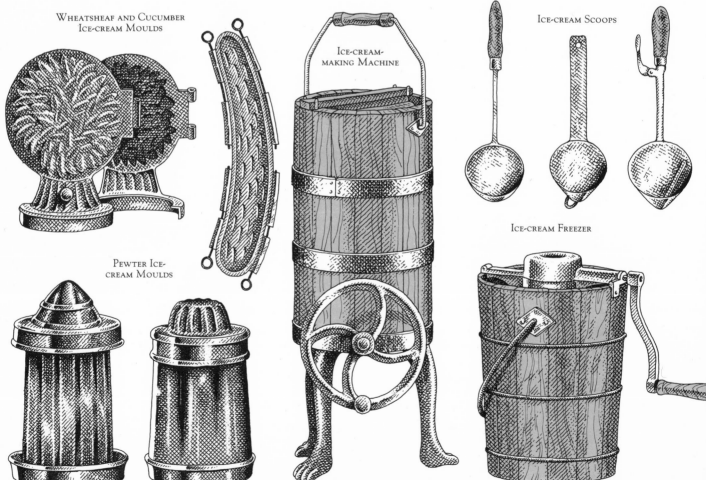

WHEATSHEAF AND CUCUMBER ICE-CREAM MOULDS

ICE-CREAM-MAKING MACHINE

ICE-CREAM SCOOPS

PEWTER ICE-CREAM MOULDS

ICE-CREAM FREEZER

LAUNDRY CRAFTS

In these days of turbo-boost washing machines and tumble driers, it is difficult to appreciate just how arduous doing the laundry was in the last century. Washing machines were not generally available until the 1880s and even then much energy was required to operate them, as they were hand cranked. In most households one day a week, usually Monday, was set aside for doing the washing and the housewife devoted the whole day to soaking, pounding, rubbing, boiling, starching, rinsing and drying the family's linen. She was lucky if she could fit in the ironing, as well. And as for ''dashing away with the smoothing iron'', such an action was very much easier said than done in the days of heavy flat irons. The rich, who owned many clothes and could afford to buy their underwear in sets of twelve, employed washer women to come and do their washing once every six weeks in a mammoth session that usually lasted four days. On the other hand, the poor, who had only the clothes they stood up in, had to wash their clothes at night, just before retiring to bed. With any luck the garments would dry overnight and be ready to wear again the next morning.

DRAWING WATER

USING A HOOP
Fetching and carrying water from the village well was a tiring daily chore for most housewives. To ease the task, the pails were often attached to a hoop before being carried, with the woman walking inside the hoop. This stopped the pails from banging into her legs.

HE ODD THING ABOUT THE adventure of Jack and Jill is that they went *up* the hill "to fetch a pail of water" instead of *down* it. Country water supplies tended to be in lower ground. Few people would try sinking a well at the top of a hill, as they would have to sink it that much further to reach the water table. So most people had to carry their water uphill, if their country was hilly, making the operation even more laborious.

CARRYING WATER
People who have never had to fetch their water imagine that carrying it would be quite unacceptably onerous, but, in fact, it is not a horrific task at all. For the first two years of living in our present house, we carried every drop of water we used up a very rough track from a spring 300 yards away and seventy feet below us on the hill. On ordinary days we required ten gallons of water for household purposes. We could each carry five gallons at a time, in two-and-a-half-gallon containers, so this meant one trip each. On wash days, which occurred twice a week, the amount was nearer forty gallons or four trips each. If we had owned a yoke we could easily have carried eight gallons at a time but we never got round to obtaining one. Bath night was once a week and meant fetching a further ten gallons, or two more trips. Each trip took perhaps twenty minutes (for we had to bail the water up from the spring and fill the containers) and few country people, I should imagine, ever had to carry their water much further.

When I was a boy, water was often carried in two buckets suspended from a yoke. Using a yoke meant that the carrier's shoulders bore the weight of the water and the buckets did not bang against her or his knees. Simple hoops made of split hazel were sometimes used, too. The carrier attached the containers to the hoop at either side, got inside the hoop and carried the

containers by hand. The hoop served to keep the buckets from bumping into the legs. In some countries—Wales was one—women carried large containers of water on their heads. Buckets were often made of wood and crafted by the village cooper. Galvanized iron sheet gradually displaced wood and the wandering gypsies or tinkers would knock up such buckets and repair them in a trice.

PUMPING WATER

I remember as a child in Essex that nearly every cottage had a well near it, generally in the garden. Often a well was actually dug in the kitchen, in which case there would be a pump over it so that you could pump the water directly into the sink. If the well was in the garden it would generally have a windlass over it and the water would be wound up in the big heavy well bucket.

Most villages had at least one village well with a pump or windlass. The task of fetching water from the village well was welcomed by the village girls because it always led to their hearing some gossip, for the well acted as a sort of women's club.

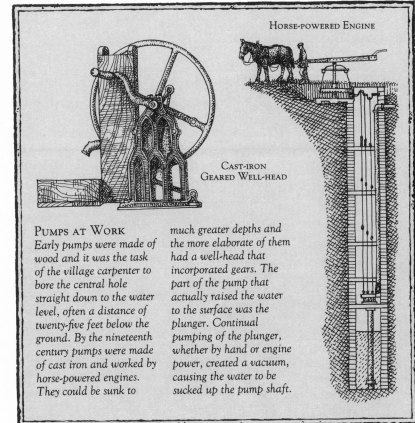

HORSE-POWERED ENGINE

CAST-IRON GEARED WELL-HEAD

PUMPS AT WORK
Early pumps were made of wood and it was the task of the village carpenter to bore the central hole straight down to the water level, often a distance of twenty-five feet below the ground. By the nineteenth century pumps were made of cast iron and worked by horse-powered engines. They could be sunk to much greater depths and the more elaborate of them had a well-head that incorporated gears. The part of the pump that actually raised the water to the surface was the plunger. Continual pumping of the plunger, whether by hand or engine power, created a vacuum, causing the water to be sucked up the pump shaft.

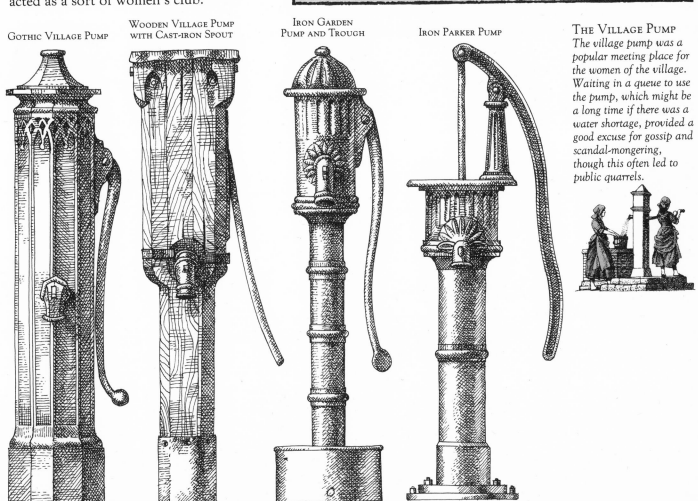

GOTHIC VILLAGE PUMP

WOODEN VILLAGE PUMP WITH CAST-IRON SPOUT

IRON GARDEN PUMP AND TROUGH

IRON PARKER PUMP

THE VILLAGE PUMP
The village pump was a popular meeting place for the women of the village. Waiting in a queue to use the pump, which might be a long time if there was a water shortage, provided a good excuse for gossip and scandal-mongering, though this often led to public quarrels.

MAKING LYE & SOAP

MY MOTHER, WHO WAS BROUGHT UP in Maryland, used to complain that her English servants drank tea "as strong as lye". When I asked her what lye was, she explained that it was an alkaline liquid made in her childhood days before caustic soda was widely available and used to wash clothes. Grease and dirt in the linen were loosened by the alkaline solution and were therefore easier to remove. Lye was made by allowing water to seep through wood ash, placed on top of a cloth on a lye dropper, into a tub. Lye could be used by itself for washing clothes in the "buck wash" or added to fat to make soap.

MAKING LYE

I made lye years later and partly experimentally. I drilled holes in the bottom of a barrel, put a layer of gravel in on top to help drainage, then filled the rest of the barrel with wood ash: hardwood ash worked best. I then trickled rain water through the ashes very slowly. After quite a long wait, the filtered water, or lye, dribbled out of the holes in the bottom of the barrel to be caught in the under-buck. I then took the liquid and "boiled it down" until it was concentrated enough to float an egg.

You could also make lye out of ferns. These were collected (free) from the countryside, half dried in the sun and burned in pots to make reddish-grey potash. In many parts of the country the ashes were not only used by the makers but also turned into balls and sold in the towns and cities.

Weeds were sometimes mixed in with the fern, burned together and formed into loaves, which would keep for up to twenty years if completely dried. This was the usual practice in Ireland.

TESTING THE LYE

To make soap with lye the housewife had to make sure the lye was the correct strength. To do this, she would make an absolutely saturated solution of brine. Then she would take a stick, weight it at one end, and float it in the salt and water mixture. Because of the weight, the stick would bob upright and she would make a notch in it at the point at which it emerged from the brine: she now had her lyeometer.

Next she dropped the lyeometer in the lye. If the stick floated so that the notch aligned with the surface of the liquid, then the lye was the correct strength for making soap. If the notch was visible above the liquid she simply added rain water until it did align. The solution was never too weak. The lye could then be used for making soap.

MAKING SOAP WITH LYE

To make soap with lye the housewife mixed one pint of lye with two pounds of clean, melted fat or oil, and simmered it gently for three hours, stirring frequently: cow, pig or sheep fat all made excellent soap, and vegetable oils could also be used. As the mixture cooled, she would stir in one pound of salt. This would fall to the bottom but still hardened the soap. Once the salt had settled she poured the molten soap into wooden moulds lined with damp cloths, leaving the brine behind. Finally she added colouring and scenting ingredients: traditionally a mixture of herbs was used. She then left the soap to set. Soap made with lye improved with keeping, but only if it was kept in a cool, but not freezing, airy place.

MAKING SOAP WITH SODA

I first saw soap made in south-west Africa, where if you didn't make it you didn't have it. I saw it made from the fat of the ox, the fat of the ostrich and, rather surrealistically, the

SOAPWORT
Soapwort is a wild plant often found growing near streams. Its leaves were boiled in water to make a lathery liquid, which was then used for washing woollen clothes.

USING A LYE DROPPER
A lye dropper was a wooden box or trough with holes in its base. It was balanced on top of a tub with a layer of drainage— twigs or gravel—arranged in the bottom of the dropper. The drainage material was then covered with a cloth, and topped up with wood ash. Water was slowly poured over the ash and, as it trickled through to the tub beneath, it took with it the alkaline salts from the ash. The resulting liquid was lye, used for washing clothes.

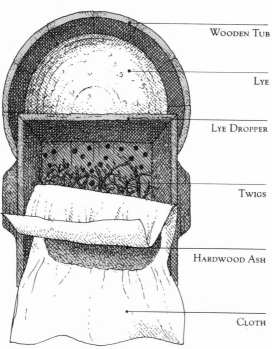

WOODEN TUB

LYE

LYE DROPPER

TWIGS

HARDWOOD ASH

CLOTH

fat of a young lioness that was shot in the act of killing a donkey. Ostriches were much hunted in the days before the Second World War for that very purpose.

The fat (acid) was boiled with caustic soda (alkaline), which neutralized it and so formed soap. There was, I was told, a bush that grew in the veld called the *seep-bosch*, which was so strongly alkaline that it would take the place of the caustic soda. However, we early settlers in that desert country, although too poor to buy soap were rich enough to lash out on a tin of soda, which cost very little and lasted a long time.

In Europe, soda was not cheaply available until the end of the eighteenth century when a Frenchman named Nicholas Leblanc found a way of producing it from salt. Before that, households that really wanted to keep clean were in the habit of using sand and brick dust, or various stone dusts, for scouring and washing clothes, which they would bash against a rock in the stream with a wooden bat called a beetle. Some people made lye and boiled the linen in that in the "buck wash".

Soap was heavily taxed in England until 1833 and ordinary households made do without it until about 1880, when cheap factory-made soap began to flood the market. This soap was used in two ways: it was rubbed on particularly dirty areas of the fabric; and it was dissolved in boiling water to form soap jelly, which mixed easily with the hot water and created a strong, soapy solution for the clothes. The American colonists certainly made it and so, as I said, did the South Africans. Soap was certainly known in England in the sixteenth century but as it was made of fat, and fat was needed for making candles and rushlights, it was always a prerogative of the rich. Many housewives economized by using soap for only some of their linen: their favourite things, perhaps, or the more delicate garments. The rest would go in the buck wash. When soda began to be mass produced, cost-conscious housewives replaced lye with it. Wealthier households used soap for all their linen and boiled it all in lye afterwards, maintaining that the lye softened the water and whitened the linen.

MAKING SOAP CAKES
The liquid soap mixture was poured into a wet wooden mould lined with a damp cloth and left to set. After twenty-four hours, the cloth containing the soap was lifted out and the soap cut into cakes with a thin wire cutter.

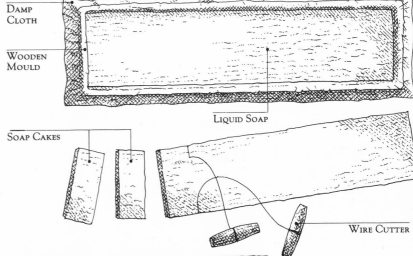

DAMP CLOTH

WOODEN MOULD

LIQUID SOAP

SOAP CAKES

WIRE CUTTER

COLOURING AND PERFUMING

Before the liquid soap set hard in the mould, colourings were added to enhance the soap's appearance, and perfumes were mixed in for a pleasant scent. Any number of ingredients could be used, provided they did not contain alcohol, which would ruin the soap. Vegetables such as carrots, spinach and beetroot coloured the soap yellow-orange, green and pink, while herbs and plants such as lavender, rosemary and lemon balm gave a natural perfume to the soap.

ROSEMARY LAVENDER

LEMON BALM

BEETROOT

CARROTS

SPINACH

WASHING LINEN

NYONE WHO HAS BEEN TO INDIA will have seen the *dhoby wallah* standing in a stream, or by a well, bashing clothes against a rock. Taking one garment at a time, he dips it in the water and slams it down hard a few times on the rock, dips it again, slams it, and so on. Off fly all the buttons if there are any but the *dhoby* man cares not a straw and bashes away regardless. In this way, without using a scrap of soap or any other chemical, he gets the clothes perfectly clean before laying them in the hot sun to dry and bleach.

Eighteenth-century artists in Europe delighted in making paintings or drawings of buxom country girls with their skirts tucked up to expose their pretty plump legs, either tramping their washing clean with their feet in washing tubs, or bashing it on the rocks of a stream with flat-headed clubs called beetles. They washed their clothes without soap or lye or anything else, bleached them in the sun, and went away rejoicing.

THE WASHING TUB

In the most engaging of autobiographies, *The Book of Boswell*, Gordon Boswell relates tales from his childhood when the family travelled around England in a horse-drawn home. His sisters each had their own washing tub, which was made of oak and had brass hoops, and the little girls used to vie with each other to see who could keep her brass hoops the most brightly polished. Whenever the "vardo", as the caravan was called, was halted for a few days in some green lane to allow the "grais", as the horses were called, to "poov", or graze, the little girls washed the family clothes, draping them on the nearby bushes to dry. Old Gordon's lyrical description brings this delicious pastoral scene to life. It is a scene unlikely to be seen again in our present world of tarmac, hooting motor cars and "authorized municipal sites for itinerants".

Some twenty years ago, when walking from one end to the other of the largest of the Irish Aran Islands (Irishmore), the most delightful singing I ever heard in my life reached my ears. Immediately I sat down and listened. It was a young girl's voice and she was singing in Irish Gaelic. She sang in that haunting melodic style that gives credence to the view held by some people that the early Irish people came from north Africa via Iberia. When finally I could restrain my curiosity no longer I got up and walked round the corner to see a little thatched cabin and before it a beautiful teenaged girl washing clothes in just such a brass-bound tub as Gordon describes, singing as she worked. She was not a bit abashed at the sight of me and willingly sang me another song at my request. Now Irishmore has an airstrip and tourists, and such an experience will never be repeated there.

WASH DAY

Before the twentieth century, washing was a job requiring strength and stamina. In large households it took a whole day to do, and that day was nearly always Monday. The

FAMILY WASH DAY
Whilst the dirtier clothes were left to soak, the more delicate clothes were washed by hand in one tub, and then rinsed in clean water in another tub. Wash day was very tiring for the housewife and she never looked forward to it.

reason for choosing Monday as the day to do the washing was not simply to honour the nursery rhyme, which designates it for that purpose, but because on Sunday the great Sunday joint was cooked and there was always plenty of cold meat left over for dinner on Monday. Consequently the housewife was saved the chore of cooking a proper dinner on Monday and could devote the whole day to washing. I remember a fine dish that was concocted on Mondays from left-over meat, cabbage and potatoes. It was called "bubble-and-squeak".

Washing wasn't merely a matter of shoving everything into a washing machine as it is now. Garments and other articles were carefully sorted, the heavier and dirtier things put to soak for a long time in lye or soda (see p.89) and then well boiled in the copper, and the lighter and more delicate articles put aside to be washed in a tub of cold or lukewarm water by hand.

Stubborn dirt was rubbed away on the fluted washboard or, more often perhaps, by agitating the material in the dolly tub. This was, in the days I remember at least, a fat-bellied tub made of fluted galvanized steel. The housewife "spun" the clothes with a peg dolly, which was a device made by a local wood turner usually out of sycamore. A wooden disc was fixed to the bottom of a rounded shaft and four pegs secured to the underside of the disc. I once heard the peg dolly called a "working woman's piano" by Mr Ellis, who was a wood turner at Boston in the county of Lincolnshire.

There was a range of remedies, some of them pretty strange ones, for getting out stains. Fuller's earth was very useful for removing grease and oil, and chalk and pipe clay were also supposed to work. Lemon juice, onion juice or even urine would all lift ink successfully and if the housewife applied a hot coal

TUBS AND DOLLIES
An effective though laborious method of washing was to spin the clothes in a wooden tub of water using a peg dolly or washing paddle. This loosened the dirt from the linen, which then collected at the bottom of the tub. The spinning action used by the housewife—first turning in one direction and then in the other—is the same as that used by today's washing machines.

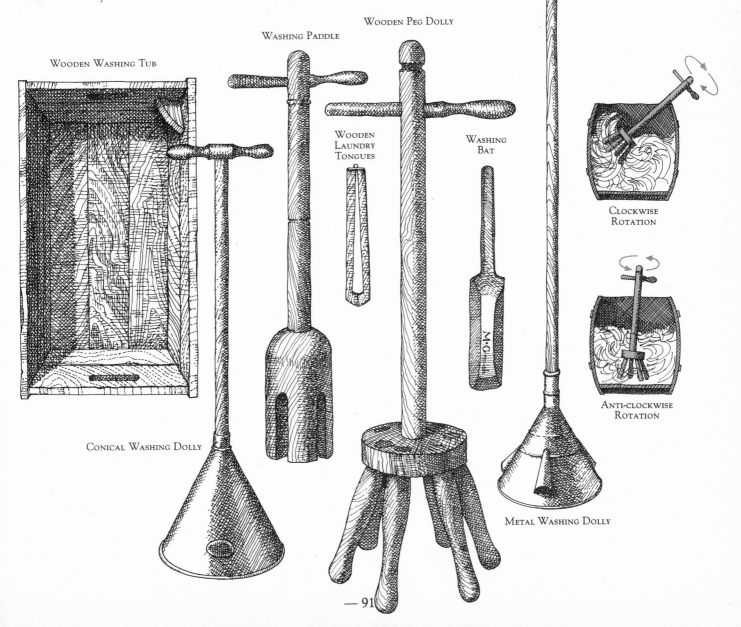

WOODEN PEG DOLLY

WASHING PADDLE

WOODEN WASHING TUB

WOODEN LAUNDRY TONGUES

WASHING BAT

CLOCKWISE ROTATION

ANTI-CLOCKWISE ROTATION

CONICAL WASHING DOLLY

METAL WASHING DOLLY

WOOD AND IRON WASHBOARD

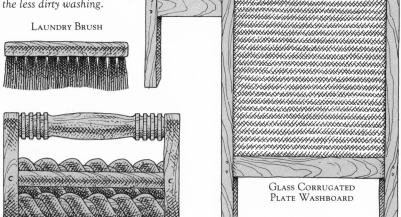

USING A WASHBOARD
The washboard was made of ridged wood, corrugated zinc or ridged glass. The washing was rubbed up and down against it in the wash tub to loosen the dirt. It was often used in conjunction with the dolly and tub, for cleaning the less dirty washing.

LAUNDRY BRUSH

GLASS CORRUGATED PLATE WASHBOARD

THE AMERICAN WASHER
This mechanical gadget was a substitute for the washboard. The machine was simply rolled up and down against the linen in the wash tub. It was less hard work and kinder to the hands and knuckles than the washboard.

THE WASH TUB
Wash tubs were made of wood and were often rectangular and trough-like in shape to make them easy to use with a washboard. Barrel-shaped tubs were also frequently used with peg dollies.

wrapped in linen to a wax stain, the wax would be removed. Milk was used to combat urine, vinegar and fruit stains. Finally there were some rather complicated recipes for multi-purpose, stain-removing liquids, which called for enormous pounding energy before the housewife had even made a start on the stain!

THE COPPER
I remember as a child in rural Essex that every farmhouse or cottage had at least one copper. The copper, which was often not made of copper at all but of thin cast iron, was a hemispherical vessel that would hold from twenty to forty gallons of water. It might be found in an outhouse (known as the "backus", or backhouse, in East Anglia, and the blue house in the Midlands), or in the kitchen. Great houses, like Tendring Manor House, where I was brought up, would have them, too.

The copper was built into a brick surround and had a fire grate under it. In the best installations the bricks were laid in such a way that the heat and smoke spiralled around the copper before reaching the chimney. Such built-in coppers were very effective. I inherited such a copper when I moved into a gamekeeper's cottage near Orford in Suffolk in the early 1950s, and was amazed by its efficiency: a fire fuelled by a few dry twigs would boil a good twenty gallons of water in no time at all.

The copper was an absolute boon. It served to wash the clothes, boil the pig food, boil the pig, provide scalding water for scalding the pig; boil the water for making beer or home-made wine, heat the water for baths, and even, in big families, boil the stew or soup. In days when bachelor farm workers lived in the house—as they commonly did in the west and north of England until fairly recent times—the farmer's wife, or her maid, would put a huge joint of beef in the copper and boil it up. This would last the extended family for several days.

BLEACHING
Linen was bleached well into the nineteenth century by the disgusting practice of soaking it in urine, which contains ammonia. Human urine was, after all, free and was collected assiduously for bleaching purposes. Hog manure was also used, mixed with a little cold water. In both cases the clothes were washed thoroughly in fresh water afterwards, of course!

The sun, too, was a great bleacher. Linen was laid out on the village "bleaching green" to be whitened by the sun. The bleach that we use today—a compound of lime, salt and oxygen—was not freely available until the late nineteenth century.

The "blue" bag was something that I remember vividly from my childhood days because, whenever I got stung by a wasp, which was not infrequently, a wet blue bag would be pressed on the sting. The "blue" was a powder containing a blue pigment made from the indigo plant or ultramarine. A squeeze of the blue bag went into the rinsing water of every white wash to make the white clothing even whiter.

STARCHING

Wheat, potato gratings, rice or another substance rich in carbohydrate was boiled in water to make starch to stiffen clothes. Starch was made commercially in England on a massive scale in the 1840s, when Reckitt and Sons Ltd was going strong.

It seems to me that our ancestors made life unnecessarily difficult and uncomfortable for themselves. The social conventions that made it necessary for a "gentleman" (or indeed a poor counting-house clerk) to wear starched shirts and collars so that he could hardly bend over or turn round, also put an intolerable burden on the wretched laundry maids. Thank God those days are over.

A SOCIAL OCCASION

As there was so much heavy work to do on wash day, from sorting and soaking the washing to pounding it in tubs and hanging it out to dry, everyone (except the men) had to help out. This often became quite a social occasion for the women of the household.

WASHING BY MACHINE

IN THE NINETEENTH CENTURY THERE WERE MANY attempts to design an effective washing machine. Most were based on the traditional method of washing—that of pounding the washing in water to loosen the dirt—and only got as far as mechanizing the pounding by the peg dolly. A lot of manual labour was still required: the washing machine had to be filled with water and then emptied afterwards, and a wheel had to be turned or a lever pushed backwards and forwards continually to operate the peg dolly.

Nevertheless, washing machines were coveted by many housewives.

The Vowel Y washing machine tumbled the washing about using wooden slats, instead of the traditional peg dolly. The Faithful machine set the washing in motion by a manually operated side-to-side rocking action.

Gradually, wooden washing machines were replaced by steel or copper ones, which were smaller and neater in appearance. At the end of the nineteenth century the first steam washing machine was invented. Water was heated in the washing tank by gas jets, and dirty washing was cleaned by the combined forces of water and steam, which proved much more effective.

TOP OF HAND-CRANKED PEG DOLLY

THE WOODEN TUB
After the dolly tub (see p.91) came the hand-cranked wooden tub. Water was added to the tub and emptied by hand. A five-legged peg and dolly was attached to the lid of the machine and this was agitated back and forth in the tub by turning the large wheel at the side. A small mangle was incorporated at the other side of the tub.

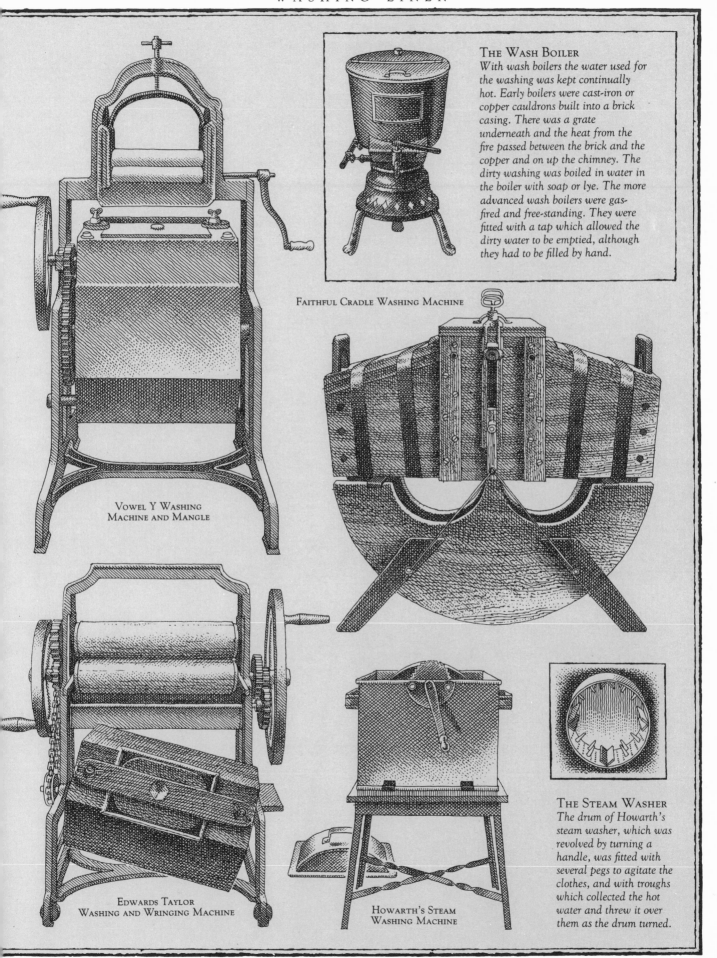

THE WASH BOILER
With wash boilers the water used for the washing was kept continually hot. Early boilers were cast-iron or copper cauldrons built into a brick casing. There was a grate underneath and the heat from the fire passed between the brick and the copper and on up the chimney. The dirty washing was boiled in water in the boiler with soap or lye. The more advanced wash boilers were gas-fired and free-standing. They were fitted with a tap which allowed the dirty water to be emptied, although they had to be filled by hand.

VOWEL Y WASHING
MACHINE AND MANGLE

FAITHFUL CRADLE WASHING MACHINE

EDWARDS TAYLOR
WASHING AND WRINGING MACHINE

HOWARTH'S STEAM
WASHING MACHINE

THE STEAM WASHER
The drum of Howarth's steam washer, which was revolved by turning a handle, was fitted with several pegs to agitate the clothes, and with troughs which collected the hot water and threw it over them as the drum turned.

DRYING LINEN

RYING LINEN WAS A TIRESOME business. The laundress was always at the mercy of the weather, for it was difficult to dry clothes indoors in the cramped space before the fire, especially before the coming of the closed range, when the atmosphere could be smoky. In the towns, housewives had to contend with the soot outside, too, and the carters that drove along the back streets where the linen was hung from one side to the other were a great hindrance, as they would often tear down any washing in their way. As a result, the laundress would try to get her washing as dry as possible before hanging it out, by wringing it.

WRINGING AND MANGLING THE LINEN
The first wringing machine emulated the traditional hand method. The sheet was fixed to two posts and one post was turned tighter and tighter to squeeze out all the water. The box mangle was a much larger and more sophisticated machine, which evolved in the eighteenth century and was used for extracting water from linen and pressing the sheets.

A heavy, stone-filled box was trundled back and forth over loose wooden rollers which rolled over the linen beneath. Only those households with a separate laundry building had the money and space for a mangle, however, and it was not until the nineteenth century, with the invention of the upright mangle, that it could be said that every cottage had something to wring out the washing. Passing clothes through the wringer or mangle got most of the water out of them so they did not take long to dry on the line (or on the hedge).

Straightforward linen, such as sheets, towels, tablecloths and pillowcases, were flattened in the mangle after they had been drying for some time and did not need ironing afterwards. Often such articles were dipped in starch water before passing them through the mangle to stiffen them slightly.

MAKING PEGS
It was a gypsy man, not Gordon Boswell but a Welsh gypsy named John Jones (alas, like Gordon, gone to the great camping ground in the sky), who taught me how to make clothes pegs, sitting before my fire in Wales.

HANGING OUT THE WASHING
If there was enough space the washing was pegged on a washing line outside and left to dry in the wind. Sagging lines were propped up with wooden clothes props, fashioned rather like large pegs. This method of drying clothes was much preferred to having wet washing draped indoors.

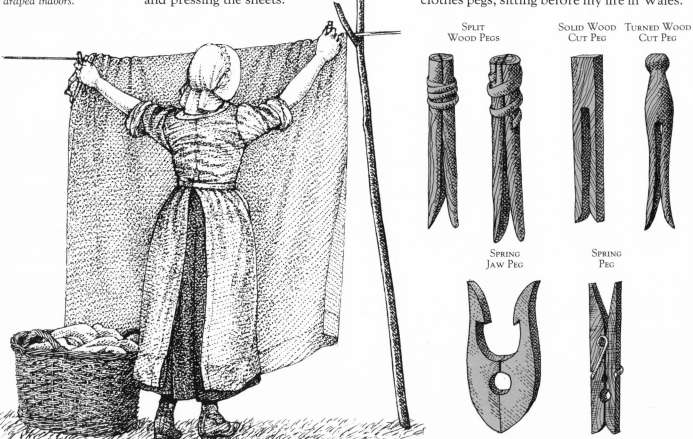

SPLIT WOOD PEGS

SOLID WOOD CUT PEG

TURNED WOOD CUT PEG

SPRING JAW PEG

SPRING PEG

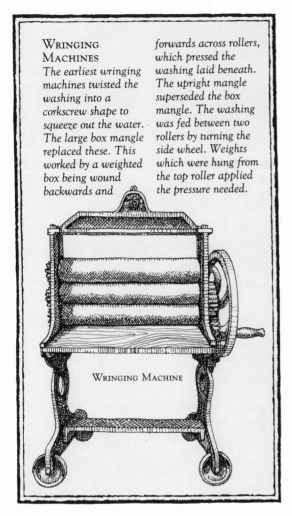

WRINGING MACHINES

The earliest wringing machines twisted the washing into a corkscrew shape to squeeze out the water. The large box mangle replaced these. This worked by a weighted box being wound backwards and forwards across rollers, which pressed the washing laid beneath. The upright mangle superseded the box mangle. The washing was fed between two rollers by turning the side wheel. Weights which were hung from the top roller applied the pressure needed.

WRINGING MACHINE

He would take willow or hazel wands, chop them with a sharp hatchet into lengths of about five inches and shape the top ends into a little knob with a razor-sharp knife. He would then wrap a strip of tinned steel (cut from an old tinned can with tin-snips) round the middle of the peg and tack it on. Finally he would split the peg at the bottom and cut out the shape of the gaping mouth with two deft slices of his knife.

Any gypsy man could make hundreds of these a day. He would clip them on to pieces of cardboard in what were called "hands" and the womenfolk would take them round when they went "calling" on householders and sell them.

HANGING OUT THE WASHING

In certain bourgeois circles it has always been considered undesirable to see other people's washing hanging out to dry. Personally, I can think of few more delightful sights. A line of brightly coloured washing flapping gallantly in the sun speaks to me of cleanliness, self-respect, and the habits of true industry. I am honoured when a member of the gentler but more competent sex entrusts me with the task of hanging out the washing. The scent of wind-and-sun-dried laundry is delightful: nothing like it ever comes out of a tumble drier.

SOCK DRIERS

So that they retained their shape when drying, socks and stockings were placed on wooden boards which were attached with string to the washing line. They were also dried on pottery sock driers. These were filled with hot water to heat the socks and dry them quickly.

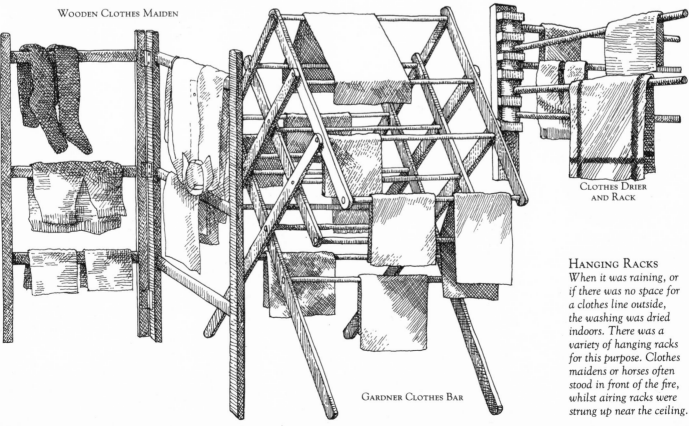

WOODEN CLOTHES MAIDEN

GARDNER CLOTHES BAR

CLOTHES DRIER AND RACK

HANGING RACKS

When it was raining, or if there was no space for a clothes line outside, the washing was dried indoors. There was a variety of hanging racks for this purpose. Clothes maidens or horses often stood in front of the fire, whilst airing racks were strung up near the ceiling.

PRESSING LINEN

THE LINEN PRESS
To ensure that sheets and table linen had precise creases and folds, they were pressed in the linen press after being ironed. The linen press worked by turning the central screw, which lowered a heavy board on to the folded linen below. Pressed linen was stored in the drawer.

IRTUALLY ALL GARMENTS HAD TO BE ironed. Flat irons were ubiquitous. They were heated on the iron hob of the kitchen range and used in turn. Generally when the ironing was being done you would see a couple standing on the hob taking the heat while a third was being used. When the ironer needed to put the iron down for a moment, she would rest it on an iron trivet. Trivets of many shapes and designs were made (see pp.100–101).

Where kitchen ranges did not exist, in such places as Africa and British India, the box iron was universally used. This was an iron-shaped box into which was placed a heated iron slug. These irons were numbered: the smaller the number the lighter and smaller the iron.

CHARCOAL IRONS
Charcoal irons were based on the same box idea. They had ventilation holes in the sides and the *dhoby wallah* in India, or the laundry boy in Africa, spent much time swinging them vigorously through the air to encourage the charcoal to burn.

I knew a man who made a fortune out of selling charcoal irons. I met him in Barotseland, in what was then called Northern Rhodesia but is now known as Zambia. He turned up at the village of Mulobesi with a Chevrolet pick-up truck full of charcoal irons. He then went to the only store in the place—the only store, in fact, for several hundred miles—and unloaded an impressive number of charcoal irons.

Later, over a bottle of whisky, he confided to me that he owed his success to a team of ladies whom he employed to go into the local store a week before he arrived and ask for a charcoal iron. They staggered their visits so that the store-keeper found himself besieged for several days by ladies demanding these, then comparatively unknown, objects. So when—providentially—a van drew up several days later with a load of the requested articles he bought up a good quantity. So my friend made his way through Africa obtaining very good sales and a great deal of money. Thus are industry and foresight rewarded.

SPECIAL-PURPOSE IRONS
In addition to the basic flat and box irons a multitude of special-purpose irons were available to the laundress. To provide a glazed or polished finish to starched garments a polishing iron was used. Similar to a flat iron, it had a convex, rounded base and the ironer would rock the iron forward with one hand while sponging an additional thin starch glaze to the material to be polished with the other: it was a highly skilled job.

The Italian, or tally, iron (see p.100) was used to iron made-up bows and bonnet strings, and to "get up" ruffs and frills. It consisted of one or more barrels of different diameter, into which were placed iron poking sticks, which the housewife heated over the fire. She would hold the tied ribbon or the top of the frilled material around the heated barrel until it was smooth and dry.

PRESSING BYGONES
Ironing boards were usually wooden and had a shelf underneath on which the pressed clothes were stacked. Very dry clothes were first sprinkled with lavender water from a clothes sprinkler before being ironed, generally with a flat iron, which came in a huge range of sizes. The fluting iron was used to crimp material. Charcoal or self-heating irons had to be fanned with bellows or swung vigorously through the air to keep the fire going inside them.

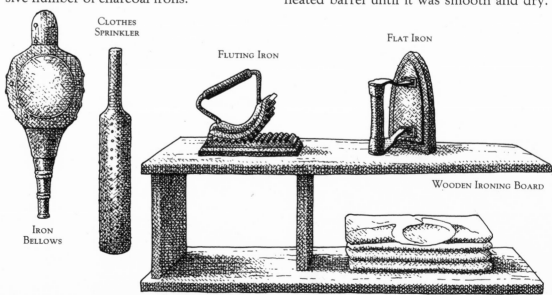

CLOTHES SPRINKLER

FLUTING IRON

FLAT IRON

IRON BELLOWS

WOODEN IRONING BOARD

The French or mushroom iron much resembled the Italian iron but had a more rounded top and was used chiefly for rounding out puffed sleeves.

Various goffering devices were developed from the late eighteenth century especially to make flutes in material. Scissor-like metal tongs called fluting or goffering tongs were popular, as were the fluting board—a corrugated wood or metal board—and ridged roller. The starched material was placed on the board when still damp and the roller run back and forth over it. The goffering stack was in use for many years: it consisted of twenty or thirty wooden or metal spills slotted into two posts. The damp material was threaded through the stack and the whole thing placed in front of the fire. The wheel goffer or crimping machine was developed from this in the second half of the nineteenth century. It operated in the same way as the upright mangle (see p.97), only the rollers were hollow, so that heated cylindrical irons could be inserted as in the tally iron, and, of course, they were corrugated on the outside.

GAS IRONS AND BEYOND
As a child I saw gas irons in use and once owned a Tilley iron. This contained a reservoir for paraffin (kerosene) and a small pump to maintain the pressure.

I remember the maids at the Manor in Essex, where I spent most of my childhood, keeping a small sprig of lavender in a bowl of water next to the ironing board. They would frequently dip their fingers in the water and sprinkle it over the material they were in the process of ironing to keep it moist and achieve a crisper finish. After it was ironed, they would fold the linen and put it away in piles, inserting lavender faggots at regular intervals to keep it smelling freshly laundered. The coming of the electric iron, and especially the thermostatically controlled electric iron with a steaming device, made ironing less of a chore and rendered the bowl of lavender-scented water unnecessary.

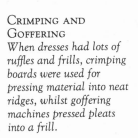

MAKING A LAVENDER FAGGOT
Lavender faggots are easy to make. Simply cut the lavender stems just before they are in full flower. Tie them tightly with ribbon immediately below the flower-heads. Bend the stems over the flowers, then weave the ribbon through the stems to make a "basket" around the flowers. Tie with a bow.

CRIMPING AND GOFFERING
When dresses had lots of ruffles and frills, crimping boards were used for pressing material into neat ridges, whilst goffering machines pressed pleats into a frill.

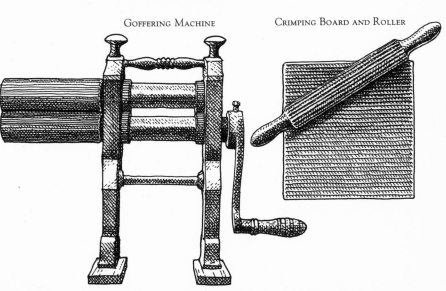

GOFFERING STACK

GOFFERING MACHINE

CRIMPING BOARD AND ROLLER

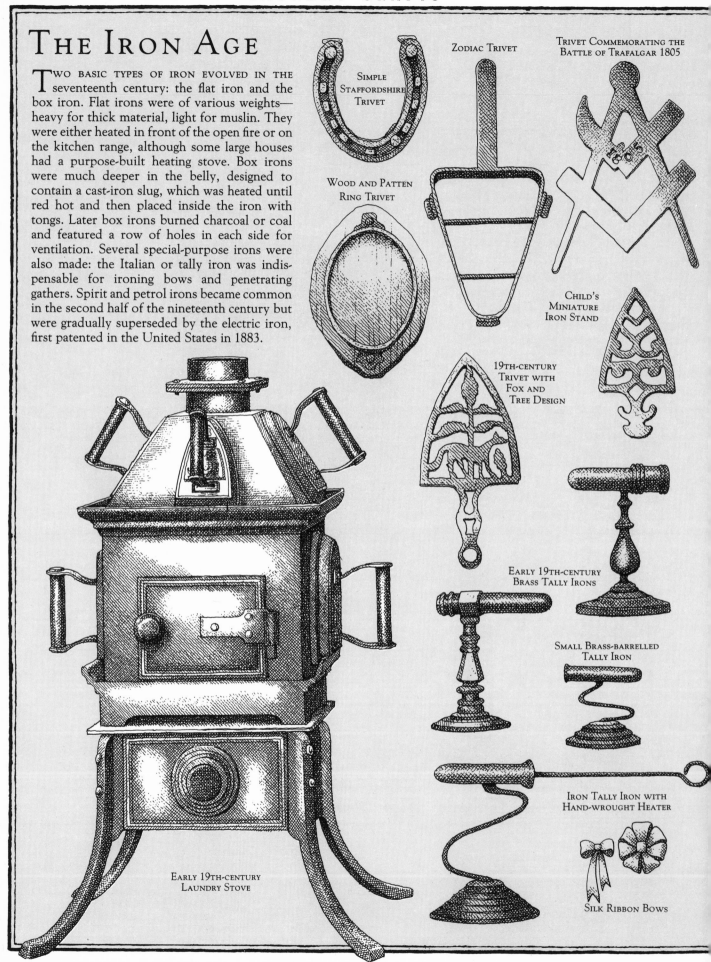

THE IRON AGE

TWO BASIC TYPES OF IRON EVOLVED IN THE seventeenth century: the flat iron and the box iron. Flat irons were of various weights—heavy for thick material, light for muslin. They were either heated in front of the open fire or on the kitchen range, although some large houses had a purpose-built heating stove. Box irons were much deeper in the belly, designed to contain a cast-iron slug, which was heated until red hot and then placed inside the iron with tongs. Later box irons burned charcoal or coal and featured a row of holes in each side for ventilation. Several special-purpose irons were also made: the Italian or tally iron was indispensable for ironing bows and penetrating gathers. Spirit and petrol irons became common in the second half of the nineteenth century but were gradually superseded by the electric iron, first patented in the United States in 1883.

Simple Staffordshire Trivet

Zodiac Trivet

Trivet Commemorating the Battle of Trafalgar 1805

Wood and Patten Ring Trivet

Child's Miniature Iron Stand

19th-century Trivet with Fox and Tree Design

Early 19th-century Brass Tally Irons

Small Brass-barrelled Tally Iron

Early 19th-century Laundry Stove

Iron Tally Iron with Hand-wrought Heater

Silk Ribbon Bows

ELABORATE METAL STAND

EARLY 19TH-CENTURY BRASS STAND WITH KEYHOLE DESIGN

LEAF-SHAPED BRASS STAND

EARLY 19TH-CENTURY BRASS STAND

19TH-CENTURY HEART-SHAPED BRONZE STAND

EARLY 19TH-CENTURY AUSTRIAN BOX IRON

CHARCOAL-HEATED FLAT IRON

EARLY 20TH-CENTURY PETROL-HEATED IRON

"DALLY" SMOOTHING IRON

LATE 19TH-CENTURY METHYLATED SPIRIT IRON

19TH-CENTURY BOX IRON

"HOT CROSS" GAS IRON

MRS POTTS' CHARCOAL IRON WITH DETACHABLE HANDLE

LATE 19TH-CENTURY BOX IRON WITH SLUG

18TH-CENTURY CHINESE PAN IRON

FLAT OR SAD IRON

DYEING

NE CANNOT CLAIM THAT THE ART OF dyeing was practised in many households in the last two centuries, but it is certainly enjoying a brisk revival now. Since the seventeenth century the story of textiles has been one of increasing specialization and industrialization. However, little by little, the modern craft weavers and dyers have unearthed the ancient lore, and begun using the many natural vegetable dyes that people used before the invention of aniline dyes during the nineteenth century.

VEGETABLE DYES

There is absolutely no doubt that the colours obtained from natural dyes are infinitely kinder than the brighter, more garish colours provided by artificial dyes. We may have to go to the tropics for brilliant natural dyes, such as indigo and cochineal, but many subtle colours can be obtained from plants of temperate countries.

Most vegetable dyes require mordanting. In other words, a chemical must be added to the dye to cause the dye to "bite" into the yarn so that it will remain permanently that colour. Chromic acid, stannous chloride (tin crystals), iron and copper sulphates, alum, and bichromate of potash can all be used as mordants. One cannot but wonder how the actions of these chemicals were discovered, nor how someone found out that the leaves of the tansy (*Tanacetum vulgare*), the birch (*Betula alba*), lady's mantle (*Alchemilla vulgaris*), cow parsley (*Anthriscus silvestris*), a kind of heather called ling (*Calluna vulgaris*) and barberry (*Berberis vulgaris*) all make beautiful yellow dyes. Red can be obtained from crottle (*Parmelia saxatilis*), and the roots of bedstraw (*Galium boreale*), while zinnia and some dahlia flowers provide a yellowish-red. The list is enormous.

DYEING FLAX AND COTTON

In the days when many cottagers spun and wove their own linen, and grew flax in their gardens, the yarn was generally bleached white by simmering it in a weak solution of caustic soda and then laying it in the hot sun. A delightful cloth was made by weaving bleached and unbleached yarn in a pattern. Unfortunately, with the passing of time, the unbleached yarn, which was a pleasant shade of fawny-grey, would become bleached and the pattern would disappear. To prevent this from happening, it was usual to soak the unbleached yarn in a strong solution of juniper juice and water.

Flax and cotton are both cellulose materials and they share a reluctance to take most vegetable dyes, although a dye made from oak-apples is effective, as is one made from several kinds of bark and twig. In any case, cotton arrived from the hot parts of the world where it is grown, too late ever to have been woven and dyed in the home on any big scale: it went straight into the factories.

DYEING WOOL

Wool is a protein fibre and takes all dyes well. There have always been black sheep as well as white sheep and spinsters and weavers have produced attractive fabrics by intermixing black and white wool. Such black and white mixtures vat-dyed in indigo result in a very pleasant-looking cloth.

DYEING WOOL

The ingredients for the dye were placed in an iron pot and the pot covered with a weighted board pierced with holes. Water was then added and the dye was boiled up. The wool was boiled in the dye for several hours.

DYEING OUTDOORS

Very early dyeing of wool and yarn took place outside. The cloth was boiled in the dye in an iron pot suspended over an open fire. This was hot and tiring work as the cloth had to be continually stirred with a wooden stick for several hours until the dye was absorbed to the strength of colour that was required. Then there was the rinsing and drying to do.

Around The Home

If you stray into one of the many ruined cottages that dot the countryside you'll probably stand on the brick or tiled floor, through the cracks of which grasses and even small trees are beginning to peep. Look up at the sky through the holes in the roof and you should feel a sense of reverence and awe. For, even though the upper floors are rotten and the smoke-blackened fireplace has long lain idle, you are standing in what was for many years a *real* home. There is far more to a home than stone and mortar, slate or thatch. The true home is a temple that has been tended and served faithfully by generations of devoted men and women. The men went out into the field, or even over the sea to provide the necessities, while the women looked after the home, cleaning and polishing, making up fires, topping up lamps. They nurtured the children, too, and saw to it that they learned the skills they would need in the future to tend homes of their own. This may not often be the way it is now but it is the way it was when that crumbling ruin was lived in, before cruel economic forces led to its abandonment.

GATHERING & MAKING FUELS

LTHOUGH MEDIEVAL LORDS OF THE manor jealously guarded their trees, almost everywhere in Medieval Europe the right of "hook and crook" belonged to the local peasants. In addition to being allowed to take any small, wind-blown timber for firewood, they could take any dead wood that could be dragged from the trees. To obtain such wood they would use either a hook tied to a piece of rope, which they flung up, so that the hook hooked over the branch, or a crook fastened to a long, wooden handle. Woodland was extensive then, especially in proportion to the human population, and there was no shortage of firewood for diligent people, however poor, and no need to cut down growing trees.

HARDWOOD AND SOFTWOOD

Not all wood makes good firewood, however. Hardwoods—oak, ash, holly, birch, beech, hornbeam, elm, maple, sycamore and lime—burn well and throw out a lot of heat. However, all except ash and holly must be well seasoned. If you are cutting down living trees for firewood you should cut down next year's supply this year. Burning green wood, unless it is ash or holly, will not warm your back or your belly. Softwoods don't throw out as much heat as hardwoods and they must be very well seasoned in the dry to give out any heat at all.

The great overhanging roofs of alpine chalets were not built just to look pretty, they serve to shelter the winter supply of firewood, which is absolutely crucial to the

FELLING TREES
The felling of trees for firewood required special tools. First a V-shaped notch was made in the tree with an axe. The trunk was then sawn from the opposite side with a two-handed cross-cut saw; more leverage was provided by driving a wedge in behind the saw with a sledgehammer. The felled tree was then split, or rived, into smaller, more manageable, logs by driving wedges into the wood until the trunk split down its length. To split smaller wood, a froe was driven into the wood, using a club, and worked from side to side to ease open the grain.

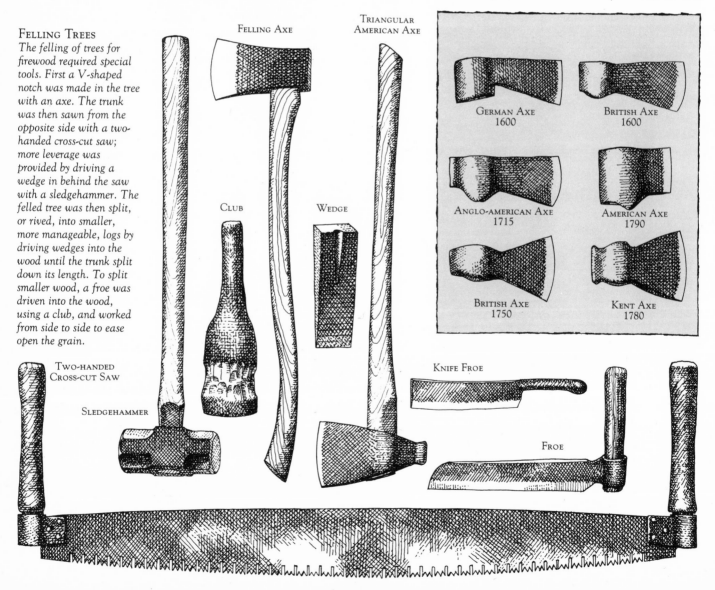

FELLING AXE

TRIANGULAR AMERICAN AXE

CLUB

WEDGE

GERMAN AXE 1600

BRITISH AXE 1600

ANGLO-AMERICAN AXE 1715

AMERICAN AXE 1790

BRITISH AXE 1750

KENT AXE 1780

KNIFE FROE

FROE

TWO-HANDED CROSS-CUT SAW

SLEDGEHAMMER

survival of the people who live in the chalet. Softwood is the only wood that grows high in the Alps and, as it spits when it burns, and as the houses are also made of wood, it cannot be burned in open fires. Instead they burn it in magnificent tiled stoves, often in every room. These stoves are massive, although the fire-box is quite small, and they store heat extremely well, so that the room remains warm after the fire has gone out.

PEAT OR TURF

It is providential that in many countries where firewood is hard to come by, peat, or what the Irish call turf, is there for the digging. Peat forms naturally in wet climates, where the drainage is poor. When the vegetation dies in such places it does not rot away aerobically but sinks into the wet bog and is preserved in its own acidity. After many centuries, deposits of peat many yards deep accumulate. Broadly there are two kinds of peat beds: mountain beds, which have formed in poorly drained hanging valleys in the uplands; and flatland beds found in the plains. Much of the centre of Ireland is composed of a huge peat bog.

Peat digging and burning has been going on for thousands of years, and has experienced a strong revival recently as oil and coal prices have rocketed. In spring and early summer you will see peat diggers all over the wetter parts of the Scottish Highlands and Islands, and anywhere in the west of Ireland (indeed there is turf digging in every Irish county). They use a special spade to dig out the peat or turf, called a slane in Ireland.

As they are dug, the brick-shaped lumps of peat are laid in windrows to dry. If the weather is wet they have to be turned frequently. When partly sun- and wind-dried they are stacked in stooks and often thereafter in high stacks. The peat is positioned in such a way that the topmost and outermost bricks are set at an angle so that they shed most of the rain.

CULM OR BOMS

A fuel now obsolete but once used widely in Wales and Ireland is what the Welsh called culm and the Irish called boms. To make the fuel clay was mixed with coal or anthracite dust (about four parts clay to one part dust). With the addition of a little water the mixture was moulded into balls. Culm had to be burnt on a raised grate to let the air get to it. It was a long-lasting and very satisfactory fuel, but rather a palaver to make!

CUTTING PEAT
A marking iron was used to make vertical cuts in the peat, which was then exposed with a paring iron. The slane cut the peat into rectangular turfs, which were transported in a hand barrow, as heavier wheeled vehicles sank in the wet and boggy ground. The peat was then stacked in loose piles to dry, before it could be used as fuel.

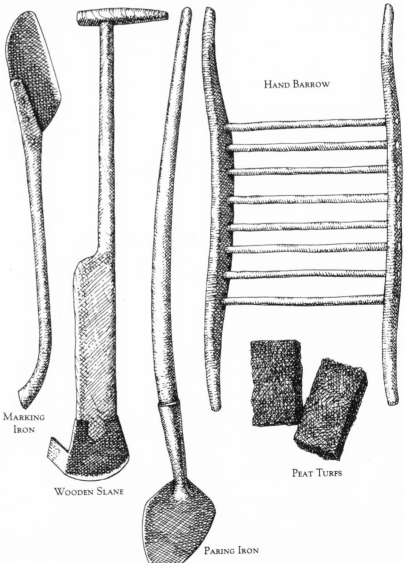

HAND BARROW

MARKING IRON

WOODEN SLANE

PARING IRON

PEAT TURFS

HEATING

T IS UNDOUBTEDLY CONVENIENT TO live in a house that has some form of central heating but, unless you have lived with one, it is hard to imagine the *magic* of spending a winter's evening in front of a great, open wood fire. True, it took a strong will on a freezing winter's night to get up, light a candle, and go up the draughty stairway to an icy bedroom, but it didn't do one any *harm* and colds were no more prevalent in pre-central-heating days than they are now. In fact, I've heard it said that central heating has caused more colds to be caught because it lowers the body's natural resistance.

BEFORE THE FIRE

Living in a house with only a single open fire resulted in a way of life that few people can imagine nowadays. I lived for many years in such a house. Every member of the family *had* to cluster close to the great fire and, in the absence of very good light, it was hard even to follow that solitary activity, reading. Consequently story telling, talking, singing and even reciting verse was the order of the long winter evenings.

My good friend Vernon Jones, who now lives in quite a modern house in Pembroke-shire (although he still has an open fire), told me how he, his parents and his grandfather used to sit around the big "simnai fawr" (large chimney) in their farmhouse in Carmarthenshire, generally with a neighbour or two, simply talking and telling stories. Late at night his great grandfather would come stalking in, having walked five miles from a pub in Carmarthen, and, without saying a word, would pull out his knife and cut a huge slice of salt bacon from a flitch hanging from the ceiling, stick it on the point of his knife and roast it in front of the fire. Four generations—and the neighbours—were united by that fire.

Nowadays great grandpop would be in a "home", grandpop would be living alone in his own bungalow, mum and dad would be silently watching the television and little boy Vernon would be in his own centrally heated room reading comics. As for the neighbours—they would not bother to visit because if they did they would only be subjected to the same TV programmes they could watch on their own telly.

KEEPING THE FIRE GOING

The secret of maintaining an open wood fire is to put really enormous logs on it that will smoulder for a week. My predecessor used to drag logs into the house with a horse. One day, when dragging a huge oak log in by this method, the log stuck between the front door posts. They tried to force it through but could get it neither in nor out and had to send a child up to the neighbouring farm to borrow a stronger horse. This animal was able to haul the log out again but meanwhile their own horse had evacuated itself liberally on the kitchen floor!

Bellows were very important for keeping the open fire going—although in parts of Ireland, where boms of anthracite dust and clay (see p.105) were burned, the fire wheel (a hand-turned centrifugal wind pump) was more common (see p.26).

WOOD-BURNING STOVES

Open fires, particularly those fuelled by spitting spruce and fir wood, are hazardous in houses built entirely of wood, and it is therefore not surprising to find that it was in the coniferous regions of Scandinavia and the Alps, that enclosed stoves were first made and developed into things of great beauty: many of them were ornamented with beautiful tiles.

In Russia and Siberia, where the largest continuous forest in the world can be found, the same conditions prevailed and it was there that the bed stove was developed. Anyone who has puzzled over references in Russian books to peasants "going to sleep on the stove" will be interested to know that the author was referring to the bed stove. Made of brick, the bed stove took the form of a massive platform with a fireplace in it, which retained its heat right through the coldest night even if the fire went out.

The American pioneers made their own enclosed stoves out of sheet metal, which no doubt burnt through rapidly. Later they were able to obtain cast-iron stoves made in foundries, which would last for several lifetimes. They tended to make great play with long iron chimneys, which radiated the heat. In severe winters in not very well insulated houses a huge supply of firewood must have been necessary to survive at all. I am told that in the north-eastern woods they would

STORING FIREWOOD
The drier the wood, the easier it was to burn. When the wood was collected it was chopped into manageable logs and stacked in a woodrick. The woodrick roof kept out the rain, allowing the logs to dry out before they were used as fuel.

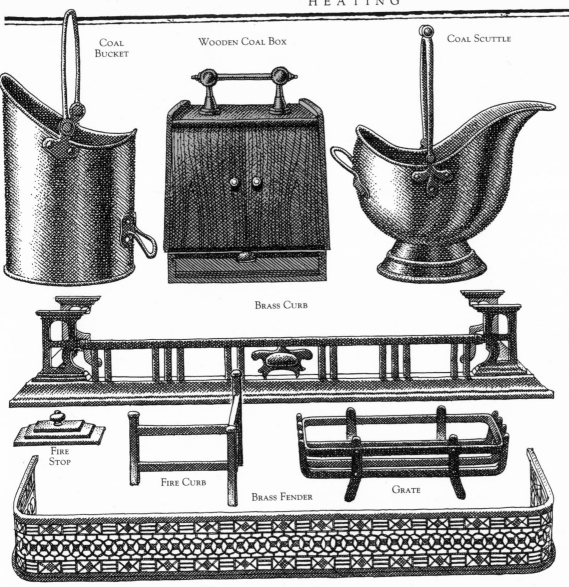

COAL
BUCKET

WOODEN COAL BOX

COAL SCUTTLE

BRASS CURB

FIRE
STOP

FIRE CURB

BRASS FENDER

GRATE

FIRESIDE APPLIANCES
Coal was kept at the side of the fireplace in a coal box or scuttle, which was made of wood, brass or copper. A fender was placed in front of the fire, and a curb at either side of the grate, to confine logs and fallen coals to the hearth. Fire kindlers were dipped in paraffin and used for lighting the fire, and bellows were used to fan the flames. Fire irons were kept within easy reach: tongs and a shovel for lifting the coal, a poker for livening the fire, and a brush for sweeping up the ash.

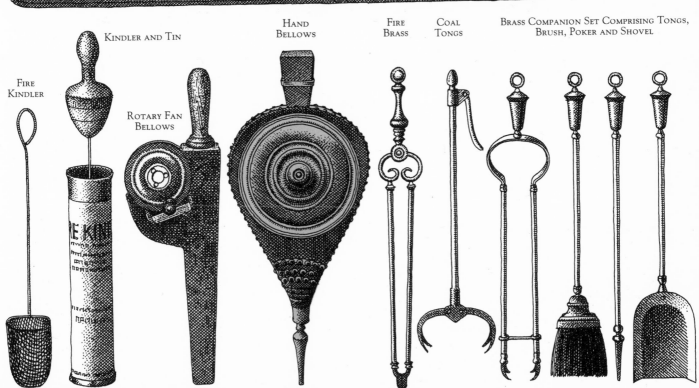

FIRE
KINDLER

KINDLER AND TIN

ROTARY FAN
BELLOWS

HAND
BELLOWS

FIRE
BRASS

COAL
TONGS

BRASS COMPANION SET COMPRISING TONGS,
BRUSH, POKER AND SHOVEL

HEAT PROTECTION
For ladies with delicate complexions, a portable heat screen made of strong canvas was used to protect them from an open fire.

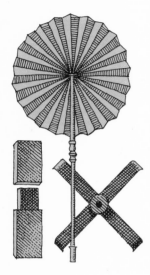

SOLID-FUEL STOVES
These stoves burned wood, coal or coke, and were designed to use fuel as efficiently as possible. They were usually made of cast iron and were conical, rectangular or sometimes tower-shaped. Often they were objects of immense beauty, ornately decorated with intricate, wrought-iron filigree designs.

fell trees in the summer and autumn and then wait for the snow before sledding them to the homestead. Storing enough firewood could be a matter of life or death.

CHARCOAL- AND COAL-BURNING STOVES
In Spain, Portugal and parts of Italy charcoal was much used for both cooking and keeping warm. Winters are very cold in Spain and I have often been amazed at the poor heating arrangements there. But the charcoal brazier under the table was not a bad device and one often used.

Anyone who was ever in the British army during the Second World War or before will remember (perhaps with mixed feelings) the "tortoise" stove. This was a pot-bellied, cylindrical monster made of heavy cast iron, which burned coal. It had a hole in the top enclosed by an iron ring and could be made (and frequently was) red hot. A kettle generally stood on top of it, bubbling away. It would keep at least the lucky end of a long wooden army hut very warm.

OIL-BURNING STOVES
A short-lived phenomenon of the early twentieth century was the oil cooking stove. This could be bought singly—a vertical cylinder of thin steel plate with a window, so that you could see the flame—or as part of a range, with as many as four burners and often an oven as well. The design varied: sometimes the burners contained their own oil reservoirs, filled with what the English call paraffin and the Americans, kerosene, and sometimes there was one large reservoir that supplied the lot.

The early burners had one or two simple wicks, which burned yellow and smoked and stank pretty disgustingly. Later burners had circular wicks that allowed the air to pass through the middle of them. Provided that you kept the wicks perfectly trimmed and the whole thing clean, the flames burned blue and were much hotter and less smelly than the early burners. However, they were still smelly enough. If the housewife was not on constant watch the blue flames would overheat, turn red and yellow and before you knew where you were, clouds of choking black smoke would emerge and everything in the room would be covered in minute greasy black smuts. Nevertheless, these stoves were popular in country districts of the United States and in what the English used to call the colonies, until the arrival of bottled gas.

The Primus stove, and its cousins, still lingers in odd corners of the world. It also burns on paraffin but with the Primus compressed air is pumped into the fuel container and the fuel is circulated around its own flame to pre-heat and vaporize it before it emerges from a jet. You must pre-heat the stove itself by burning methylated spirits under the coil and the jet has to

FREE-STANDING COKE AND COAL STOVE

CYLINDRICAL SLOW COMBINATION STOVE

OPEN-DOOR FRANKLIN STOVE

TORTOISE WORKSHOP STOVE

DOWNWARD-BURNING STOVE

be pricked with a fine wire from time to time to clear it or the flame will go out and the thing will hiss and spit raw paraffin all over you. The Primus is somehow rather an endearing thing to be with in the small cabin or fo'c'sle of a boat. A turn at the wheel or tiller in a freezing wind is made all the more bearable by the friendly hiss and cheering heat of this machine as hot soup bubbles on the jet. The Primus makes up for a lot of struggling with the wheel in my opinion. Sadly, bottled gas has almost completely wiped out the Primus stove and you would be hard put to buy one today.

PORTABLE TABLE
HEATING STOVE

OIL, GAS AND
ELECTRIC HEATERS
*Oil-burning stoves
contained a reservoir of
paraffin, which was
burned to keep the wick
alight. The flame was
visible through a window
in the side of the stove.
Gas heaters operated by
the gas being drawn
through an open chamber
at the base of the heater.
This was then mixed with
air, which resulted in
combustion. In electric
heaters, electricity flowed
through spirals of wire, or
heating elements, to
provide heat.*

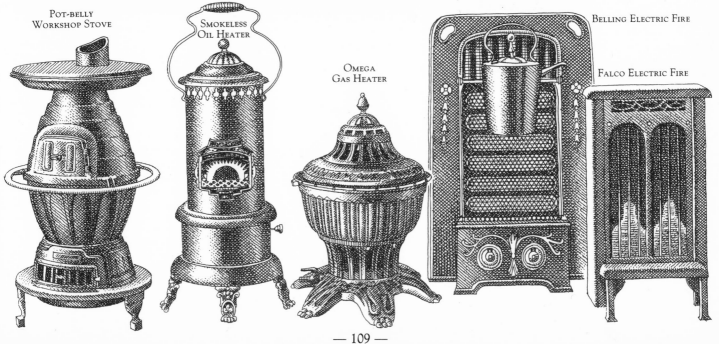

POT-BELLY
WORKSHOP STOVE

SMOKELESS
OIL HEATER

OMEGA
GAS HEATER

BELLING ELECTRIC FIRE

FALCO ELECTRIC FIRE

BEDS & BEDROOMS

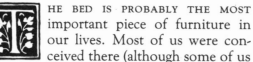

THE BED IS PROBABLY THE MOST important piece of furniture in our lives. Most of us were conceived there (although some of us may happen to have been originated on the chaise longue), most of us were born there, and most of us will die there. And, if we know what is good for us, we will spend a third of our lives there.

THE SETTLE-BED
The settle-bed was the forerunner of today's sofa bed. During the day it was used as a sideboard, and at night its seat folded forwards to create a wide trough in which the bed was then made.

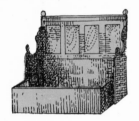

THE VARIETY OF BEDS
Odysseus built the bed that he shared with Penelope with his own hands. He laid out the bedroom around an old olive tree. Then he lopped off the silvery leaves and branches and hewed and shaped the stump into a bedpost. It was the memory of this marriage bed that kept him steadfast when the goddess Calypso offered to make him immortal if he stayed and married her.

In India, the string-bed, or charpoy, is ubiquitous but strangely most people in that country sleep on the floor. The charpoy is often kept on the back porch, or under the shade of a tree, for sitting cross-legged on during the heat of the day. It was an Indian maharajah who owned that strange and

BED WRENCH

BED BASES
Bed bases were either made of ropes, which were stretched between the sides of the bed frame, and tightened with a bed wrench, or laced canvas, which was strung between the head and foot of the bed. The tension could be adjusted by turning a handle at the bed head.

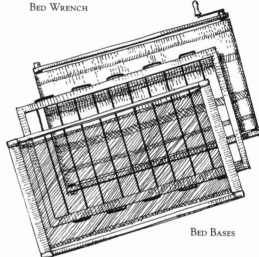

BED BASES

PERSONAL HEATING
Upon arriving at a country inn in England during winter, a warming pan filled with hot ashes was placed between the sheets of your bed to allay *some* of the damp, cold clamminess of an unslept-in bed. If the inn was a good one the landlady would also light a coal fire in the little bedroom fireplace. If not, you suffered the full rigours of the untempered climate.

The stationmasters of many country railway stations used to supply delicate passengers with hot bricks wrapped in flannels to warm their feet when travelling. With a hot brick under your feet, and a rug around your knees, you would be as warm as toast. Hot stone foot warmers and foot stoves were also common.

In Kashmir, high in the mountains, you see women walking about with their hands under their dresses. They look as though they are pregnant, but they are, in fact, clutching small charcoal braziers in front of their tummies.

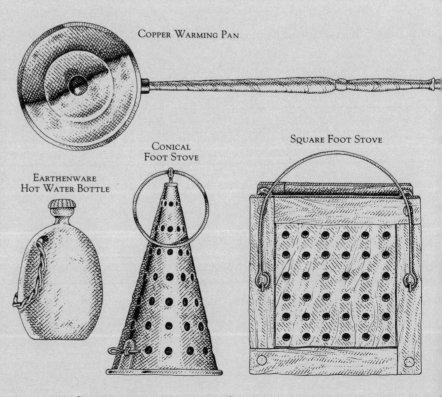

COPPER WARMING PAN

CONICAL FOOT STOVE

SQUARE FOOT STOVE

EARTHENWARE HOT WATER BOTTLE

extravagant bed made of solid silver. It had four life-sized nude female figures painted in realistic colour and detail, fitted with wigs of real hair, and equipped with feathered fans and fly-whisks. The maharajah had merely to lie down and the fanning would automatically commence.

The bed of Louis XIV was held to be so sacred that visitors to the room that contained it had to salute it even if His Majesty was elsewhere. This reminds me of a particularly demanding officer in command of a training camp I was in during the Second World War. So punctilious was he about those of the lesser ranks saluting those of the more important ones that he insisted that we salute the jakes as we passed by if we knew that an officer of higher rank was inside. So we all saluted it anyway just in case.

The stately four-poster bed provided privacy as well as freedom from draughts. Small cottages often had cupboard beds, which folded into the wall after use to look just like the door of a cupboard. I knew an old man in North Pembrokeshire who made cupboard beds to order until recently. In the Highlands of Scotland beds were built into recesses in the wall and shut off by sliding doors. They provided complete privacy as long as you did not mind being half suffocated. There was a disease well known in the Highlands and recognized by doctors and clients alike, which only afflicted husbands. Only ever obliquely referred to by the words, "He's ta'en to his bed", the disease struck only in the dark days of the winter, when the good man, stricken with it, would retire into his box bed together with a bottle of whisky and, despite all the tonics passed to him, remain there until the days grew longer again. It was never fatal.

MATTRESSES

Sailors used to sleep, like countrymen, on feather-bed mattresses if they were lucky or on "donkey's breakfasts" if they were not. These were no more than hessian sacks containing straw or hay. I knew an old "flat" man—a mate on a Mersey flat (the equivalent of the east coast barge, the Humber keel, or the Severn trow)—who saved his vessel from sinking after she had been holed due to a collision with a steamer by stuffing his donkey's breakfast in the hole.

Feather beds, incidentally, were very difficult things to clean. By far the best way was to take the feathers out and dry them, very carefully, in a slow oven or even, if one was available, in a malt kiln (a perforated iron plate) over a slow fire. Feather beds *could* be washed whole but drying them was a hideous business, necessitating endless shaking and fluffing and hanging in the wind. If you didn't dry them thoroughly you would invariably end up with a putrifying mess.

MOVABLE BEDROOMS

Gypsies, who came from India, lived for a couple of centuries in vardos or horse-drawn living wagons—the "gypsy caravans" of the story books. The vardo was simply a movable bedroom, for almost all the cooking was done on the open fire outside. You entered the vardo by climbing gaily decorated steps, placed between the shafts after the horse was taken out. To your left, just through the door, you would see a "Queen" or "Princess" stove—a small, highly ornamented, cast-iron enclosed stove. Such stoves threw out an enormous amount of heat and one would keep the vardo very cosy. In front of you, taking up the whole width of the living space and much of its length, too, would be a great bed, enclosed by shuttering and extremely colourful curtains. Below this bed you would find another bed in which all the children slept, regardless of age or sex: it held an enormous number of children.

THE BED-WAGON
The bed-wagon was a device for warming damp and cold beds. Like the warming pan, it was inserted into the bedding shortly before the bed was to be used. It consisted of a small brazier which was enclosed in a metal cage.

ADVERSE CONDITIONS
Damp beds were a frequent hazard for early travellers. To overcome the problem they measured the humidity of a bed with a damp bed detector before agreeing to stay at the inn!

STONE FOOT WARMER

HAND WARMER WITH CHARCOAL REFILL

HOT WATER BELLY WARMER

CHAMBER POTS
Before houses had indoor bathrooms, a chamber pot was always kept under the bed in case of "emergencies". Its presence must have saved many a long and cold walk to the privy at the bottom of the garden! Far from being plain and inconspicuous, many chamber pots were often very prettily decorated.

DECORATED CHINA POT

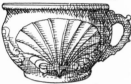

PLAIN MARBLE POT

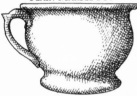

LEAD-GLAZED EARTHENWARE POT

BOW DESIGN POT

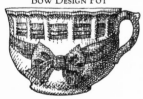

STATIC BEDROOMS

The cottager's bedroom tended to be virtually just that. In addition to the bed there would be a chamber pot, placed underneath it or concealed in a cheaply made piece of wooden furniture with a door, a wash stand with ewer and basin and slop bucket, a few pictures and possibly some poker-work, religious texts or sentimental messages hung on the papered walls.

People who were born in this central-heating age can have no idea of the rigours of an unheated English bedroom in the middle of an old-fashioned English winter! You would often have to break the ice on the washing water in the jug on the wash stand—that is, if you were foolhardy enough to want to wash! You were lucky if you had a feather bed, with a big feather-filled eiderdown, and luckier still if you managed to get your hands on at least one of the brown glazed porcelain hot water bottles that were common in my childhood days.

In wealthier households the bedroom was far more than just a place to sleep. In a lady's bedroom there was always an elaborate and beautiful dressing table, which supported and contained a mass of material most mysterious to a man. There were hairpins, ribands, bows, make-up and face powder, a selection of combs and hair brushes, bottles of scent and other lotions; there might also be mementoes and photographs of members of the family; and there would be mirrors set at angles, so that my lady could view herself from every direction, and, in addition, at least one silver-backed or tortoise-shell-backed hand mirror, too.

In this bedroom you would also probably find an elegant escritoire, or small writing desk, on which my lady would write her diary, compose poetry, and write secret notes to her lovers. She may also have had a couple of chairs set in front of the fireplace, and maybe a small occasional table, in case she wanted to have a little tête-à-tête with a close acquaintance. In larger houses, too, there were often dressing rooms attached to the main bedrooms: perhaps two, one for him and one for her. There would also be a bell pull, which would probably take the form of a tasselled rope hanging down from the ceiling. It was connected by a secret Heath Robinson-like system of ropes and pulleys to the great kitchen or the butler's pantry, or the hall between the two, where there was an array of small bells upon the wall, each struck by little hammers on springs. When the servants heard a bell they would rush to the place to see which little hammer was still swaying about to discover the room in which they were required.

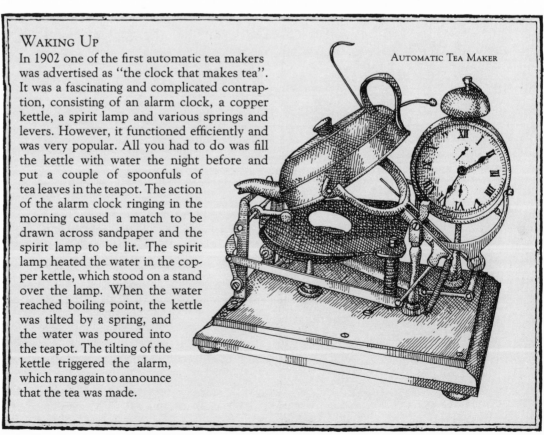

WAKING UP

In 1902 one of the first automatic tea makers was advertised as "the clock that makes tea". It was a fascinating and complicated contraption, consisting of an alarm clock, a copper kettle, a spirit lamp and various springs and levers. However, it functioned efficiently and was very popular. All you had to do was fill the kettle with water the night before and put a couple of spoonfuls of tea leaves in the teapot. The action of the alarm clock ringing in the morning caused a match to be drawn across sandpaper and the spirit lamp to be lit. The spirit lamp heated the water in the copper kettle, which stood on a stand over the lamp. When the water reached boiling point, the kettle was tilted by a spring, and the water was poured into the teapot. The tilting of the kettle triggered the alarm, which rang again to announce that the tea was made.

AUTOMATIC TEA MAKER

HOME DOCTORING

P UNTIL THE EARLY NINETEENTH century the still room was a part of every country mansion. In it the lady of the house presided at the distilling of, not only perfumes, spirits and cordials, but also essences of many plants used as remedies for a vast range of ailments. The body of knowledge that the well-bred countrywoman was expected to have in this respect was immense.

HERBALISM

It is remarkable how many of the medicines in the modern pharmacopoeia owe their origins to the old herbalists. Many old country people still use herbs or, more frequently, talk of using herbs. I know an old wind-miller in Suffolk who swears that every part of an elderberry tree is good to cure some disease, and I knew an old gypsy man, God rest his soul, who used to dig up mandrake roots for a living. Some mandrake roots, he assured me, were male and others female, and if you found a specimen of the one there was sure to be a specimen of the other nearby. According to him, when you hauled a root out of the ground it would "shriek like a man in torment, frightening a man's heart to hear it". Mandrakes, he believed, and so did many another old countryman, only grew on the ground over which a man had been hanged.

BEFORE ANTIBIOTICS

The Victorians were usually equipped with all kinds of medical knick-knacks, for they took sickness very seriously. Much of it was self-inflicted: the frequent fainting fits, the "vapours" and the wastings-away that young ladies were prone to then were largely due to the frightfully restrictive clothing fashion forced them to wear. Consumption, or pulmonary tuberculosis, was extremely common among both rich and poor, largely because of an absolute phobia about opening windows to let in fresh air.

I am old enough to remember the thick mat of straw laid on the public highway in front of a house containing a sick person. The straw deadened the noise of the wheels of passing horse-drawn traffic and I remember the sense of foreboding and awe when being driven over such a straw mat. Sickness —a very grave thing indeed!

MEDICAL PARAPHERNALIA
In Victorian times sickness was taken very seriously and houses were equipped with much medical paraphernalia. There were bed pans, throat sprays and brushes, inhalers, eye baths and smelling salts, plus, of course, a well stocked medicine chest.

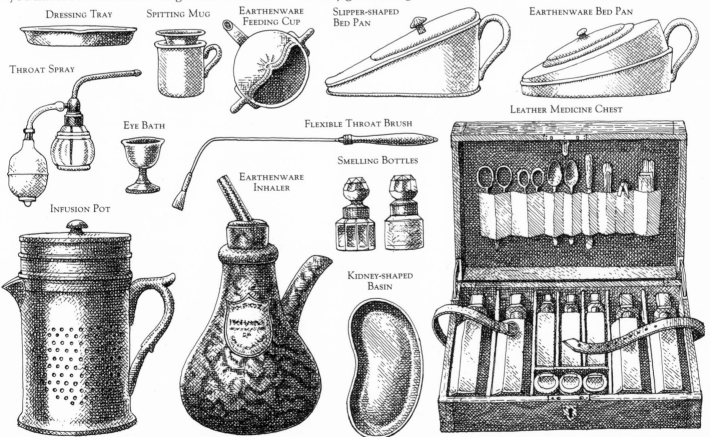

DRESSING TRAY SPITTING MUG EARTHENWARE FEEDING CUP SLIPPER-SHAPED BED PAN EARTHENWARE BED PAN

THROAT SPRAY

LEATHER MEDICINE CHEST

EYE BATH FLEXIBLE THROAT BRUSH

SMELLING BOTTLES

INFUSION POT EARTHENWARE INHALER

KIDNEY-SHAPED BASIN

BATHING & THE JAKES

HEN I WAS A BOY, IF YOU WERE A guest in any decently appointed household you would always be woken in the morning by a house-maid tripping into the room and opening the curtains to let the sun come stream-ing in. A cup of tea and a plate of white bread and butter would be placed on the side table, with the bread cut thinner than the butter. A copper jug with a lid hinged to the main part of it and another tiny lid hinged to the spout was set next to the plate. Full of hot water for washing, the jug would have a clean towel draped over it to keep the water warm in case you were reluctant to get out of bed.

BEFORE PLUMBING

Such a house would probably have a per-fectly good bathroom, and it was *de rigueur* for the trendy set to take a hot bath every morning. I think this strange idea emanated from the United States, where personal cleanliness was an obsession. Young Ameri-can ladies were coming to England in increasing numbers in those days and their influence was making itself felt.

The bathroom tended to be a splendid affair. The bath would be long and encased in mahogany, and there would be a network of massive pipes made of galvanized iron or copper that made the place look like the

THE BATH

A popular bath for horsemen was the hip bath, as it eased any saddle-soreness! It was a very comfortable bath to sit in, with its rounded base and armchair shape, and you could dangle your legs over the side and lean back and soak in the steam. A jug of extra hot water was kept alongside the bath for topping up the water as it cooled.

The tin bath was a larger version of the hip bath. Long enough to allow you to immerse your whole body in the water, it required more hot water than the hip bath and was therefore more work for the chambermaid. This oval-shaped bath has remained the stan-dard shape for baths ever since, though styles have altered: some early baths were decorated with engraved bows and clawed feet.

Bath heaters saved the constant tramping up and down stairs with pails of hot water. The gas heater could heat a bathful of cold water in about twenty-five minutes.

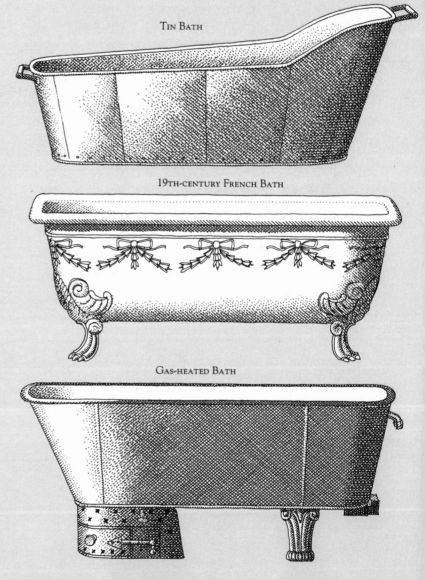

TIN BATH

19TH-CENTURY FRENCH BATH

GAS-HEATED BATH

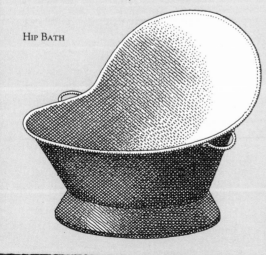

HIP BATH

engine room of a submarine. This was the age of the early gas geysers that would roar and hiss in a terrifying manner and spurt steam like a trans-Canadian locomotive.

Plumbed baths didn't make an appearance until the 1880s, but even after plumbing became fairly common, every big country house was sure to have a hip bath stored away in some box room. Hip baths posed a problem for the guest. For if you availed yourself of a hip bath it meant that some overworked housemaid had to lug several buckets of boiling water up several flights of stairs.

Plumbing took longer to creep into the bedrooms, which were equipped with a hideous wash stand. At least, I thought they were hideous but perhaps my general aversion to washing at all at that age accounted for this aesthetic judgement. Most wash stands were simply tables with marble tops to them, the latter sometimes with holes cut out of them to hold a porcelain basin. In the basin would be a big jug, generally also made of porcelain but sometimes of white enamelled steel. This would be filled with cold water and a towel tastefully draped over it. Somewhere on the wash stand there would be a glass flask of drinking water, alas generally stale, with a glass tumbler inverted over it, and under the whole arrangement would be a slop bucket, usually of white enamelled steel. A concave disc with a hole in it covered the top of the slop bucket. You poured your dirty water into the hole, together with any urine from the chamber pot.

Commodes were fairly common in those days, for many a grand house would have only one jakes and that at a great distance from where you were likely to be. The commode was a large and stately mahogany chair. You lifted up the seat to reveal the top of a large pot; you were supposed to sit over this and relieve your nature. I am glad to say that I never availed myself of this device. I never used the potty either if I could possibly reach, and open, the window.

WOODEN SHEDS

Perhaps the most reprinted book in the world next to the Bible is a little book called *The Specialist*. The specialist of the title is an American country carpenter who specialized in building little wooden sheds at the bottom of people's gardens. They had little ventilation holes cut in a variety of shapes, according to the genius of the specialist; these often doubled as spy holes.

These sheds contained a seat with a bucket underneath and a box of earth or ashes next to it. You sprinkled some of this on top of the slowly mounting contents to protect the seat from the flies. Hopefully, before the bucket was full to running over the man of the house would carry it into the garden and tip the contents into a trench, where it would be buried to await the planting of next year's potatoes. It was such bucketfuls that contributed to the burgeoning fertility of country gardens.

There were even simpler methods of disposing of the wastes of the human body. One was used up to a very few years ago in a certain Shropshire farmhouse. The wooden shed was there, together with the seat with a hole in it, but there was no bucket. Spring water oozed out of the ground underneath

THE FOLDING BATH
This was ideal for those with a cramped bathing area. When not in use, it looked like a bedroom cabinet.

The front opened outwards to the floor, revealing a zinc-lined bath, water tank, heater and waste water outlet.

THE MOSELY BATH TUB

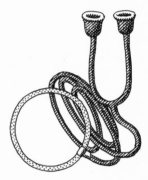

THE SHOWER RING
A novel way of taking a shower was to use a shower ring. You stood in the bath, attached the shower nozzles to the bath taps, and slipped the pierced ring over your head. This method of showering prevented any splashing over the walls and floor, and also stopped your hair from getting wet.

FOOT BATHS

If you got your feet wet while out in the rain, use of a hot foot bath was considered essential to ward off colds and fevers. Foot baths were generally oval-shaped and made of tin. Some had a ledge to rest your feet on while you dried them.

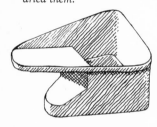

WASH STANDS

Early wash stands were simple wooden frames containing a basin, jug and soap dish. As their design improved, shelves, drawers and mirrors were added, and some wash stands were enclosed in elegant cabinets.

the seat and gently washed whatever was dropped into the hole down the adjoining hillside, where it fertilized the grass. The owners, not without a perverse sense of humour, had installed the snarling head of a stuffed fox hard by the hole and I remember my initial shock as, gingerly lowering my latter end past the head, my eyes slowly becoming used to the darkness, I suddenly became aware of those needle teeth.

FLUSH TOILETS

Sir John Harrington invented a flush toilet as early as 1596, and one was installed for the use of Queen Elizabeth I. Except for the one that disposed of the royal bodily wastes we do not hear of any others until, in 1775, a watchmaker named Alexander Cummings patented a water closet with a "U" bend in the outlet pipe. Because the water always remained in the "U", noisome odours were prevented from rising from below. Joseph Brahmah, a cabinet maker, further improved the design as did another installer of these useful devices, who had the almost unbelievably apt name of Crapper. Many of the very early water closets, with their accompanying overhead cistern, are still in use—some nearly two centuries old—whereas the latest plastic objects are apt to be broken or out of order within weeks of being installed. Certainly not one of them will still be in use in a hundred years' time.

EUPHEMISMS

Euphemism after euphemism has been invented to convey the meaning of the harmless jakes. The one I like most is the "thunder-box", which I believe is a British India expression. "W.C." is simply a shortened form of the words "water closet", which is what the thing was called when water-borne sewage was common in the nineteenth century. Water closets were born much earlier, however.

The monks of the Middle Ages had water closets: they cunningly sited their necessaria over a running stream, downstream, of course, from where they extracted their drinking water. The Cistercians used the water from their stream to drive their corn mill, and sometimes also a sawmill; provide their drinking water; fill their stewpond (in which they reared carp); provide their lavatorium (the place where they washed, *not* what we now call a lavatory); supply their tannery, their laundry and their brewery; and finally act as their sewer. Whether this depressed riparian property values downstream, we are not told.

Another euphemism born in Medieval times was the word "garderobe". This term originated because of the practice of hanging costly furs in the necessaria of castles and palaces: the ammonia gases did a great job of keeping away the moths!

MARBLE WASH-BASIN CABINET

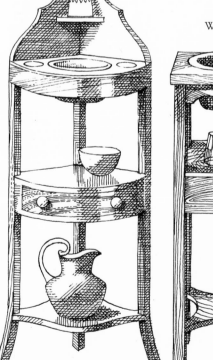

CORNER WASH STAND

WOODEN WASH STAND

THE PRIVY

THE EARTH CLOSET PRECEDED THE WATER closet as a household privy, yet they both followed the same principles of operation, one using dry earth, and the other water. The earth closet consisted of a wide wooden seat with a hole in the middle, under which stood a large pan. Dry earth was stored in a hopper-like container above the seat; a chute led from the hopper to the pan. After using the earth closet, the side lever was pulled, which released a measured amount of earth from the hopper into the pan. The pan was emptied manually. The earth in the pan absorbed and retained any offensive odours, so that the pan could remain unemptied for a week or more!

Water closets were developed from these early privies and are still used today, albeit with some refinements of design. They were usually built against a wall, with boxed-in sides, and often had highly decorated seats and china pans. The more ornate water closets had a sunken, pull-up handle on one side and a sunken box to hold paper on the other. The large cistern was mounted on the wall above the closet; the two were attached by a pipe. A long chain hung from the cistern and was pulled to release a measured amount of water down the pipe to flush the closet pan. The cistern then slowly refilled. Early water closets were often extremely noisy. It was said that if a burglar broke into the house, all he had to do was flush the water and no one would suspect he was there!

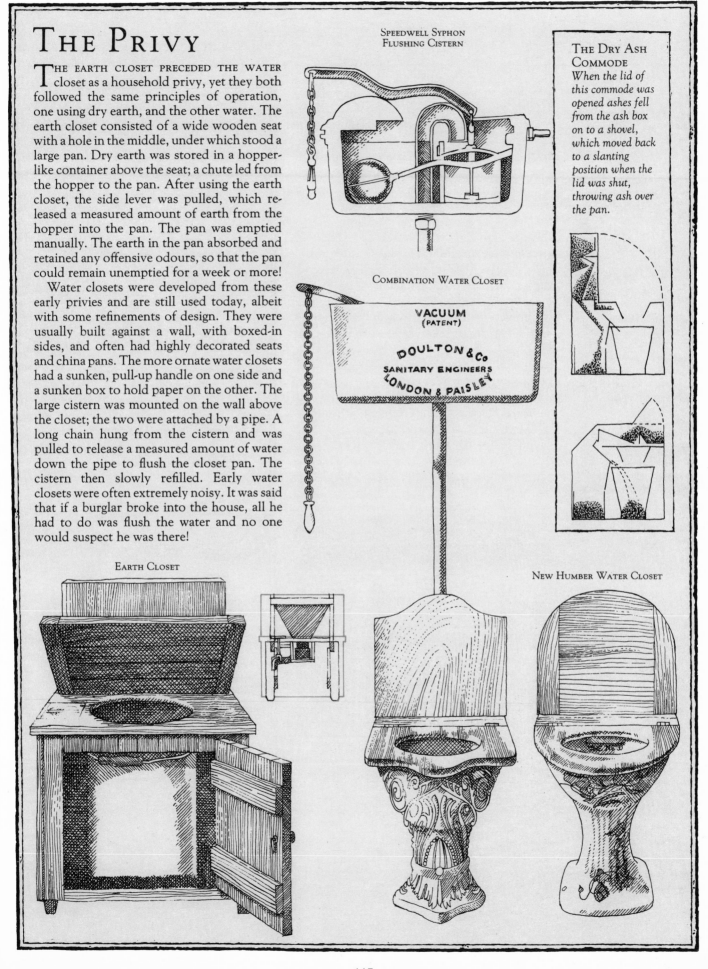

SPEEDWELL SYPHON
FLUSHING CISTERN

COMBINATION WATER CLOSET

VACUUM
(PATENT)

DOULTON & Co
SANITARY ENGINEERS
LONDON & PAISLEY

THE DRY ASH COMMODE
When the lid of this commode was opened ashes fell from the ash box on to a shovel, which moved back to a slanting position when the lid was shut, throwing ash over the pan.

EARTH CLOSET

NEW HUMBER WATER CLOSET

DINING & ENTERTAINING

NLY TWENTY YEARS AGO I KNEW A wealthy sheep farmer in Wales who used to dine, together with his wife and many children, sitting round one huge bowl of cawl (mutton soup). Everybody was armed with a spoon and they all dipped into the same bowl. Washing up was a speedy business: everyone would swish his spoon in a bowl of water and the washing up was done. It seemed to me an eminently sensible arrangement, much more so than the ludicrous elaborations of the rich in Victorian times, when far more dishes of food were put on the table than anybody would possibly eat and spoons, knives and forks lay in serried ranks beside the plates, upon the snow white table cloth. Reading Victorian menus leads one to suspect that the wealthier people of that era dug their own graves with their knives and forks. They cannot have eaten that much food!

The meals of the working class in Victorian times were a stark contrast to those of the rich. Instead of the lush family breakfast of the rich, in which there was a choice of ham in jelly, chicken, potted shrimp, potted

GOBLETS AND TUMBLERS
Drinking water was always provided at the table, together with vessels such as goblets and tumblers. Goblets were made of thick glass and were heavy to hold. Crystal glass tumblers were made of a finer glass and were easily broken.

CUTLERY CANTEENS
Traditionally, a canteen, or chest, of cutlery was given as a wedding present. As the newly married couple usually had very little in the way of cutlery, the canteen included a set of everything, from knives and forks to mustard spoons and sugar tongs.

THE DEVELOPMENT OF CUTLERY
In the fifteenth and sixteenth centuries knives were long, narrow and rather skewer-like. Handles were made from amber, ivory, agate or bone, and were elegantly decorated with silver filigree. Forks were introduced in the seventeenth century and, as a result, knife blades became less pointed. The handles also became thicker and stouter. From the eighteenth century onwards, cutlery started to become more utilitarian and much less exquisitely fashioned.

SILVER HANDLES WITH COLOURED ENAMEL 1670

IVORY HANDLES WITH TORTOISE-SHELL PANELS 1710

POTTERY AGATE-WARE HANDLES 1740

RESIN-FILLED SILVER HANDLES 1770

SILVER HANDLES 1805

PRESSED-HORN HANDLES WITH BRASS RIVETS 1835

DECORATED IVORY HANDLES 1880

salmon, boiled eggs, hot rolls, toast, muffins, butter, preserves, caramel custard, sponge cake, tea and coffee, the poor ate only bread and butter and always drank tea (see p.53). They ate their main meal of the day at lunch time and called it dinner. However, it bore no relation to the evening dinners of the rich, with their four or five sumptuous courses. Instead, they ate mostly roast mutton, broth and pease pudding. Their supper nearly always consisted of bread and cheese or bread and jam, although occasionally the man might have fish for tea, and at Sunday tea time, as a special treat, there might be enough cake for everyone.

THE CEREMONY OF DINING

In Medieval times in the noble households of Europe the dining table consisted of a simple board on trestles. If the household was very grand they might have several such tables in the Great Hall. The older Oxford and Cambridge colleges feature some magnificent Great Halls. Two long tables run down the length of the hall for the hoi-polloi to sit at and a smaller table is set at right angles to these on a higher level at one end: this is the high table, where the dons and fellows sit. The hall is separated from the kitchen by a passage called the screens across which the food is carried.

The tables were not "laid" with cutlery as we lay tables today, as each diner owned his own nef, or eating utensils, which consisted of a knife, a spoon and a drinking cup. Forks had not yet come into use. The only permanent embellishment on the trestle table was a huge and ornamental salt cellar. You sat below it or above it according to your social status—at least everybody knew where they were. There were no plates as we know them today. Instead, trenchers of bread (see p.35) were used. These were brought in with the first course and given to those at the top of the table or at the high table if there were several. The diners with

bread would cut their trenchers to make as many plates as there were to be courses and lay their own knives and spoons ready to eat. Once they had finished the first course, which at an elaborate feast might consist of a choice of boar head and pudding, game and fish, they would pass their trenchers, now soaked with gravy, to the lesser orders sat further down the table or at the lower tables, who could then start eating.

As each course was brought in—held aloft by servants—it was heralded by a fanfare of trumpets. In the church of St Margaret in King's Lynn, Norfolk, there is a splendid depiction of a magnificent feast on the funereal brass of Robert Braunche, erstwhile Mayor of King's Lynn, who died in 1364. The brass depicts a long board, with eleven guests sitting along one side, and a twelfth guest in such a hurry to get at the victuals that he is leaping over the table! The main course of the meal is a splendid peacock, complete with feathers. Of course, the peacock had been skinned and roasted first, and then the skin placed over the bird again just before it was brought to the table: a glorious sight. At the flank of the board stands a group of musicians.

The scene highlights the difference between the Medieval attitude to the gifts of the good Lord and the attitude shown by many today, who sit down in front of the telly to eat some processed rubbish from the supermarket. Maybe we cannot all have a group of musicians playing to us as we eat our sausages and mash but we could at least approach the whole business of eating with some degree of respect.

HOUSEHOLD DEMOCRACY

It was not until late Tudor times that the fine old tradition of dining in hall—everybody together from the highest to the lowliest in rank—began to be replaced by the lord and lady eating separately from the workers in a "solar"—a private apartment upstairs. This

WARMING PLATES
To warm the plates before a meal, they were stacked on a plate warmer, which was then set in front of an open fire. The four corner rods prevented the plates from falling off the stand and breaking.

THE VASE THE BISHOP

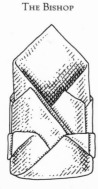

THE MITRE

THE ROSE AND STAR

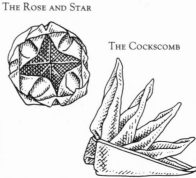

THE COCKSCOMB

NAPKIN FOLDING
Napkins provided the finishing touch to the set table and if they were untidily or badly folded, the meal could well be ruined! All competent housewives were expected to master the art of napkin folding and produce designs like these with the minimum of fuss.

began the end of the tradition of the Great Hall. Cobbett bitterly regretted the tendency in his time (the early nineteenth century) of yeoman farmers to eat with their families in the dining room instead of at the great scrubbed kitchen table with the maids and farm workers, many of whom "lived in". He realized that this practice would mean that the servants would no longer eat the same quality or quantity of food as the master and mistress. He knew that it signalled the end of the true democracy that made English farming so splendid and gave the farmer's boy the chance that befell the hero of the song of the same name:

> They left the lad
> The farm they had
> And their daughter for his bride!

His fears were well-founded: the farm men and lasses have all gone to the cities, the boy who would have been "the farmer's boy" is on the dole, and the master and mistress sit alone in a tiny "modern" kitchen. The big mahogany table in the dining room now gathers dust and the great old farm kitchen is used as a store room.

THE ARRIVAL OF SIDEBOARDS

By Georgian times the master and mistress sat at opposite ends of a wide, heavy table and the other members of the family along each side. The sideboard became common then and often, like the dining table, was made of mahogany. Magnificent silver vessels and dishes, made along classical lines, adorned the table: it was not until the Victorian age that silverware became over-ornamented and vulgar.

Even in my childhood the sideboard was an important feature of the dining room. Breakfast was placed on it every morning, each dish set over a spirit stove to keep it warm for late arrivals. There would be bacon, eggs, sometimes mushrooms, and often kedgeree: a mash-up of fish and rice, which was excellent. Finally there would be a coffee percolator, which would be kept bubbling away throughout breakfast.

As my mother was American she made waffles for Sunday breakfast at the table, using an electric waffle iron. We ate them with maple syrup sent to her from America by her relatives and I remember never being able to eat enough of them. We boys could have gone on eating them all day or, I suppose, until physical illness intervened to save us from bursting.

VICTORIAN DINING ROOM
In a middle-class establishment, while the guests drank sherry and the master and mistress entertained them, the children, dressed in their Sunday best, were expected to help the maid lay the table for dinner; at least, that was what my mother used to tell me.

SERVING AIDS
A dinner carrier kept food hot until it was needed, proving an ideal serving aid for dinner parties and picnics. It was made of china in separate sections which fitted on top of each other, and was specially designed to carry four separate courses.

CANDLE & OIL LIGHTING

I N THE TROPICS THE SUN RISES AT six in the morning and sets at six in the evening and that's that. There is very little twilight. As you go further north or south of the equator, the differential between winter and summer daylight hours increases until you reach those unfortunate latitudes where the sun never sets all summer or rises all winter. To spend a winter in such a place without artificial light would surely drive you mad.

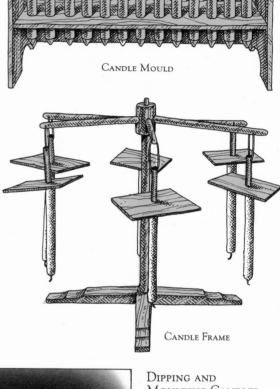

CANDLE MOULD

THE LIGHT OF THE OPEN FIRE

You can see to cook and eat, and to perform simple or straightforward tasks by the light of an open fire and you can always pick up a burning stick from the fire and use it as a torch: I have done so many times in the African bush. Until the introduction of oil lamps most African people would use and enjoy the twelve hours of daylight, gather around the fire for three or four hours and then sleep for the rest of the night. At the time of the full moon they would sometimes dance all night. Even without a full moon, a leaping fire of dried sticks sends out enough light for plenty of dancing.

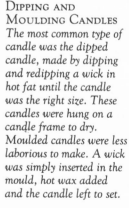

CANDLE FRAME

THE WICK MEASURE

The wick measure was used to cut the candle wicks to an exact length— usually eighteen inches. It was a flat piece of board with an upright rod at one end and a piece of bent wire at the other. The wick was doubled round the rod, held to the wire, and then cut with scissors.

PRODUCTION LINE

An economical method of candle making was to dip several wicks at a time, setting up a kind of production line. As some were being dipped, others were hardening on a makeshift drying rack. The consistency of the tallow was important to the final result: too hard and the candles would crack as they dried; too soft and they would splutter as they burned. The method of making the wick was also crucial. If the wicks were plaited and then flattened out they tended to burn to one side of the candle. In this way, as the wick burned and collapsed, the charred portion did not smother the flame.

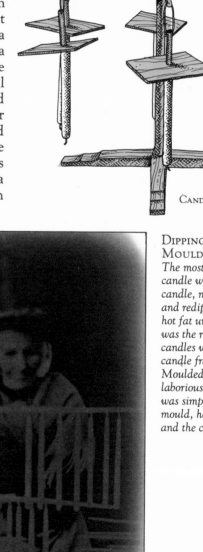

DIPPING AND MOULDING CANDLES

The most common type of candle was the dipped candle, made by dipping and redipping a wick in hot fat until the candle was the right size. These candles were hung on a candle frame to dry. Moulded candles were less laborious to make. A wick was simply inserted in the mould, hot wax added and the candle left to set.

THE DEVELOPMENT OF RUSHLIGHTS

Further north sustained indoor lighting was essential, particularly if people wanted to read (or paint pictures on cave walls). The first lamps were probably made from stones or rocks with natural depressions in them. The dips would be filled with animal fat, and a rush or a chewed twig laid in the fat and lighted. People learned to press oil out of plants, render fat from animals and, eventually, extract it from fish, whales and even sea birds. Early crafted lamps, found by archeologists in nearly every dig, were made of pottery, soap stone and other soft, natural stones. Sometimes they found lamps made of such beautiful hard stones as quartz, serpentine and lapis lazuli. They all had a small reservoir for the oil or fat and a lip on which the wick could be laid.

A natural progression from these simple lamps was the traditional rushlight. Rushes can be found in abundance. Peeled of their hard outer skin the inside pith makes a fine absorbent wick. If you peel a rush nearly all the way round, leaving a strip of skin the length of it to give it sufficient strength, and dip it in hot animal fat, once it is cooled you have a primitive candle. If you then devise a grip to hold it—perhaps a paperclip mounted on an upright stick—you have illumination. You can even read by the light of several of them. A rushlight fifteen inches long will burn for half an hour. They smoke and smell of burning fat but in 1700 they probably didn't mind, especially as it was the one light that was absolutely free: everyone who killed a pig or a fat sheep occasionally, or who could scrounge some rancid dripping, could have rushlights for nothing. Mutton fat made the best rushlights; pig fat was awful.

THE ARRIVAL OF CANDLELIGHT

Candles were certainly used in Elizabethan times and noblemen attending a banquet at the French court of Louis XIV used to carry a candle in order to appear subservient to the king. The first candles were often made by dipping a rush wick into fat, drawing it out for the fat to cool, then dipping it in again, and so on until the required thickness was reached. Alternatively the wicks were hung and hot fat was repeatedly poured over them. Occasionally they were moulded in a long rounded mould with a small hole in the closed end. You poked the wick into this hole and then simply poured in the fat from the other end and allowed it to cool.

When cotton began to be imported from hot countries it replaced rush wicks and linen was sometimes used, too. At first, bleached, twisted yarn was used but this had the disadvantage that it stuck above the candle fat as the fat burnt and had to be constantly clipped with scissors or candle snuffers. Eventually it was discovered that if the cotton wick was braided it curled over and was consumed in its own fire. Modern candles have braided wicks.

Beeswax makes the finest candles and candles burnt in churches have long been made of beeswax. This partly explains why monks obtained a reputation for being jolly. For to get beeswax they had to keep bees,

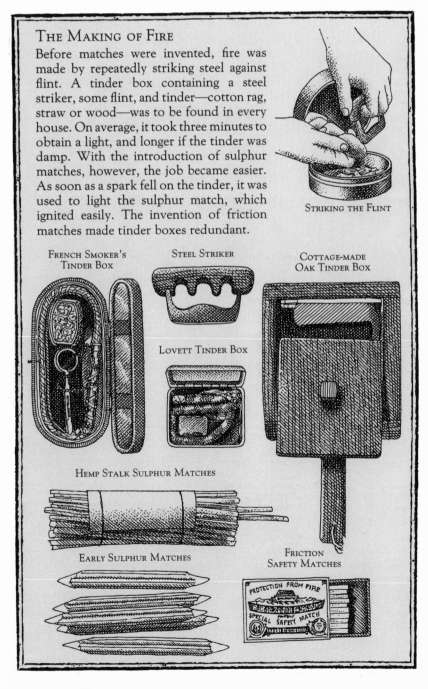

THE MAKING OF FIRE

Before matches were invented, fire was made by repeatedly striking steel against flint. A tinder box containing a steel striker, some flint, and tinder—cotton rag, straw or wood—was to be found in every house. On average, it took three minutes to obtain a light, and longer if the tinder was damp. With the introduction of sulphur matches, however, the job became easier. As soon as a spark fell on the tinder, it was used to light the sulphur match, which ignited easily. The invention of friction matches made tinder boxes redundant.

STRIKING THE FLINT

FRENCH SMOKER'S TINDER BOX

STEEL STRIKER

COTTAGE-MADE OAK TINDER BOX

LOVETT TINDER BOX

HEMP STALK SULPHUR MATCHES

EARLY SULPHUR MATCHES

FRICTION SAFETY MATCHES

CANDLESTICKS AND RUSHLIGHT HOLDERS

Candle and rushlight holders were invaluable. Rushlight holders were made of wrought iron, and held the taper of rushes firmly in the middle by spring jaws mounted on a stand. Candlesticks had small sockets in which the candles were inserted. Rushlight holders often had fittings for candles as well. As light was needed principally for getting up before dawn and going to bed after dark, many candle holders were designed specifically for bedroom use. Known as chamber-candlesticks, they had handles and extinguishers. For the kitchen, there were broad-based candlesticks, as these could not be knocked over very easily. The upright, columnar candlesticks, made of pewter or brass, were mainly used at the table. Wealthier families possessed silver candlesticks bearing one or two branches; these were known as candelabra.

A USEFUL "CONTRIVANCE"

To prevent a candle from wobbling in a large candlestick, this useful gadget was wedged in with the candle.

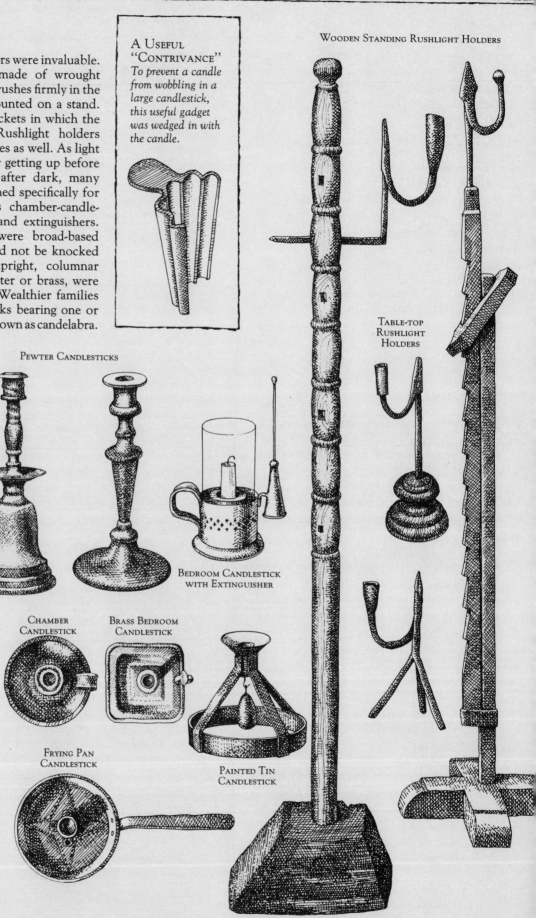

WOODEN STANDING RUSHLIGHT HOLDERS

TABLE-TOP RUSHLIGHT HOLDERS

EGYPTIAN-STYLE CANDLESTICK

PEWTER CANDLESTICKS

BEDROOM CANDLESTICK WITH EXTINGUISHER

WALL CANDLE SCONCE

CHAMBER CANDLESTICK

BRASS BEDROOM CANDLESTICK

FRYING PAN CANDLESTICK

PAINTED TIN CANDLESTICK

and to use the surplus honey they had to make mead: the rest follows. Paraffin wax, distilled from coal and oil shales, was first made in the United States by Abraham Gesner in 1846. The use of this made the candle a much cheaper and therefore much more common article.

A candle becomes shorter as it burns, of course, and lamps were soon made with a spring set below the candle to push the candle gradually upwards, so that its flame was always at the same height. The hole through which the candle was pushed was slightly smaller than the candle itself, so it was only as the top of the candle was consumed that it could be pushed through. I once had a pair of trap lamps that worked on this principle. I drove many miles of roads on dark nights with them, although the amount of light they shone on the road in front of the horse was—well—minimal.

THE DEVELOPMENT OF OIL LAMPS

The mighty Greenland whale of the Arctic and north Atlantic was nearly made extinct by the demand for lamp oil in northern Europe almost two centuries ago. Between 1753 and 1850 an estimated 2,761 whales were brought into one little whaling port alone and boiled down for lamp oil. Even the street lamps of some Dutch and English cities were lit by the oil of the whale. Oil from rape seed filled many a lamp as whales became scarcer, and vegetable oils were used before the widespread use of mineral petroleum in 1859.

The original oil lamp had a closed reservoir for the oil with a wick sticking out of the top. The wick hardly burned at all, as the oil, constantly rising by capillary action, cooled it. As the oil burnt, and smoked and stank, some light was emitted. The wick gradually wore away and you had to "turn it up" by operating a handle.

In the early 1780s, a Frenchman named Ami Argand invented a circular wick which allowed air to pass up the middle of it and resulted in a brighter flame. But the major improvement of oil lamps came with the invention of the glass chimney by Count Rumford. A draught was forced up the wick, causing the flame to burn bright yellow instead of smoky red. This invention was more beneficial to human civilization than the motor car or the aeroplane as, for the first time, ordinary people, who could not afford to buy batteries of candles, could read in the winter time.

CANDLE STORAGE
Candles were kept in tin or wooden candle boxes which hung horizontally on the wall. They were usually cylindrical in shape and had a hinged lid for easy access.

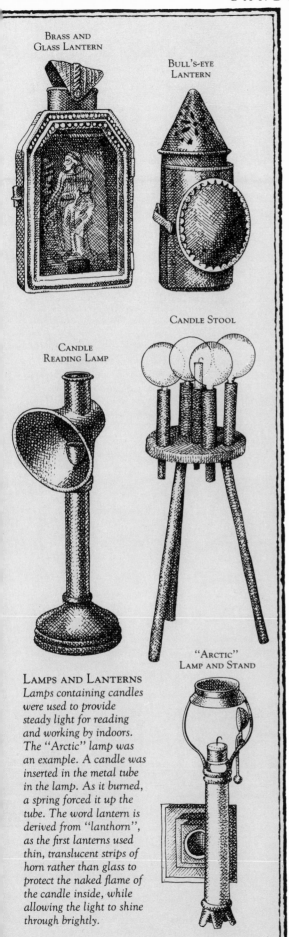

BRASS AND GLASS LANTERN

BULL'S-EYE LANTERN

CANDLE STOOL

CANDLE READING LAMP

"ARCTIC" LAMP AND STAND

LAMPS AND LANTERNS
Lamps containing candles were used to provide steady light for reading and working by indoors. The "Arctic" lamp was an example. A candle was inserted in the metal tube in the lamp. As it burned, a spring forced it up the tube. The word lantern is derived from "lanthorn", as the first lanterns used thin, translucent strips of horn rather than glass to protect the naked flame of the candle inside, while allowing the light to shine through brightly.

The final breakthrough in oil lighting came with the invention in 1884, by a German named Dr Karl Auer, of the incandescent mantle. The mainspring of this cunning device was a little balloon of fabric impregnated with asbestos. The fabric was quite flexible to begin with—like silky cloth. You simply put it in the lamp, lit it and, behold, the fabric burnt away, leaving a balloon of brittle white asbestos. A moth could destroy this delicate stem (in which case you would have to buy another one) but if nothing touched it and nothing shook it, the asbestos would become white hot and give out a brilliant white light as strong as that emitted by a 100-watt electric light.

ALADDIN AND TILLEY LAMPS

The Aladdin lamp was the primary illuminating lamp of the nineteenth century. Hanging Aladdins swung in gimbles from the cabin tops of sailing ships and barges; resplendent table ones stood on every Victorian table (whose owner could afford one). Overheating was a problem with these. When this happened flames shot out of the top of the chimney and tiny black smuts covered the whole room.

I don't have to delve back very far in my memory to recall the business of lamp filling, mopping up the inevitable spillages, wick trimming (if the wick was not perfectly trimmed it smoked and stank to high heaven), washing glass chimneys, smashing them and buying new ones, because our house was wired for electricity only the year before last. Cleaning oil lamps was a time-consuming business. You had to take apart the lamp and wash inside with soda dissolved in water and the chimney had to be wiped at least once a day, as you could lose a considerable part of the light through having a dirty chimney window.

I still have a brace of Tilley lamps, those fine pressure lamps that you pumped up, and which hissed as they gave light. Occasionally, too, the oil inside would fail to vaporize and great red flames would arise within, belching vast amounts of smoke, so that their glasses became sooted up. However, when in good order and using good paraffin, your Tilley would emit a brilliant light and would never go out even outdoors in a gale. I have gutted fish by their light on the deck of a small fishing boat in a gale in the south Atlantic. I'll tell you a secret, though. It's very nice to be able simply to switch on an electric light!

WIRE COIL NIGHT LAMP

LAMP WITHOUT A FLAME
This night light produced a small glow of light, not from a flame, but from a red-hot wire coil, wrapped around its wick. The wick was lit for a few minutes to heat the wire coil, and then the flame was extinguished. The wire stayed red and glowing due to the heated vapours of spirits of wine that rose from the base of the lamp.

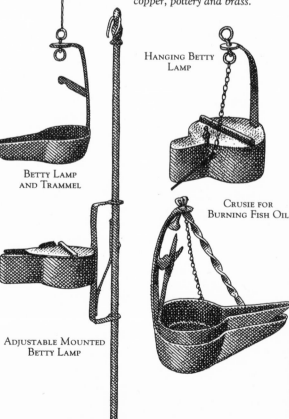

LIGHTING WITH OIL
The earliest oil lamps were shallow earthenware dishes containing oil and a wick of twisted flax, which rested in a pointed lip at one end of the dish. Crusies, or betty lamps, were similar except that they were usually made of iron and had a tray underneath to catch the dripping oil. Crusies burned fish oil and were hung on the wall. When whale oil became too expensive to use, lard was discovered to be a good substitute and many lamps were designed specifically for burning this fuel. Half a pound of lard burned for sixteen hours! As oil lamps became more sophisticated and varied in design, so they became more popular. There were ornate hanging lamps, small portable lamps, free-standing and table-top lamps, made of tin, iron, copper, pottery and brass.

HANGING BETTY LAMP

BETTY LAMP AND TRAMMEL

CRUSIE FOR BURNING FISH OIL

ADJUSTABLE MOUNTED BETTY LAMP

BRASS SLIDING
BALANCE BALL

HANGING LARD
OIL SOLAR LAMP

BRONZED SUSPENSION LAMP

LARD-BURNING
TIN LAMP

OIL LANTERN
WITH SHOE

TWIN COLZA
OIL LAMP

WHALE OIL
LANTERN

BRASS
SUSPENSION LAMP

BULL'S-EYE PEWTER LAMP

BRASS
SPIRIT LAMP

PEWTER OIL LAMP
WITH DRIP TRAY

GLASS AND SILVER
SPIRIT LAMP

GAS & ELECTRIC LIGHTING

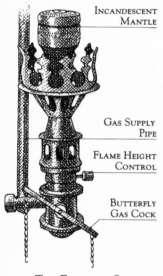

INCANDESCENT
MANTLE

GAS SUPPLY
PIPE

FLAME HEIGHT
CONTROL

BUTTERFLY
GAS COCK

THE ELECTRIC SOCKET
*Domestic electric lighting
was much safer than gas,
as there was no naked
flame, and it was much
cleaner, as there was no
smoke; the flex made it
possible to put lamps
wherever they were
needed.*

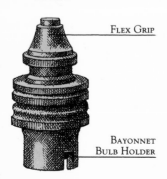

FLEX GRIP

BAYONNET
BULB HOLDER

CELIA FIENNES, THE DIARIST, RODE from Wigan to Warrington in 1698, and her guide "set ye water in ye well on fire and it burned just like spirits and continued a good while..." Thirty years before that a man named Thomas Shirley described how a well near Wigan took fire when approached by a candle. These were the very first references to natural gas.

COAL GAS LIGHTS

Apparently, as early as 1782, curious noblemen discovered that you could obtain an inflammable gas by heating coal. For a long time they put this discovery to no practical use, but in 1792 we hear that one William Murdoch lit his own house at Redruth in Cornwall with gas made from coal. By 1807 a German called Winsor lit up part of Pall Mall with coal gas: the first mention of gas street lighting. It was not until 1812 that the first Gaslight and Coke Company received a charter in London; after that gas lighting spread quite quickly throughout the towns and cities of the land. Piped gas never penetrated the countryside, and the large country house in which I was brought up had an acetylene gas plant: a noisome room tacked on to the house, containing large steel cylinders encrusted with carbide. Water dripped into the carbide, causing it to release the gas, which was then distributed throughout the house by iron pipes.

PORTABLE GAS LAMPS

Carbide and water provided the gas for the lamps of bicycles, motor cycles, and motor cars for several decades. Our great ambition when boys was to be challenged by a policeman (he on foot of course) as we careered past him on our bicycles in the darkness without any lights. He was to shout after us: "Where are your lights?" To which our triumphant reply was to be: "Next to our livers!" ("Lights" is the term for animal lungs.) Although I cycled many a mile through country lanes without lights this final felicity never befell me.

My old Triumph motor bike had an acetylene headlight. On a smooth road the light would shine only dimly but when you hit bumps and potholes it would brighten considerably. The agitation would shake

down more water into the carbide. I came upon carbide lamps again when I worked down a copper mine in northern Rhodesia just before the Second World War: each of we "whiteys" carried one. A little naked flame spurted out of the middle of a silvered concave mirror: it was a touch better than the candles that the black miners had to put up with. The famous Davy lamp used in British coal mines worked on the same principle, but the flame in this was protected by a piece of wire gauze because of the presence of fire damp—the inflammable gas found in coal mines.

PIPED GAS

Gas lighting, although used in mills and factories for many decades, and in street lights widely, did not really penetrate the homes of many people until around the 1880s. The fact was that it wasn't really much good until Dr Auer invented his incandescent mantle (see p.126). Until then gas lights gave out as much smoke and stink as they did light.

Widespread gas lighting for homes was short-lived. From the beginning of the twentieth century electricity made great strides and finally eclipsed its chief rival. Nowadays you might find some bottled gas lighting in some yachts and caravans, and perhaps in a few remote country houses.

THE SLOW SPREAD OF ELECTRICITY

Although electric arc lamps were available from the middle of the nineteenth century, it was not until the invention of the first practical incandescent light bulb in 1879 by Sir Joseph Swan and Thomas Edison that electric lighting was taken seriously. By the 1890s, many streets and large buildings were being lit by electricity but few people could afford to have electric lighting installed in their homes. The perfection of metal filament lamps in 1911 made it cheaper but cable laying and installation was still a costly business and electricity was still confined to the rich. Not until the standardization of the generation of electricity did electric lighting become cheap enough for everyone to have it installed. However, once it took off, electric lighting soon outstripped gas in popularity, for it was clean, silent and emitted no nasty smells.

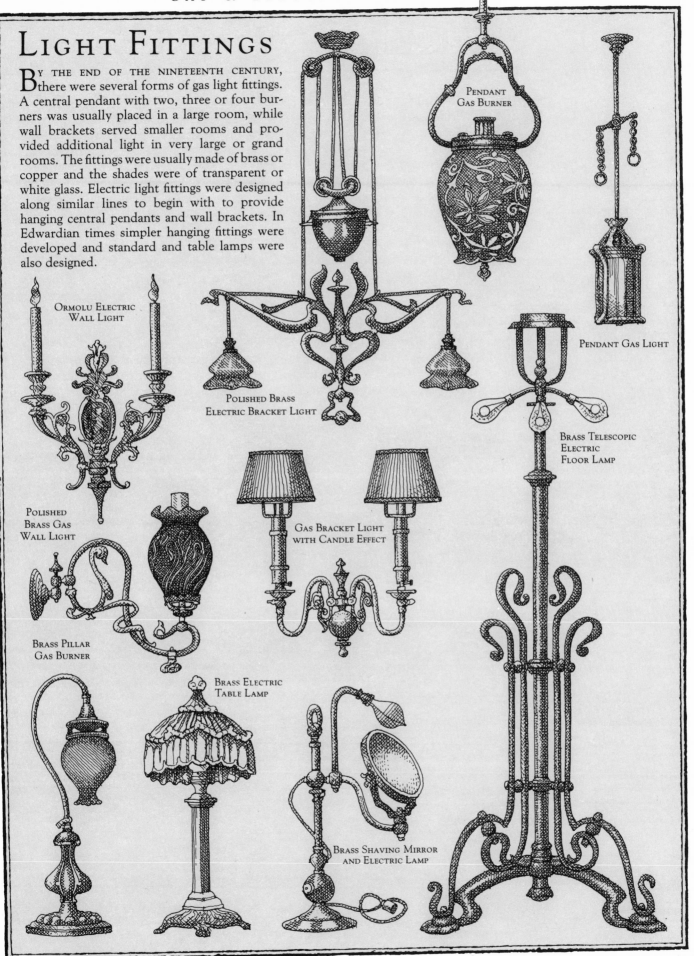

LIGHT FITTINGS

By the end of the nineteenth century, there were several forms of gas light fittings. A central pendant with two, three or four burners was usually placed in a large room, while wall brackets served smaller rooms and provided additional light in very large or grand rooms. The fittings were usually made of brass or copper and the shades were of transparent or white glass. Electric light fittings were designed along similar lines to begin with to provide hanging central pendants and wall brackets. In Edwardian times simpler hanging fittings were developed and standard and table lamps were also designed.

PENDANT GAS BURNER

PENDANT GAS LIGHT

ORMOLU ELECTRIC WALL LIGHT

POLISHED BRASS ELECTRIC BRACKET LIGHT

BRASS TELESCOPIC ELECTRIC FLOOR LAMP

POLISHED BRASS GAS WALL LIGHT

GAS BRACKET LIGHT WITH CANDLE EFFECT

BRASS PILLAR GAS BURNER

BRASS ELECTRIC TABLE LAMP

BRASS SHAVING MIRROR AND ELECTRIC LAMP

CLEANING

BRUSHES AND BROOMS
Cleaning was considered by many to be a moral duty. Indeed, there was a different brush available for every cleaning task in the house. Stiff-bristled brushes were used for scrubbing floors and carpets, while a range of soft-haired brushes was used on furniture, hearths and banisters, and for light dusting. There were also different types of broom that could be used, depending on how dirty the floor was!

HERE ARE STILL CABINS IN Ireland with earth floors. These are generally swept clean every day with a birch broom and become as hard (nearly) as concrete. They cannot be wetted or they turn to mud, so the only way of cleaning them is to sweep them. In India even better floors are made by laying a mixture of cow dung and mud. These, too, are fine if kept swept.

SWEEPING THE FLOORS

The birch broom, or brooms of heather, ling or other vegetation, has held sway to the present day. In England there still exist "broom squires"—people whose sole source of livelihood is derived from making besom brooms. Besoms are marvellous for sweeping the rough floors in most barns, out

buildings, or yards, and for spreading the worm casts on lawns (instead of resorting to the dastardly use of worm poisons to destroy what is really the gardener's best ally; to say nothing of murdering the birds which eat the poisoned worms).

As artificial floors began to take the place of earth floors, brooms became more sophisticated. The harder and smoother the floor the softer the broom you need to clean it with. Hogs' bristle brooms became popular (the coat of arms of the Brush-makers' Guild had wild boars as supporters): most of the hogs' bristles were imported from Russia and eastern Europe.

The widely held opinion that people in former ages kept their houses in a filthy condition is, like so many other popular beliefs, mostly nonsense. True, different

DOUBLE BRISTLE FURNITURE BRUSH

BANISTER BRUSH

DRAWN BASS BROOM HEAD

SET BASS BROOM HEAD

BRISTLE SINK BRUSH WITH WING

DOUBLE BANISTER BRUSH

RED POLISHED BROOM HEAD

STIFF FURNITURE BRUSH

WHISK BANISTER BRUSH

RAISED CENTRE BROOM HEAD

WHISK CARPET BROOM HEAD

WARDROBE BRUSH

WHISK WARDROBE BRUSH

HAIR BROOM HEAD

CARPET BROOM HEAD

DANDY WHISK BRUSH

MATTRESS WHISK BRUSH

TURNOVER LIBRARY DUSTER

LAUNDRY BRUSH

WALL BROOM HEAD

WHISK BROOM HEAD

standards of cleanliness befit different types of house. I lived for eight years in a cottage in Suffolk that had brick floors. Brick is porous and if the floors were scrubbed too often with water they would remain wet for ages. A dry sweep every day with a broom was sufficient to keep the place perfectly habitable. Glazed tile floors can be washed as often as you like, of course, as they do not absorb water, and wooden floors such as parquet can easily be given a high polish.

In Medieval times the sensible practice of strewing the floor with rushes, or sweet-smelling herbs and grasses, was a very clean habit, and far less wasteful of resources than at first appears, for cow byres or pig-sties were inevitably attached to the Medieval country house and these needed to be heavily littered with dry vegetable matter. So the house rushes were raked up fairly frequently and simply thrown to the animals. They turned them into good farm-yard manure, which fertilized the land.

MAKING BESOMS
Besoms, or brooms, were made from birch twigs. A number of twigs were clamped together while hazel wands or willow rods were bound around one end. The broom handle—often a stout ash branch—was then rammed into this end, which tightened the bundle further. To secure the broom handle, a peg was driven into it through the birch twigs.

HAND WHISK BRUSH

DUSTING BRUSH

POLISHED BRASS OVAL BRUSH

TOY SLIPPER BRUSH

TELESCOPIC HEARTH BRUSH

TOY HEARTH BRUSH

LARGE BRASS HEARTH BRUSH

A DAILY CHORE
Every morning housewives swept their backyards clean and whitened their doorsteps with hearth-stone. Those housewives who were especially diligent also scrubbed their windowsills, as well as the pavement immediately in front of their houses.

Sawdust, too, is a very hygenic floor covering. Even now all the best butchers use it on their floors and so do many of the best pubs. In times of old, kitchen floors and the like were often sanded (see p.47), and there were such people as sand men. They travelled round the towns with their donkeys loaded, and cooks and housewives bought sand off them to sprinkle on the floor. Traditionally the sand was renewed once a week and the old swept out with the dirt.

THE COMING OF THE VACUUM CLEANER

The electric carpet sweeper or vacuum cleaner was predated by the mechanical carpet sweeper. In 1876 Melville Bissell of Grand Rapids, Michigan, invented the first carpet sweeper; he called it the Grand Rapids and it swept, in both senses of the word, America. The English equivalent was manufactured by Thomas Ewbank in 1889.

The first practical private household vacuum cleaner was invented by J. Murray Spangler in Ohio in 1907. The prototype comprised a tin can, a broomstick, a flour sack and an electric motor. He sold the rights to William Hoover shortly afterwards and Hoover brought it to England in 1912, where by 1927 a thousand a week were being sold and the verb "to hoover" was born.

I well remember, as a small boy, living in a rented house in London for a few months. While we were there a man knocked on the door and came in carrying a strange device. My mother immediately summoned the housemaid, who looked on with wonder, as no doubt I did, too.

With horror I watched as the man took a bag off the back of the device and shook a whole load of filthy dust on the carpet! Then, before anybody had time to summon the police, he put the bag back on again and plugged the device into a socket in the wall. Straight away it started humming and the pile of dust was gone in an instant! Not content with this he lifted a corner of the carpet and dumped some dirt underneath it. Behold! His device sucked the dirt up right through the carpet. My mother did not need any further demonstrations. She bought the device straight away and there and then we entered the Hoover age.

This happened in the early 1920s at the very same time that we bought our first wireless set, another magical machine. It had a crystal that you had to "tickle" with a cat's whisker (a fine wire). You had to listen to it through ear-phones and when, if you were

SPRING CLEANING
In the nineteenth century spring (and autumn) cleaning really did mean cleaning the whole house. Carpets were taken outside and beaten and shampooed, curtains and covers were washed, paintwork was scoured and washed, ceilings were rewhitened, glass, furniture and ornaments were polished: all in all, a monumental task.

THE PERFECT CARPET-BEATER
Before the invention of vacuum cleaners, carpets and rugs were taken outside and beaten to get rid of the dust. This carpet-beater, made from woven cane, was so effective that its design was left unchanged for over a hundred years!

THE EFFECT OF COAL
The use of coal as a fuel increased the amount of cleaning housewives had to do. As well as the smoke and smuts produced when coal was burning in the grate, everything was covered in coal dust when the coal was delivered.

CARPET SWEEPERS
The mechanical carpet sweeper consisted of a brush, fitted inside a box, which rotated as the sweeper was rolled backwards and forwards over the carpet, sweeping dirt into the box. Some sweepers also had "side whiskers" for cleaning skirting boards.

lucky, you had "tickled" it correctly, you would hear a very faint voice saying "2LO calling!" Then if you were even luckier you might hear some ghostly music: it was superb.

SCRUBBING AND SCOURING

In addition to the sand men there were men who hawked whitening stone, brownstone, holy stone (so-called because it was supposed to be stone taken from the walls of old churches), and donkey stone (a proprietary reconstituted stone with the figure of an ass impressed on top of it). All these substances were used for scrubbing, scouring and colouring the indoor environment. Stone doorsteps in towns had to be rigorously scrubbed very early every morning, and then often whitened with chalk or white stone. This practice served as a sign to the outside world that the housewife (or her

servants) was a hard-working moral woman without a spot on her character. This almost excessive scouring and scrubbing was all, no doubt, part of the Protestant work ethic, although there was a practical reason for all this cleanliness, too. In pre-vacuum cleaner days fleas were ubiquitous; lice, too, were common and so was the disgusting bed bug. They all thrive in dust and dirt. So keeping the place reasonably clean was essential.

MAKING POLISHES AND POLISHING

Before the age of proprietary polishes people used to make their own. For example, you could make a metal polish with two ounces of rottenstone, one ounce of emery powder, half a pound of soft soap, one teaspoon of vinegar, one teaspoon of olive oil and half a pint of water. The mixture had to be boiled for three hours.

One cannot imagine that there was much polishing to do in the Medieval household, except perhaps in connection with arms and armour. The simple trestle table did not need much polishing, the floor was probably strewn with rushes, and there was not a great deal of other furniture. When polishing did come into vogue, beeswax was the thing. Even today there is nothing to beat it and it is sad that it is almost unobtainable. Beeswax has always been a most desirable commodity and its present dearth is due to the invention of the modern bee hive, which conserves the wax that the bees make so that they can use it again next year. In the old days of the straw or rush bee skeps (see p.67) the honey cells of the bees, which are made of wax, were destroyed in the annual extraction of the honey, and could not be used again by the bees. Instead, the bee-keeper used it for making candles and polish. It is a magical substance and has a nice smell. Mrs Beeton recommends mixing three ounces of common beeswax with one ounce of white wax, one ounce of curd soap, one pint of turpentine and one pint of boiled water to make a furniture paste. For polish she recommends mixing equal portions of turpentine, vinegar, spirits of wine and linseed oil. She doesn't mention the elbow grease!

All English schoolboys of the cricket-playing classes come in contact with linseed oil early in life when they are exhorted to put it on their cricket bats. Many of we prep-school boys thought it had magical powers. I was always swamping my cricket bat with it, although it didn't improve my performance at the wicket in the least. Linseed oil is a product of the flax plant (*Linum usitatissimum*). To make the best linen, flax should be pulled before the seed is ripe, but you can wait until the seed is ripe and harvest the flax for both its seed and stem. In fact, much flax was, in better times than these, grown especially for seed. The oil was crushed out of the seed to be used in polishes, varnishes and substances for preserving wood, while the residue was made into that marvellous stuff, linseed cake, the best foodstuff there is for putting a bloom on beef cattle.

As for turpentine, another common ingredient of polishes, it is obtained from the sap of coniferous trees. Originally it came from the terebinth tree (*Pistacia terebinthus*).

Shellac was also much used in polishes and in varnishes, too. It is a dark, transparent resin produced by the action of an insect on the twigs of certain trees that grow in India. The word "lac" comes from the Hindi "lakh", which means 100,000. These little coccid insects swarm in lakhs, so there is never a shortage of shellac in India. It is perhaps a measure of the wide-ranging scouring of the planet for anything of use that the exudations of twigs irritated by insects in far-away India should have played a part in Victorian housekeeping.

French polishing was the rage in Victorian times and was made by dissolving shellac in methylated spirits. It was very laborious to do and required great skill. Furthermore, although a table that had been French polished looked very posh, the finish was destroyed if you put hot things on top.

POLISHING
A useful tool for cleaning windows and wooden furniture was this chamois leather brush. It combined the easy grip of a regular scrubbing brush with the softness of leather.

HOUSEMAIDS' BOXES
The most essential item of equipment required by the housemaid was the housemaids' box—it contained all the cleaning tools she needed, from leathers and black lead to brushes and emery paper. When cleaning the fire grate, the housemaid put the ashes in a cinder pail, which was sometimes built into the housemaids' box. The pail contained a wire sifter for separating the cinders from the ash, so they could be re-used.

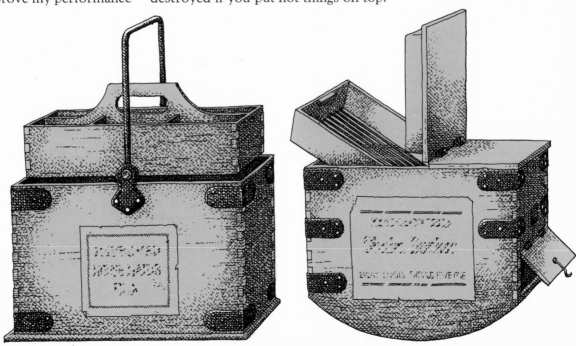

Dustless Cleaning

The first step towards dustless cleaning came with the invention of the carpet sweeper in 1876 by Melville Bissell. In addition to the main brush, Bissell's early designs also featured small rotary brushes to clean along the edges of skirting boards and furniture. There was also a knob that enabled the operator to adjust the main brush to various floor levels, and the dust box could be opened for emptying by pressing a lever. It worked very well and soon became very popular.

However, the cleaning power of the vacuum cleaner, when it arrived, greatly exceeded the efforts of the carpet sweeper. Hubert Booth devised the first suction cleaner in 1901 and coined the term vacuum cleaner. His machine was huge and powered by a petrol-driven engine. As it was too large to enter the house, it was parked outside and yards of flexible hose fed through the windows to reach every room (see below). King Edward VII and Queen Alexandra were greatly impressed with the machine and bought two, but clearly for ordinary household use a much smaller and cheaper machine was needed. Booth produced the Trolley Vac in 1906, which was driven by a

(rather large) electric motor and featured a glass section so that you could see the dust as it was sucked up. It came with a vast array of hoses and attachments and was an excellent vacuum cleaner, but it was still far too heavy—nearly a hundredweight.

Many bellows-operated vacuum cleaners were produced, such as the Harvey cleaner, patented in the 1890s. These were smaller and lighter but required two people to operate them: one to push the lever up and down that worked the bellows, and one to position the hose over the areas to be cleaned. The foot-operated cleaner, such as the Griffith, marketed in 1905, also required two people to work it, and even the plunge suction pump vacuum was difficult to work by yourself. It was not until J. Murray Spangler successfully fitted a light, compact vacuum cleaner with a small electric motor in 1907 and sold the rights to William Hoover that the upright domestic vacuum cleaner was truly born. In 1920 a revolving brush was added to agitate the carpet so that dirt was loosened deep in the pile. In 1926 revolving bars were added to help the brush by beating the carpet on a cushion of air.

Portable Vacuum Cleaners
In the race to design a portable vacuum cleaner, several machines were developed. The Trolley vacuum cleaner worked by an electric motor; the Griffith was operated by a foot pedal; while the "Baby Daisy" used a lever and bellows. The last two both required two people to operate them.

The First Vacuum Cleaner
Hubert Cecil Booth invented the vacuum cleaner in 1901. Powered by a petrol-driven piston engine, it was a massive and cumbersome machine, measuring four-and-a-half-feet wide, four-and-a-half-feet long and three-and-a-half-feet tall. It had to be transported on a horse-drawn cart and worked by a team of men.

The Cleaner at Work
Painted bright red, the horse-drawn machine was parked outside the house to be cleaned and a team of liveried operatives entered the building dragging long pipes behind them. A crowd often gathered in the street to watch the extraordinary sight of several hundred feet of pipe being slung from the windows. Then the dust from the carpets, curtains and furniture was sucked down the pipes into the vacuum cleaner outside. The suction was so powerful that the weight of some carpets was reduced by fifty per cent after their first vacuum cleaning!

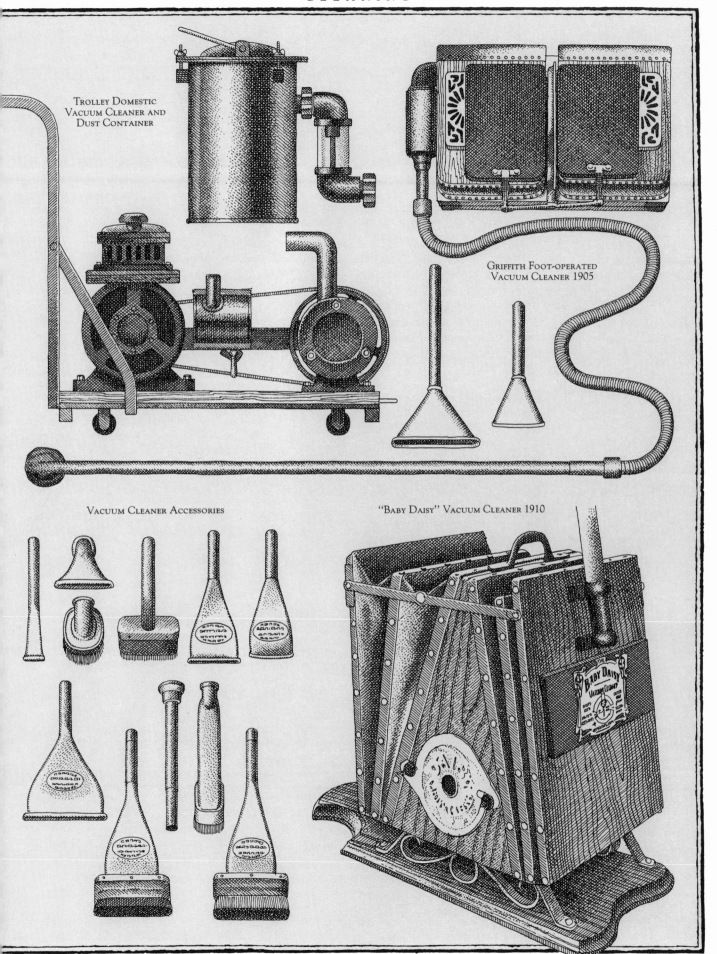

Trolley Domestic
Vacuum Cleaner and
Dust Container

Griffith Foot-operated
Vacuum Cleaner 1905

Vacuum Cleaner Accessories

"Baby Daisy" Vacuum Cleaner 1910

CHIMNEY SWEEPING

PROFESSIONAL CHIMNEY SWEEPS have always been objects of, if not awe, certainly superstition: seeing one is supposed to bring good luck. In some countries, particularly Germanic ones, the sweep used to be an extremely dignified figure. He wore a black frock coat and a top hat and, of course, his face tended to be black, too. Riding solemnly along on his sit-up-and-beg bicycle, with his rods and brushes strapped to the crossbar, he was a noble sight.

All those who have grown up with smokeless fuel cannot imagine just how extremely dirty a fuel coal is and the huge amount of soot coal fires used to produce. The chimneys in prosperous houses, where many fires were burned, had to be swept at least once every three months, otherwise some of the soot was bound to fall down of its own accord, making a huge mess on the probably just whitened hearth below. Even most of the poor had their chimneys swept twice a year. For all that, even when the chimney was being cleaned regularly by a professional sweep, and the housewife was prepared for the descent of the soot, it was impossible to contain it all in the fireplace. Soot particles wafted out into the room and settled on every surface, creating an enormous cleaning task for the housewife after the sweep had left.

Chimney sweeping was a dreadful experience for the small boys who used to clean them in the early nineteenth century. They were often forced to climb up chimneys against their will and many got stuck and died as a result. Fortunately, this barbarous practice was outlawed in the middle of the last century.

PECULIAR CUSTOMS

A strange custom was observed in remote areas of Wales many years ago. In such areas it was supposed to be bad luck for a corpse

A DEJECTED SWEEP
The chimney sweep's lot was not a happy one. He performed a dirty and dangerous job in dreadful conditions, and often sustained burns, falls and chronic chest disease, caused by the dust.

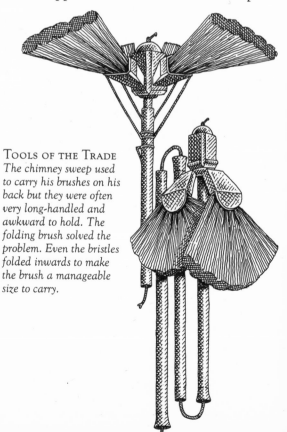

TOOLS OF THE TRADE
The chimney sweep used to carry his brushes on his back but they were often very long-handled and awkward to hold. The folding brush solved the problem. Even the bristles folded inwards to make the brush a manageable size to carry.

to pass through the door. As the windows were generally too small, the coffin—and its occupant— used to be hauled up the chimney! If anyone has seen the typical "simnai fawr" (large chimney) of a Welsh farmhouse they will know that it would provide passage for a very large coffin. I had such a chimney in my own house in Wales (fortunately, I did not have to avail myself of its right of passage) together with a smaller, ordinary-sized chimney, which served an Aga cooker.

The highlight of our calendar in that part of the world was "Hen Nos Galan"—the Old New Year. New Year's Eve, according to the old calendar, falls on 12th January. One 13th January found me very much the worse for wear (libations always went on all night) and, to add to my miseries, the Aga began to smoke: the chimney was blocked.

I clambered on to the roof and fired several rounds from a twelve-bore shot gun down the chimney. This filled the room below with soot but had absolutely no effect on the blockage. A neighbour came in and, on seeing my plight, fetched a holly bush. I lowered a cord down the chinmey and he tied the holly bush on the end. However, as he was in a similar state to me, he did not tie it on very well. Consequently, when I had pulled it half-way up the chimney the bush fell away from the cord. My friend went away again and this time returned with "the rods". Fixing a brush to the end of them he poked the rods up the chimney. "Keep turning the rods!" I shouted down the chimney, meaning that he should turn them clockwise to keep the threads engaged. Dutifully he turned them but, alas, he turned them in an anti-clockwise direction. Needless to say the brush joined the holly bush half-way up the chimney.

Desperate situations call for desperate remedies. After refreshing ourselves with home brew we both climbed on to the roof armed this time with four gallons of petrol, so that we could burn a hole through the blockage. Not realizing that the chimney was still very hot and the Aga, in fact, still just alight, we poured down the petrol without further ado. As we peered down the chimney to see if anything was happening before chucking down some lighted paper, we were thrown back by an immense explosion. The house shook, our eyebrows were blown off and we never found out what happened to the holly bush and the brush. Perhaps they were atomized. At all events the chimney worked perfectly well after that.

HOME-MADE METHODS
Those households that did not or could not employ chimney sweeps devised other, somewhat unorthodox, methods of cleaning their chimneys. One way was to throw a live hen or goose down the chimney: its flapping wings dislodged all the soot! People with more respect for their poultry lowered a cord down the chimney and tied a bundle of holly twigs half-way along it. Then, man and wife, one at the top, the other at the bottom of the chimney, worked the cord up and down, so that the twigs scraped the sides of the chimney. Eventually it was clear of soot.

KEEPING HOLD OF THE CORD

BUNDLE OF HOLLY TWIGS

PULLING THE CORD

WASTE DISPOSAL

H ORROR IS EXPRESSED BY MOST people, used to the regular visit of the dust cart or garbage truck, that even now in many parts of the countryside in even the most "developed" countries there is no rubbish collection. I live in such an area and truly I do not find this deprivation very serious at all. I do what all good country people have always done: classify my rubbish and dispose of it.

I have a bin with a lid on it for organic waste that will rot down into a compost. When it is full I empty it on the compost heap. If I had a pig I would give it to him but just at present I have not. I have a box for inflammable rubbish. I empty this into a perforated steel drum at the bottom of the garden and put a match to it. Lastly I have a box for non-inflammable, non-organic rubbish. When full, I empty this into plastic bags and once a month drive a load of these in the back of a car to the local land-fill dump.

Nowadays great rubbish trucks come along and seemingly eat the rubbish as complicated machinery forces it into their reeking interior. Not so long ago, before the age of the black plastic bag, men had to carry the full galvanized dustbins to the lorries

ORGANIC WASTE
Organic household waste, such as vegetable parings, dish scrapings and tea leaves, was collected throughout the day in a domestic refuse holder. This was a metal pail containing a sieve. At the end of the day, the waste was either thrown on the compost heap or fed to the pig to fatten it up.

and empty them. I remember the dustmen of my childhood as jolly men, banging and rattling and shouting and laughing, and even singing. They wore special hats with leather flaps hanging down the back. I remember thinking that if I was a city person and had to have a job, I would rather be a member of their merry company than sit in a stuffy office, and I still would now.

BEFORE THE WASTE AGE

What happened before people had cars and plastic bags? Well, the fact of the matter is that they had hardly any rubbish! They lived before the age of waste: they possessed no tinned cans, no plastic, hardly any glass jars, and any metal utensils that they owned they made last as long as they could. They didn't throw things away just because they were broken either. Travelling tinkers would repair leaking pots and pans and even staple together broken china objects.

It must also be remembered that up until roughly the Second World War, tatters—rag-and-bone men, or any-old-iron men—penetrated everywhere in town and country. Everything salvageable was salvaged. An old gypsy man once told me that the thing he liked to discover most was an old feather bed. This could be sold to the tatter's yard for five shillings, which was a fortune to him in those days. Bones went to the super-phosphate factory (to be dissolved in sulphuric acid and turned into phosphatic fertilizer). Rags went to make paper. Iron found its way back to the foundry to be melted down again and recast. And then there was what the gypsy folk called "jewellery" by which was meant any metal that was not iron. This could be sold for much more than iron and went to whatever smelting works dealt with that particular kind of metal: brass, copper, bronze and gun metal all came into this category.

THE DUMP AND THE PIG

Any non-rottable, non-edible rubbish people did have they quite simply dumped, maybe in the edge of a piece of woodland near the house or even in a ditch. I have twice had the task of excavating such an ancient rubbish tip in order to create a garden on its site. It was interesting to note the frugal contents: old hand tools like bill-hook

blades worn down by use and sharpening until there was hardly anything left; an occasional rusty kettle or saucepan; the heel-irons off old boots, worn down nearly to extinction; and, nearer the top, the occasional Bovril bottle, bottles that had once contained somebody's famous cure-all elixir, Tate and Lyle's golden syrup tins, baking powder tins and the odd Camp coffee bottle. Coffee bottles were the first portent of the throw-away age to come not many years later.

In days of old, in the country at least, the pig was your great consumer of rubbish! Any rubbish that was remotely edible was given to him, and thus was rubbish turned into good bacon and ham. The pig was your compost heap, too. Any food that he ate that he couldn't turn into meat, and any organic material that he could not eat, he turned into the finest manure with which to fertilize the garden.

SEWERS AND NIGHT CARTS

Before this century and the advent of the night cart, sewage disposal was a terrible problem and many people, especially in the cities, lived in extremely unsanitary conditions. In London, cholera mortality was very high in the middle of the last century as a direct result of women obtaining cooking, washing and drinking water for their families from disgusting foetid ditches. They knew that sewage was dumped into these streams, indeed they were guilty of the same crime themselves, for they had nowhere else to dump it, but they had to use it, as piped water was not provided to the poor districts in the towns and cities. The profit-making water companies only laid on piped water to rich households and even

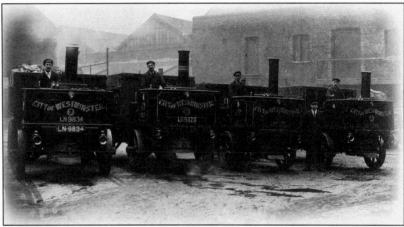

then it was not usually adequately filtered (see p.52). Piped water and mains drainage didn't begin to come to the poor until the second half of the nineteenth century. They arrived in the country even later but at least country people had access to springs and plenty of earth in which to bury their sewage (see p.115). From the beginning of the twentieth century they also had night carts.

The night cart was an institution in many a village and small town up to the Second World War and I even knew of one that worked a Suffolk village after the war. The cart was pulled by an old horse and driven generally by an elderly man. Sometimes it had a big tank on top but more generally there was a collection of steel drums. Late at night you would hear the friendly rattle of the iron-shod wheels of the night cart, as its driver stopped and started through the village lanes, emptying sewage buckets into the tank or drums. He was known as the "muck snatcher" in many a village and was, quite rightly, much respected. I, for one, mourn his passing.

REFUSE COLLECTION
Sewage was collected every evening in the night cart. This was a horse-drawn cart carrying a large steel drum (top). Early dust carts were much smaller than they are today and were operated by only one man (above).

CONTROLLING PESTS & VERMIN

N THE DAYS OF THE RAT CATCHER, before "rodent officers" came on the scene, there was a multitude of ways of catching mice and rats. Keeping cats was one of the ways of keeping the rat population down, although there was no guarantee that they would catch the wretched things. I knew a miller in Suffolk who kept forty cats, which seemed to do a good job. To see them all lapping milk out of saucers in the mill yard at the same time was truly hypnotic. I pointed out to him once that the cats must have cost far more to feed than the rats would have done. His abstruse reply was that he couldn't stop them making love and his wife wouldn't allow him to drown the subsequent kittens.

As for traps—they were many and various. By far the commonest trap was the ubiquitous "gin" trap, no longer allowed in England, thank heaven, which caught any wretched animal that walked over it by the leg. It was used extensively in farm buildings for catching rats and was usually set in a drain pipe, where the cats and dogs couldn't fall foul of it but the rats certainly would.

MOUSE TRAPS

Mice were generally caught in the little spring mouse traps that you can still buy from any village store. The base used to be made of wood: nowadays the whole thing is stamped out of steel. These little traps gave currency to the term "mouse-trap cheese", which describes British factory cheese so eloquently. Although it might be a cause of wonder why any self-respecting mouse would be drawn to the stuff; certainly no French mouse would.

I once had a simple and most effective wooden mouse trap that I bought from an old Danish man. It was an ingeniously simple device—the mouse ran up a little wooden ramp to get to the bait and its weight caused the ramp to pivot. When the mouse stepped off, the ramp, relieved of its weight, returned to its normal position, so trapping the mouse, which could not reach the end of the ramp to return by it. It was highly effective but to me completely useless. It caught mice by the dozen but I had not the heart to kill them and simply let them out again—on somebody else's land.

RATS AND MICE
Rats and mice were a constant hazard in the days of poor sanitation, and many ways were devised to get rid of them. Most of the traps contained bait to lure the animals, and then either a cage to entrap them, or, more harshly, a wooden block to crush them.

OTHER HOUSEHOLD PESTS
Wasps, flies and cockroaches were common pests, and there were numerous ways of dealing with them. Cast-iron fans were supposed to drive flies and wasps away, while cockroaches were lured into traps with sloping sides, which prevented any escape.

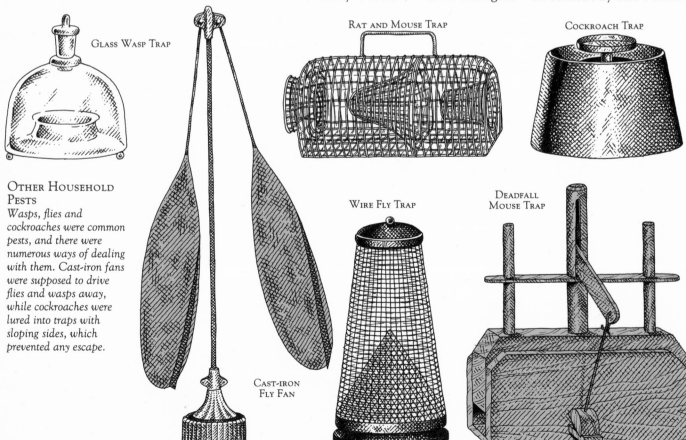

GLASS WASP TRAP

RAT AND MOUSE TRAP

COCKROACH TRAP

WIRE FLY TRAP

DEADFALL MOUSE TRAP

CAST-IRON FLY FAN

TEXTILE CRAFTS

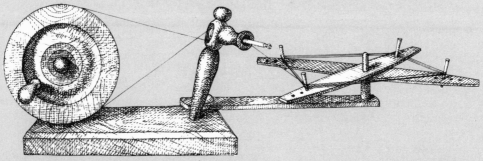

The arts of spinning and weaving are so old that I will not even try to guess exactly when they were invented. I imagine, however, that it was very early indeed in the history of man- and womankind that people learned to twist vegetable fibres together to make string or rope, and, probably enough, not long after that, someone (my guess is a woman) learned to weave such yarn into cloth. Unfortunately, few early examples of textiles are left for us to see, but I knew a man, alas now gone from this life, a great writer and philosopher named Lanza del Vasta, who never wore anything that he did not make himself out of pieces of wool that he pulled off bushes and fences. He turned this wool into excellent cloth, using, as he used to boast, only six sticks. One stick formed his spindle, four others, a simple weaving frame, and the sixth, his shuttle. It was a very effective method of making cloth that could have been taught to a child in a very short lesson. However, it was rather slow: he should have used those excellent inventions, the spinning wheel and the loom, and saved himself some time.

SPINNING

WAYS OF SPINNING
There are two ways of allowing the twist of the yarn to form. For a slightly shaggy yarn, which makes a soft woollen cloth, the fibres are allowed to spiral together. For a smooth yarn, which makes a finer worsted cloth, the fibres are combed straight.

WOOLLEN-SPUN

WORSTED-SPUN

 HAVE TO TRAVEL BACK IN TIME well before I was born to find the age, in industrialized countries at least, when spinning was a common household activity. It has lingered on in the more remote and peasant parts of Europe and in Greece and the Balkans you can still see women spinning with the spindle as they walk. They tuck the distaff that carries the wool under their left arm, and spin the spindle against their thigh with their right hand: a tricky operation.

COTTAGE INDUSTRY

There is nothing more soothing, at the end of a hard day's work, than the sight and sound of a treadle spinning wheel whirring away in front of the fire. And for the spinner, too, how much more enjoyable is spinning in the comfort of one's own quiet home than spinning in the dark satanic mill with the constant roar of machinery! The good news is that home spinning is enjoying a vigorous revival in every country in Europe and in North America, too.

It is easy to see why home spinning died out so speedily and so absolutely when industrial spinning was introduced. For non-industrial spinning is a very slow job. It takes twelve spinsters to keep one weaver going and, in my opinion, they would be hard put to do even that if the weaver was any good. Also, the preparation of the fibre, whether wool or flax, is a skilled and extremely time-consuming job.

Gandhi realized all this when he wanted to free India from industrialism. Village weavers wove quickly enough for India to be able to do without the weaving mills, but spinning was a problem. So Gandhi exhorted every Indian to spin and even invented a small portable spinning machine which people could take into railway trains or to the office. I have seen members of the Indian Parliament in New Delhi spinning away as they listen to debates. Perhaps our Western assemblies would be wiser and more thoughtful in their deliberations if they did the same. Can you imagine the President of the United States or our own beloved Prime Minister spinning as they worked? It could have a calming effect on their counsels. Maybe they could start with the contents of the woolsack.

PREPARING WOOL FOR SPINNING

Wool can be spun "straight from the grease" and I have seen good yarn spun without first being carded. However, for fine thread you must break up the fleece, mix it together to make it more uniform, wash the grease and dirt out of it, and then grease it artificially with anything from goose grease (the best) to butter, vegetable oil or even paraffin (the worst).

After all this, the wool has to be carded. This is an extremely time-consuming process. Made from small planks of wood, hand carders have handles attached to them and each is set with hundreds of fine,

CARDING

Before raw wool can be spun, it must be carded. The raw sheep's wool is pulled apart a little by hand and then placed between two hand carders—small, wooden tools covered on one side with fine, hooked wires. The carders are pulled across each other, with their hooks opposing one another, so that the wool is combed, or scarified, and the fibres are teased apart. The wool is then collected on one carder and the process repeated. The combing process is repeated a further five times for the wool to be properly carded. The untangled wool is then removed from the carders and rolled into rolags—long, sausage-like shapes of fluffy wool—ready for spinning.

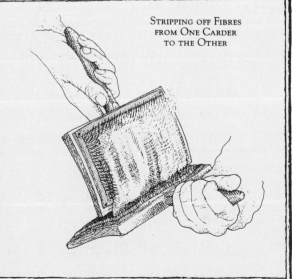

STRIPPING OFF FIBRES FROM ONE CARDER TO THE OTHER

SPINNING METHODS
The basic method of spinning is to use a hand spindle. Raw wool is hooked on to the end of the spindle and, as the spindle is turned, the wool fibres are twisted together to form a continuous length. The weighted end of the spindle gives momentum to the spinning. The spinning wheel is a sophisticated mechanization of the hand spindle, and produces spun wool of a much more even thickness.

HAND SPINDLE

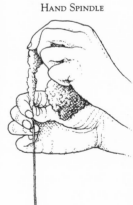

hooked wires. The wool is thoroughly scarified between two hand carders to produce rolags—little cylinders of very fluffy wool. The yarn is spun from these.

SPINNING WOOL

The ancient method of spinning wool while walking, using a distaff and spindle, is now nearly completely gone and use of the spinning wheel is universal. The fine slivers of wool are held in the hand and a thread fastened to the wheel and spindle. The spinster turns the wheel, drawing the thread out to a considerable length. When the spindle is filled, the thread is wound on to a reel and removed in a skein. Wool winders take the skeins and wind two or three together to make a single thread.

PREPARING FLAX FOR SPINNING

The preparation of flax for spinning requires even more hard work and skill than preparing wool. First, the fine fibres (known as the line) have to be cleaned of all the connecting tissue. To do this you must first "ripple" the fibres to remove the seeds of the flax plant, and then "ret", or rot, them by steeping the sheaves of flax in water for several weeks. Next you must "scutch", or beat, the fibres to break them, and "hackle" them—drag them through a bed of nails—to remove the "tow", or short fibres. Finally, the line must be "dressed", or arranged in successive layers of fans. Only then can it be placed on the distaff—the wooden batten that stands above the spinning wheel—and the spinning can begin.

THE SPINNING WHEEL

THE SPINNING WHEEL WAS A NATURAL progression from the hand spindle. At some stage it was realized that the hand spindle could be held horizontally in a frame and turned, not by twisting with the fingers, but by a wheel-driven belt.

One of the first spinning wheels was the great, or walking, wheel. This consisted of a low table above which were mounted a drive wheel at one end and a spindle mechanism at the other. The wheel was turned by hand and drove the spindle mechanism by means of a drive belt. Many spinning wheels were fitted with a distaff, which held the wool fibres ready for spinning.

The invention of the U-flyer spindle enabled the yarn to be twisted and wound in one combined operation. As both the bobbin and the flyer spindle rotated at different speeds, the spun yarn was wound on to the bobbin. As the bobbin became full of yarn, its speed of rotation altered, so to spin a consistent thread, either the tension of the drive belt was adjusted, or friction was applied to slow the bobbin or flyer.

Early spinning wheels were operated by hand and it was not until the seventeenth century that foot treadles were invented. The foot treadle was condemned by some because the spinner could pedal a rhythm with the foot irrespective of the requirements of the yarn. However, the spinner welcomed the treadle as it freed both hands to guide the yarn.

AMERICAN WHEELS

American spinning wheels were similar to the European counterparts on which they were based, but with a few differences. The wheels were often mounted on three legs instead of four, a design that proved to be more stable on uneven floors. In addition, the spindle mechanism was removable, so there was a great variety of spinning wheels with similar types of spindle head.

SPINDLE POST

DRIVE WHEEL

SPINDLE

UNSPUN YARN

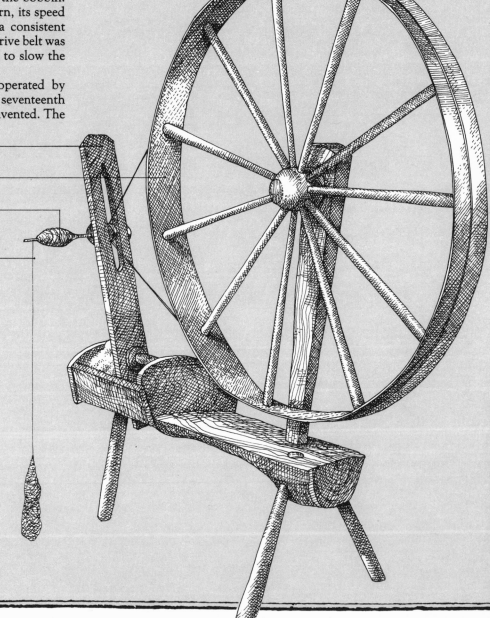

THE GREAT WHEEL
This was sometimes known as the wool or walking wheel. It consisted of a wooden drive wheel which had a flat rim. This drove the spinning mechanism by means of a drive belt or cord of tightly twisted linen or cotton. The wheel was mounted on a post which rose from a low table. At the other end of the table a spindle post supported the spindle. The spindle post had a slot cut into it to allow room for movement of the pulley. Some types of great wheel also had a storage tray mounted on the table to hold the unspun yarn .

THE U-FLYER

With the development of the bobbin and U-flyer, the twisting and winding of raw wool were combined in one operation. The spun yarn passed through an orifice at the end of the spindle on to the U-shaped arms of the flyer. On each arm a line of hooks distributed the yarn evenly on to the bobbin. The bobbin and flyer were then rotated by means of pulleys. The relative speeds of rotation (the bobbin rotated at a higher speed) caused the spun yarn to be wound on to the bobbin. The speeds were maintained by adjusting the tension of the drive belt.

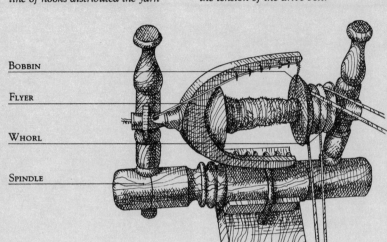

BOBBIN

FLYER

WHORL

SPINDLE

DIFFERENT TYPES OF SPINNING WHEEL

Spinning wheels were made in many different shapes and styles, the free-standing and table-top wheels being the most common. Early wheels were usually made from oak, beech or sycamore, and had heavy, wide-rimmed wheels. In the eighteenth century, when spinning had evolved into a fashionable drawing-room activity, spinning wheels were elegant items of furniture made from mahogany, rosewood or satinwood.

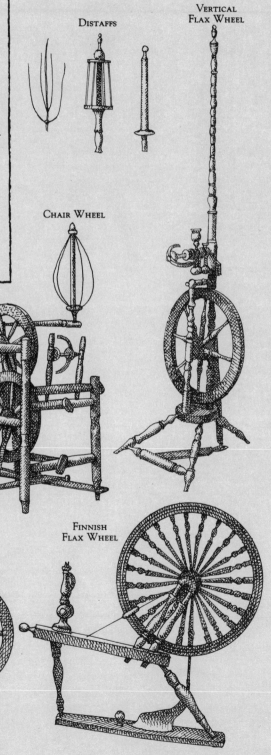

DISTAFFS

VERTICAL FLAX WHEEL

CHAIR WHEEL

TABLE WHEEL

DOUBLE TREADLE ACCELERATING WHEEL

HORIZONTAL WHEEL

FINNISH FLAX WHEEL

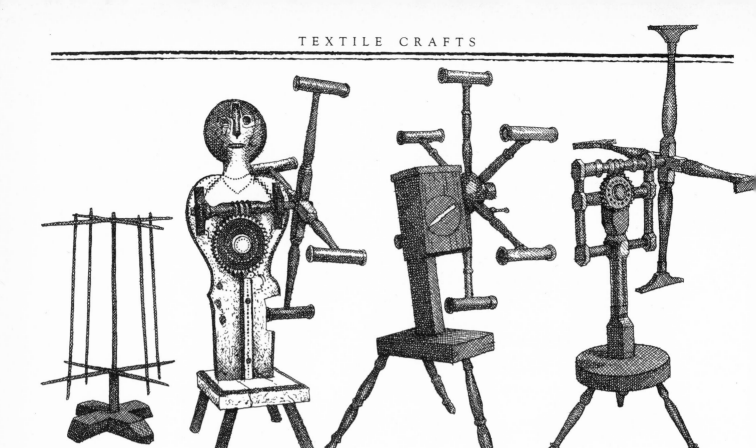

PRIMITIVE REEL   WEATHER VANE   CLOCK REEL   TURNED REEL
WOOL WINDER

WINDERS AND REELS
Once spun, the yarn was removed from the bobbin to be measured and skeined. This was a tedious task which involved winding the yarn round and round the wooden arms of a reel or winder. Some reels had a geared cog that clicked every ten rounds; others had a clock face that indicated the number of rounds wound on the reel. The circumference of the skein varied according to the locality.

Linen yarn, when woven, makes the finest, strongest, longest-lasting cloth, whether for the mainsail of a sailing ship or the finest shirt. Linen cloth has been recovered from Egyptian pyramids still in good condition.

SPINNING FLAX
The simplest method of spinning flax is by using the distaff and spindle. The flax is lapped around the stick or distaff and the spinner draws off a few fibres at a time with her thumb and forefinger to form a thread. She attaches these fibres to the spindle, which is round and pointed at one end, and twirls the spindle in her hand, twisting the thread together as she goes. The very able Flemish spinners used this method to great effect. They wound the thread on to the spindle by rolling it against their knee or against a leather strap, specially made for the purpose, hanging from a belt on their waist. Although a surprisingly fine thread can be wound by this very simple method, it does take a very long time to spin sufficient yarn to weave into, say, a sheet or an article of clothing such as a shirt.

The flax wheel speeded things up considerably and increased the evenness of the twisted thread. It is a simple machine to use: the spindle on which the thread is wound is turned by the motion of the wheel, which in turn is rotated by a treadle moved by the foot. A flyer makes sure that the flax is wound on to the spindle pole or bobbin regularly. When the spindle or bobbin is full of wound thread, or yarn, it is taken off, thrown into the basket for the weaver and replaced by an empty one.

It is very sad that the cultivation of the flax plant, whether used for producing cloth or for making linseed oil, has almost entirely died out in the British Isles. Even the famous Ulster linen industry is entirely dependent now on foreign flax. In *Irish Traditional Crafts*, David Shaw-Smith describes how a group of young girls in County Donegal used to carry their spinning wheels to the house of one of them every evening and sit and spin flax together. They would also spin stories and sing the night away. Then every evening, when the spinning session ended, in stormed the young men with violins and bagpipes and dancing would take over.

Unmarried girls, by the way, were called spinsters because they were always spinning. They had to spin enough yarn to fit out their households with cloth when they got married: it was more than a full-time job, but one which they were mostly happy to do. The weaving tended to be done either by travelling weavers or professional male weavers resident in the towns.

WEAVING

N CRETE EVERY DECENT MOTHER weaves cloth for her daughters. Not only does she weave the cloth but she often weaves skilful patterns into it, or embroiders designs on it once it is woven. When I visited Crete I was shown chests full of beautiful woven articles, which had been set aside for the day the daughters of the family got married. For every daughter, on marrying, is supplied with an heirloom. This is her right. If there is no heirloom that has been handed down in the family, then one is made for her by one of the loom makers on the island. We met such a man in the village of Margherites. His looms were so beautiful that we simply had to buy one to bring home.

HAND WARPING
Before the weaver can begin weaving she or he has to prepare the warp threads so that they don't tangle in the loom. You can do this by hand by placing two sets of three pegs the distance of the intended length of the piece of cloth plus three feet apart. You then wind the yarn round the pegs in a figure-of-eight fashion until you have the right number of threads. You then tie the threads together where they cross and pull them off the pegs. Finally, you pull them into a chain until you are ready to thread them through the reed and heddles of the floor loom.

For longer warps a warping mill is much easier to use. With these you wind the warp up and round the framework and back again, from one set of pegs to the other. If your warp is still too long then you will have to resort to machinery.

HAND WEAVING
A simple square frame made out of wooden sticks probably served as the first loom. The warp was wound round and round the frame and weft or wool thread passed alternately under and over the warp threads from one side to the other round the end and back again with the fingers or a makeshift shuttle.

The first shuttle was simply a stick with a notch each end. The weaver took a spindle full of spun yarn and rewound the thread around the shuttle. The boat shuttle was a great improvement, as you did not have to rewind the yarn: you could place the loaded spindle in the middle.

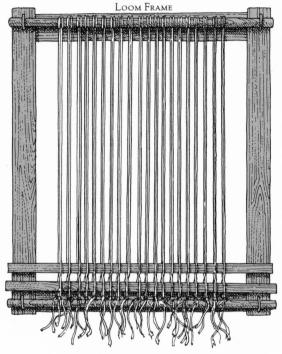

LOOM FRAME

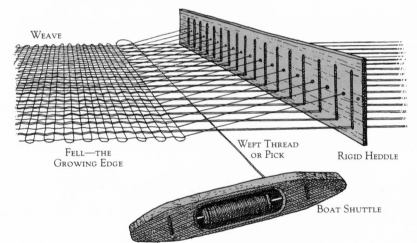

WEAVE

FELL—THE GROWING EDGE

WEFT THREAD OR PICK

RIGID HEDDLE

BOAT SHUTTLE

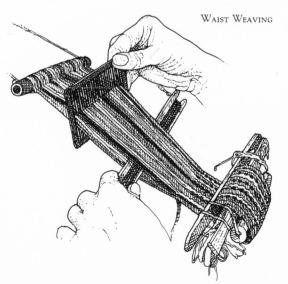

WAIST WEAVING

EARLY LOOMS
Early looms were simply square frames made by lashing four sticks of wood together. The warp was wound tightly round the frame and the weft woven through it, using the fingers or a simple shuttle to separate the threads. One step up from the simple square frame was the backstrap loom, which also featured a hand-operated heddle.

SHUTTLES AND HEDDLES
Developed from the basic shuttle, the boat shuttle incorporates the wound spindle inside it. This contraption makes unnecessary the tedious process of unwinding the spindle each time the shuttle needs reloading. The heddle is a wonderfully simple device that separates alternate warp threads on the loom, thus allowing the shuttle to be passed through quickly and easily.

LOOMS

THE SIMPLEST LOOMS CONSISTED OF A BASIC wooden framework that held the warp threads steady while the weaver laboriously wove the weft threads in and out. Free-standing floor looms were fitted with up to ten heddles, making the weaving process easier and quicker. To operate the loom, the warp thread was first rolled round the warp beam and secured with a weight. Then the warp was stretched to another roller called the cloth beam, so called because the cloth was wound around it when completed. Every warp thread passed through the holes and sections of the heddle, which was connected to the pedals via lams or marches. When the weaver pressed the pedals, the heddle raised and lowered each warp thread alternately, thus creating a gap for the weft to pass through. The weft was driven from one side of the warp to the other by means of a shuttle, and then packed up close to the last weft thread by the batten.

FAMILY TRADITION
The Dougherty family of Russellville, Tennessee, have been spinning and weaving excellent cloth "since the first settlers came westward across the Blue Ridge". Their cloth is characterized by fine workmanship and thoughtful designs.

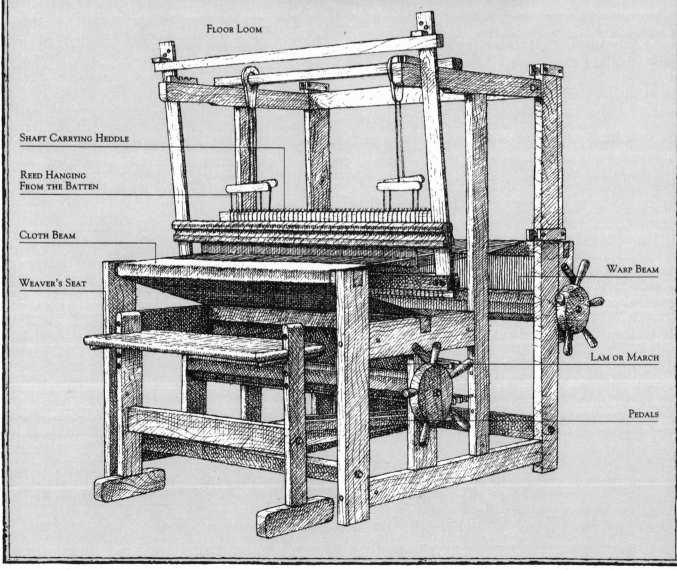

FLOOR LOOM

SHAFT CARRYING HEDDLE

REED HANGING FROM THE BATTEN

CLOTH BEAM

WEAVER'S SEAT

WARP BEAM

LAM OR MARCH

PEDALS

Weaving was still a laborious business until the invention of the heddle. This ingenious device lifted every other warp thread, so that you could pass through the shuttle with the weft thread in one easy movement, rather than weaving through every other warp thread. The gap created by the heddle that you pass the shuttle through is referred to as the "shed".

To make sure the weft threads were kept tightly packed the weaver poked a "reed" or hand-held stick under and over the warp threads and pulled it towards his or herself every so often. The later floor looms incorporated a fixed reed, which looked rather like a large comb. With the floor loom the weaver operated the heddle or heddles by pressing down a foot pedal, leaving his or her hands free to catch the shuttle. The width of the weave was determined by the distance the weaver could throw and catch the shuttle. Consequently, until the development of the flying shuttle, cloth widths were always narrow—certainly no more than twenty-six inches.

PROFESSIONAL WEAVERS
Weaving in England, and also in the United States, long ago became the work of men. Women spun, men wove. There were sedentary weavers in towns and villages to which housewives would bring the yarn that they had spun during the year.

There were also travelling weavers. If we are to believe early nineteenth-century novelists, such as George Eliot, many large farm houses and country houses had looms that were used by itinerant weavers, who would come and stay for the time it took them to weave up the yarn that the spinsters of the household had spun. For before the widespread introduction of the mule and the jenny—the first mechanical spinning machines—spinning was the activity that took up most of a woman's time. Weaving was a comparatively quick and productive activity: it did not take a weaver long to weave up all the yarn spun in a household during the entire year. As a result, hand weaving was able to compete much better with the big mills than spinning. It survives quite competitively even today in such places as County Donegal in Ireland and the Western Isles of Scotland, although hand weavers have to use yarn that has been spun in the factories: they would be unable to compete with industry if they had to rely on home-spun yarn.

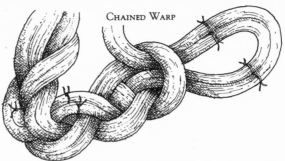

CHAINED WARP

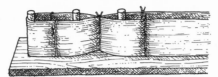

FIGURE-OF-EIGHT LOOPING

WARPING FRAME

WARPING
Warping means preparing the warp threads for weaving. The warp is first wound round sets of pegs in a figure-of-eight looping, and then pulled into a chain shape for safe-keeping, ready for threading on to the loom.

COOPERATIVES
It was the invention of the flying shuttle loom that saved Irish and Scottish hand weavers. This enabled them to step up their production enormously with only a very small investment of capital. A sling caught the flying shuttle as it emerged from the shed and flung it back again through the next shed; the motive power being provided by the weaver's arm.

Today, Scottish and Irish hand weavers work in cooperatives. They weave at home, or in small sheds next door to their homes, usually using warps that have already been made up for them in a warping shed owned by the cooperative. For, the making of the long warps that they need requires special equipment for which most of them don't have the space. Many of the weavers are crofters, who weave only part of the time. If you compare the quiet and peaceful atmosphere of the cottage weaving shed with the dust and deafening din of the mechanical weaving factory you cannot but mourn the coming of the power loom.

Hand weaving is coming back as a pastime and at the moment the demand for looms is not being fully met. So far, the new generation of hand weavers has not discovered the flying shuttle. Maybe the new weavers won't take to it: weaving is quieter and more pleasant without the jerky movement associated with it. Perhaps, when the huge clattering weaving mills grind to a halt, there will be enough skilled hand weavers to meet moderate demands of the people of the world for cloth. I hope so, for there is no comparison between the lovely living feel of hand-woven cloth and the lifeless monotony of that made on a machine.

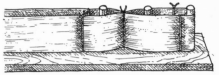

THE WARPING MILL
The warping mill is an alternative to the warping frame, and is more convenient for long lengths of warp. It has pegs at the top and bottom for the warp to be looped around.

MAT & RUG MAKING

RUGS HAVE BEEN WOVEN SINCE 2000 BC. The first woven rugs were made by tying short lengths of yarn to the warp threads of a loom. A piled fabric was created, using the "Ghiordes" knot, which was later developed into the rya knot by the Scandinavians, who also developed a special canvas backing for it. Today these shaggy rugs can be worked on the Scandinavian backing with a continuous length of yarn and a blunt-ended rug needle. Bed rugs were developed from rya rugs and became very popular in America, where they always provided the top cover of the bed in the nineteenth century. Needle-tuft rugs are also made with a blunt-ended rug needle and a continuous length of yarn. It is a good idea to stretch the even-weave canvas backing on a frame when working this type of rug to make sure that the pattern comes out as expected!

RUSH AND STRAW MATTING

Floors were usually covered with rush or straw matting up to the eighteenth century. Such mats and mats made of other natural fibres, such as sedge, flags, jute and coir, were woven. Later, the housewife covered floors with straw matting in the summer, while the wool carpets were being cleaned, and sometimes used them to cover the "best" carpets to protect them.

STRAIGHT- AND PUNCH-HOOK RUGS

Although the technique for making simple hooked rugs was known for centuries in Scandinavia, it was the Americans and especially the New Englanders in the nineteenth century, who raised hooked rug making to such a high art. A hooked rug is made by holding a long strip of fabric under a backing of canvas or hessian and plunging a straight hook through the backing and pulling a loop of fabric strip to the top.

PLAITED RUSH MATS

Plaited rushes made very good mats. The rushes were first dried. Then three rushes were folded over a hook and plaited together to form a long, thick plait. Several of these plaits were shaped into a coil and stitched together with strong thread or twine. A variety of patterns could be worked into the design of the mat.

PLAITING RUSHES   RUSH MAT

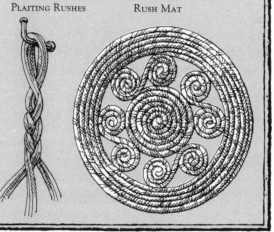

TYPES OF RUG

The straight-hook rug is the most common type of rug. It is made by pushing up yarn through the backing fabric to form loops on the surface. The traditional rag rugs were made in this way. The punch-hook rug looks similar but is easier to make. The backing fabric is stretched on a frame and the loops of yarn are then pushed through, using a punch hook. The latch-hook rug, which is a dense pile rug, is made by knotting lengths of yarn on to open-mesh canvas. Needletuft rugs have a very thick pile. They are worked on even-weave canvas using a long, blunt-ended rug needle and continuous lengths of strong yarn.

STRAIGHT-HOOK RUG

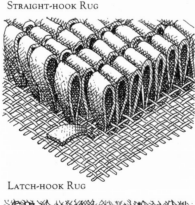

PUNCH-HOOK RUG

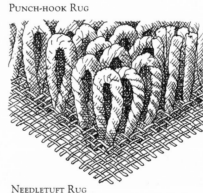

LATCH-HOOK RUG

NEEDLETUFT RUG

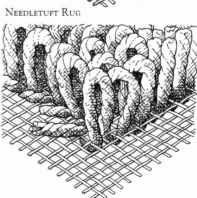

HEMMING BIRDS

These were used to keep material taut while it was being sewn. The bird was clamped to a table, and the material inserted into its beak, which was opened simply by pressing the tail.

Punch-hook rugs look similar but can be worked more quickly. You simply thread the yarn through the punch hook and punch the hook through the back of the canvas to the front: this special hook regulates the size of the loops on the top. For straight-hook rugs and punch-hook rugs a frame is used to ensure even hooking.

These were the most common sorts of hooked rug and an American housewife might well make two each winter using a simple, repetitious design. More elaborate floral patterns might grace the living room but simple geometric designs were more commonplace. You could make simple patterns with a latch-hook or rag rug.

LATCH-HOOK OR RAG RUGS

There was a time when you would find a rag mat in front of the fireplace of every English country cottage. Generally, a cat or dog would be lying on it.

I first came into intimate contact with a rag mat as a child when my mother let me live in the cottage of the father of one of our maids. The family lived near Landemeer in Essex, and Annie's father was head horseman on a farm. I remember the couple of stays I made with them with the most intense pleasure. The kitchen-cum-living room was a small room with religious oleographs and texts around the walls. The fireplace was set in a recess and contained a substantial iron range on which all the cooking was done. Winter or summer, there was always a glowing coal fire on this range and I used to be bathed (I was only seven or eight years old) in a galvanized iron tub in front of it. After bathing, I would stand, dripping, upon the rag mat and dry myself. This did not take long because the heat of the fire dried me as well as the rough towel.

MAKING A RAG MAT

I once watched Annie's mother making a rag mat. She used a jute sack for a base: the sort of sack that you found in their hundreds on every farm in those days, before horrible plastic bags had been invented. I didn't know it then but the jute was grown in faraway Bengal, and years later I saw a huge stand of it as I went up the Brahmaputra in a troop-carrying paddle steamer.

The sack was opened out and then pieces of rag, all cut to the same length, were woven through the "fabric". This was done with a rugging or latch hook, which was a small steel hook with a wooden handle. The hook

had a latch across its mouth to enable the hook to be pulled out of the sacking without catching in it. Knotting was extremely simple and quick, and you were left with the two ends of the bit of rag sticking up.

The rug would be kept clean by bashing it against the outside wall of the house every day, and when it had gone beyond remedy, as you might say, it would be thrown on the compost heap and another one made. The sacks were free—no farmer ever missed a sack and rags cost nothing.

For all that my recollection of the Fisher household is one of contentment and happiness. In the autumn, all the children were sent blackberrying and searching for mushrooms. For a treat I used to be taken down to the tidal creek at Landemeer to fish for little crabs by dangling a length of string with pieces of meat on the end of it into the water. These were simple joys and contented people and whenever I think of the word "home" I think of that place.

THE HOOK
The hook is an essential tool in rug making. The straight hook has an end shaped like a crochet hook to pull the yarn into loops. The punch hook is first threaded with yarn and then pushed through the backing fabric of the rug to form loops.

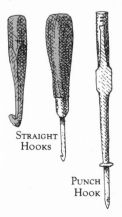

STRAIGHT HOOKS

PUNCH HOOK

LACE MAKING

HORTLY AFTER THE SECOND WORLD War, when walking along the shore in south Devon, I came across the little village of Beer, which is where the last chalk cliffs can be found as you wander westward. Going up into the village in search of a pub I found two ladies sitting outside a cottage door busily making lace.

They sat with lace-making cushions, or pillows, on their laps and worked complicated stitches with large pins and small wooden bobbins: they were making Honiton lace. Beer, they told me, was one of the last refuges of the true lace makers of England: the lace for Queen Victoria's wedding dress was made there as was that of Queen Alexandra and Princess Alice.

FROM NEEDLEPOINT TO BOBBIN LACE

Needlepoint lace was developed from the pulled linen decoration found in the wrappings of Egyptian mummies. The designs gradually became more complicated and needlepoint lace reached its zenith at the time of the Renaissance with Venetian gros point. This sophisticated needlepoint was mostly used to decorate heavy ecclesiastical cloths at that time but was gradually adapted to be used on finer personal materials.

As the Renaissance spread across Europe, so did needlepoint lace making. By the time it reached the Netherlands finer threads were being spun and the bridges, or brides—the bars between the flower shapes—were replaced by thread twisted into net, using bobbins. Soon after this the needlepoint patterns were dropped and the flowers and foliage created with bobbins, too. It was but a small step from assembling the shapes to weaving the whole pattern as one piece.

TYPES OF BOBBIN OR PILLOW LACE

Lace-making techniques developed differently in different countries and the various forms of lace came to be named after their original place of manufacture.

In that best of all books on needlework, *The Encyclopedia of Needlework*, Thérèse de Dillmont provides descriptions in easy-to-

MAKING LACE PATTERNS

Whatever the type of bobbin lace the woman of the household made and however simple the pattern, she would always have to prick the design on to a piece of parchment first. The pricker below was made by fixing a needle into a broken bobbin. The pins on which to hang the threads were always made of brass, which did not rust. Instead of being stored in a pincushion they were sometimes inserted in a special sheet of paper for safe keeping.

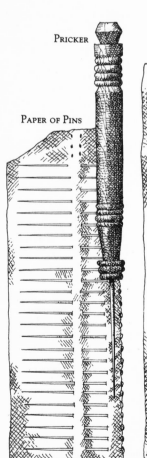

PRICKER

PAPER OF PINS

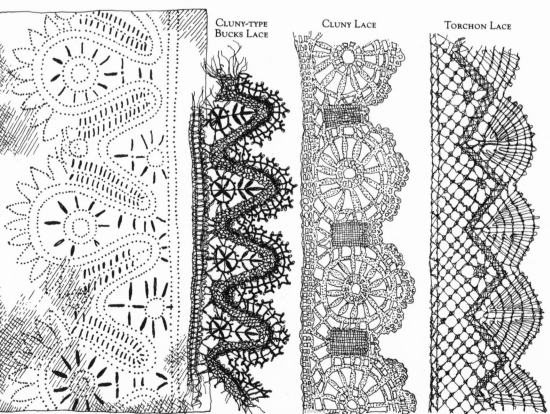

PARCHMENT PRICKED FOR MALTESE LACE

CLUNY-TYPE BUCKS LACE

CLUNY LACE

TORCHON LACE

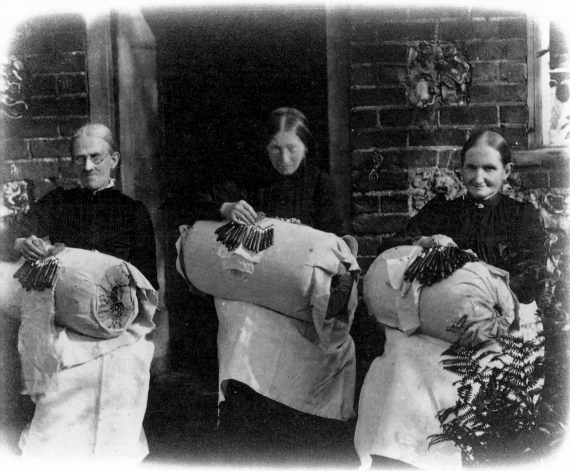

A SOCIAL OCCASION
Before machine-made lace took over in the second half of the nineteenth century, it was a common sight to see lace makers, both men and women, sitting together so that they could talk at the same time as they worked. In this photograph, the lace makers are using bolster pillows. These were stuffed hard with straw so that they held the pins firmly. When the central strip grew soft with use, they were "new-middled".

LACE PILLOWS
Some lace makers preferred to work with the pillow supported on a stand or horse. A special stool held candles at lap height and individual glass domes were placed on top of each to soften and diffuse the light.

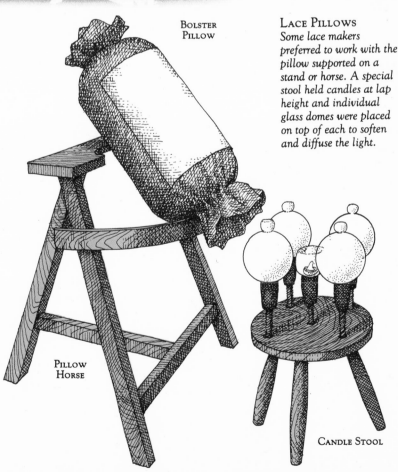

BOLSTER PILLOW

PILLOW HORSE

CANDLE STOOL

follow steps of how to make lace of every degree of delicacy and elaboration, including Venetian, Netherlands, French, English, Irish, Chantilly, Brussels and Sedan point lace: "names", as she says confidently, "familiar to everyone".

Brussels lace found its way from the Low Countries in the sixteenth century to Devon, in the south-west of Britain. From Devon it came to London, inevitably on the Honiton coach, and has been called Honiton lace in Great Britain ever since. With their sprigs and leaves joined with bobbin net, Brussels and Honiton lace are identical to this day.

French lace from Lille, Chantilly and Mechlin was brought to Britain by fleeing Huguenots and took root in Buckinghamshire. Bucks lace differs from Honiton lace in that each piece is surrounded by a thicker thread called a gimp or trolly, which is woven into the main piece.

Demand for a coarser, cheaper lace in the last century was met by lace made in Bedfordshire and known as Beds lace, based on Maltese, Torchon and Cluny lace patterns.

All these different laces were derived from the same basic lace-making techniques, using a pillow and bobbins.

BOBBINS AND SPANGLES

MOST BOBBINS WERE MADE OF HARDWOOD or bone. Wooden ones were more common as they were cheaper but bone bobbins lasted longer. Occasionally you might come across a thin brass, iron or pewter bobbin and glass and silver bobbins were given as presents. To provide extra weight a "spangle" or "jingle" was fitted on the end of most bobbins. The spangle was simply a ring of attractively coloured beads wired on to the end of the bobbin to give it extra weight and hold it steady against the lace pillow. Some of the beads on the spangle were spherical and some were square-cut, and there was usually a larger spherical bead at the bottom. Sometimes the lace maker would detach the beads from the wire and thread her own charms and mementoes on to it instead. Bobbins used for making Honiton lace were pointed and light so that they could be passed easily through a loop of very fine thread to connect different parts of the motif.

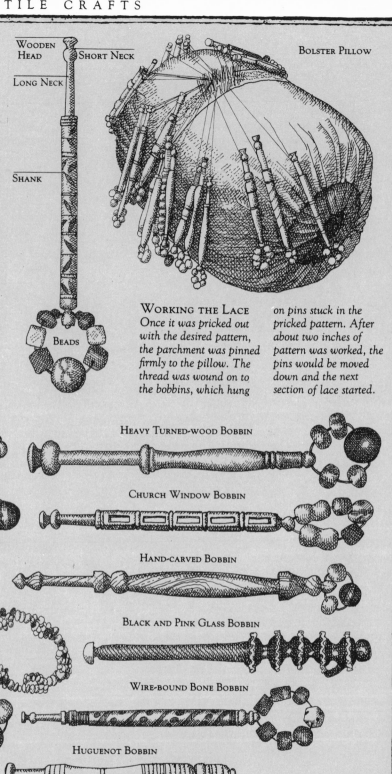

WOODEN HEAD — SHORT NECK
LONG NECK
SHANK
BEADS
BOLSTER PILLOW

WORKING THE LACE
Once it was pricked out with the desired pattern, the parchment was pinned firmly to the pillow. The thread was wound on to the bobbins, which hung on pins stuck in the pricked pattern. After about two inches of pattern was worked, the pins would be moved down and the next section of lace started.

"OLD MAID" BOBBIN

HEAVY TURNED-WOOD BOBBIN

TURNED WOODEN BOBBIN

CHURCH WINDOW BOBBIN

COLOURED BONE BOBBIN

HAND-CARVED BOBBIN

BITTED WOODEN BOBBIN

BLACK AND PINK GLASS BOBBIN

INSCRIBED BOBBIN

WIRE-BOUND BONE BOBBIN

HONITON "LACE STICK"

HUGUENOT BOBBIN

MALTESE BOBBIN

AUSTRIAN BOBBIN

NORMANDY BOBBIN

HAND-CARVED FRENCH BOBBIN

MAKING BOBBIN OR PILLOW LACE

The art of making lace with a pillow and bobbins was invented by a German lady—one Barbara Uttman—in the middle of the sixteenth century.

To make pillow lace—sometimes called bone lace because the bobbins were often made of bone—cotton or silk thread was first wound around little bone or ivory bobbins. A pattern was then drawn up and the design pricked on to a piece of paper or parchment. This was placed over the pillow, or cushion, which sat firmly on the lap of the lace maker or was supported by a pillow horse. She would then fasten the ends of the thread together, stick pins into the holes of the first part of the pattern and twist the threads over and under one another and around the pins, according to the design.

As soon as the first part was finished, the lace maker would move the pins down to the next section of the pattern and begin winding the threads around those. So she would continue until the whole piece of pillow lace was completed.

THE VALUE OF LACE MAKING

Lace making requires greater concentration than knitting and is an extremely rewarding occupation. During the last century there were lace schools to which children would be sent from the age of four to learn the rudiments of lace making in addition to the three Rs. A heart-shaped pincushion hung at the side of each pillow and the children had to stick ten pins a minute. They chanted "lace tells" as they worked to keep up the momentum. If they could not work fast and accurately enough by the age of seven, they were apprenticed to another trade.

Lace making was a skill that provided women of very poor countries with profitable employment. I remember seeing groups

IMITATION LACE

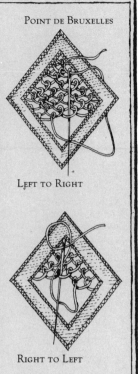

POINT DE BRUXELLES

Point lace experienced a revival in the Victorian age. Many Victorian ladies decorated cushions, bonnets, handkerchiefs, parasol covers and dresses with this attractive imitation lace. They traced out the pattern on glazed calico, which they then sewed to a piece of card. Pink calico was recommended so that the worker could see the traced pattern more easily by gaslight. With a large needle and some fine linen thread they sewed the point lace braid firmly along the lines of the pattern. When the braiding was completed, an open overcast stitch was worked into the outside edge. Finally, the open parts of the design were filled with fancy stitches. Of course, it was only with the braiding stitches that the needle passed through the calico and paper: the fancy stitches were done on the surface. Here, point de Bruxelles is shown being worked first from left to right and then from right to left—row upon row of buttonhole stitches are worked to fill the braided area.

LEFT TO RIGHT

RIGHT TO LEFT

of Sinhalese women in remote Ceylon villages sitting making splendid lace—the craft having been taught to them by a helpful English lady several years before.

MACHINE-MADE LACE

Unfortunately men learnt how to make something resembling lace with a loom and this, aided by the general decline in taste, has led to the elimination of most delicate handmade pillow lace.

The "lace" hawked around by gypsy women, when they are "calling" or "dukkering", as they call it, is not made by them at all (I will wager that no proper gypsy lady has ever made an inch of lace) but comes from the large factories in Nottingham.

USING A BOBBIN WINDER

Bobbin winders greatly speeded up the process of winding thread on to bobbins. The skein of thread was positioned around the pegs on the crossed blades and the end of it wound round the neck of the bobbin a couple of times to secure it. The neck was then placed in the spool of the winder and the fly-wheel turned.

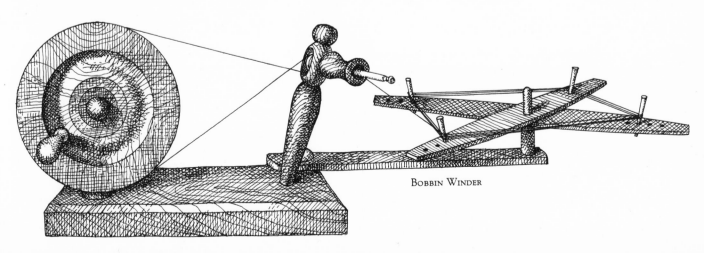

BOBBIN WINDER

CROCHET

VERY CHILD HAS AT SOME TIME made a chain of closed stitches out of a long piece of string. He or she makes two loops in the piece of string, and inserts the second loop through the first loop and pulls the latter tight. He continues in this manner until he has created a chain of closed stitches. Then comes the fun: the child pulls both ends of the chain at once and the chain miraculously disappears, so that he is left holding the ends of an ordinary piece of string again.

This is the basis of crochet. If the child had tied a knot in the end of his chain so that it could not unravel and then worked back along it, pulling more loops through the loops of the chain, he would have ended up with a piece of fabric. If he used a hook fashioned out of a piece of wood, he could do the job more quickly and more neatly.

Variety of Stitches

Needless to say, crocheters soon found ways to elaborate the basic crochet stitch and there is now a long list of crochet stitches, including: single, rose, Russian, ribbed, chain, picot, slanting, crossed, Russian crossed, counterpane, knotted and loop. In addition, elaborate patterns can be worked incorporating large holes.

So-called granny squares, or hexagons, can be crocheted out of left-over bits of coloured wool and subsequently sewn together to make bedspreads: a fine use of left-over yarn much employed by pioneering white Americans. In Tunisian crochet many stitches are held at once on a long crochet hook and then cast off in the same way as knitting. Perhaps this gave rise to the practice of working the stitches from one needle to the other. Not that I wish to incur the wrath of the crocheters of the world by implying that their skill is one whit less sophisticated than that of knitting: not a bit of it. The Victorians took crocheting to great elaborations, effecting lace-like crochet work with tiers of tassels. Victorian ladies tended to cover the nether limbs of tables and grand pianos with tasselled crochet work, as bare legs, whether belonging to humans or pieces of furniture, were considered most indecent.

Crochet Stitches
There are half a dozen basic crochet stitches; the long double crochet stitch is shown below. The basic stitches provide an endless variety of patterns for mats, ornamental laces and for fancy articles of clothing like shawls.

Crochet Edgings
Many different crochet edgings can be used to finish off pieces of crochet, knitting or other fabric. When worked in fine cottons and with a small hook, crochet edgings look extremely pretty, often resembling old lace made with needles and bobbins. Edgings are worked directly on to the fabric or are worked separately as a strip and joined on.

CROCHET EDGING

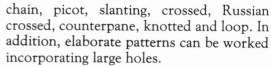

SCALLOP EDGING

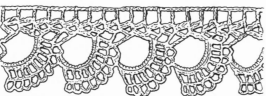

PLAIN PICOT EDGING

ARCH EDGING

PICOT ARCH EDGING

TATTING & MACRAME

OU NEED A SHUTTLE FOR TATTING. You simply wind the thread around the spool between the two pieces of boat-shaped wood or ivory. Then weave the shuttle in and out of the work, leaving a line of thread behind, much as a spider spins a web behind her as she goes. Tatting can be used for making quite fine lace-like fabrics.

THE ORIGINS OF TATTING
Like many arts, tatting found its way to Europe from the East. It is still practised in Arabic countries today, where it is called "makouk". In France it is called "frivolité" which a philistine might think just about describes it. Certainly it is not a useful art—you could not, for example, make a barge's mainsail with it—but it does create delightful borders on the collars of girls' pretty blouses and is often found decorating peasant costume. For peasants, perhaps the most practical people in the world, are nevertheless fond of decoration. Tatting had its heyday in the eighteenth century and would have died out if it hadn't been for the nuns, who carried on the craft to embellish church furnishings and vestments. It is now enjoying something of a revival.

MACRAME
Macramé is the art of tying knots in threads of string that hang from a horizontal string or strings. It is very easy to learn and quite useful, too, as practical items such as curtains and screens can be made using macramé, in addition to decorative fringes. Very complicated and often beautiful patterns can be created using the simplest of macramé knots. The half-hitch and the clove hitch are often used, and so, strangely enough, is the granny.

The granny knot, anathema to scout masters and girl-guide leaders, is a more decorative knot than the reef, which it is often mistaken for. It is also not a very good knot, which is why the granny knot is the one chosen by the gypsies for tying their neckties, or dicklos. If, in a fight, you grab a man's neckerchief and it is tied with a reef knot, it will not come undone and you might strangle the man. If it is tied with a granny knot, it will simply come loose in your hand and he will be free to counterattack.

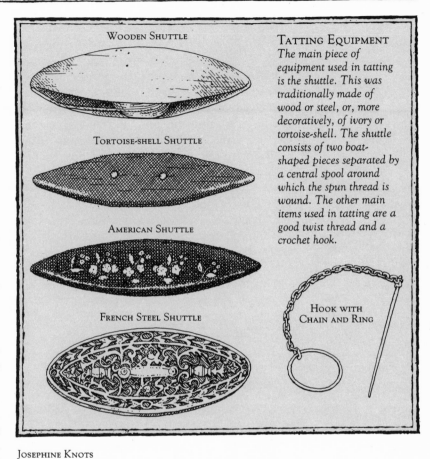

WOODEN SHUTTLE

TORTOISE-SHELL SHUTTLE

AMERICAN SHUTTLE

FRENCH STEEL SHUTTLE

HOOK WITH CHAIN AND RING

TATTING EQUIPMENT
The main piece of equipment used in tatting is the shuttle. This was traditionally made of wood or steel, or, more decoratively, of ivory or tortoise-shell. The shuttle consists of two boat-shaped pieces separated by a central spool around which the spun thread is wound. The other main items used in tatting are a good twist thread and a crochet hook.

JOSEPHINE KNOTS

JOSEPHINE SCALLOPS

DETACHED SCALLOPS

DETACHED RINGS

SCALLOP BRAID

CHAIN AND RING BRAID

TWO-COLOUR BRAID

VARIETIES OF TATTING
Although tatting looks quite complicated, it is really made up of only one knot. The design varies, depending on the way the knots—or stitches—are combined. The picot is a loop between double stitches and is often used to join motifs.

MAKING A PICOT

MAKING A JOIN

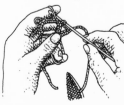

KNITTING

HILE SOME OF THE MEN OF THE world have been posturing like peacocks, fighting with each other and flying to the moon, many of the women have been quietly engaged in an activity that is completely harmless, peaceful, non-polluting and, above all, useful. They have been turning woollen or other yarn into garments of the utmost utility and beauty with the help of nothing more complicated than a couple of pointed sticks.

This is not to give the impression that knitting is necessarily a restful pastime, although no doubt it is when performed as a leisure activity. In the past much knitting was done by hard-pressed women to help pay the rent. I have a photograph of the wretchedly poor inhabitants of the island of

A FAMILIAR SCENE
The once familiar scene of all the women of the household busily knitting is now relatively rare. Knitting is still a popular activity, even though ready-made woollen garments are so easily available, but it is now more likely to be a solitary one.

KNITTING SHEATHS
Knitting sheaths were first used at around the end of the eighteenth century. Women discovered that by using a stick to support their knitting needles, their fingers were left free to manipulate the wool. The knitting sheath was hooked into the wearer's belt and a needle was slotted into a hole at the end of the sheath. The more knitting needles being used, the more knitting sheaths were needed. Sometimes up to six sheaths were slotted into the knitter's belt at one time. They were about eight inches long, made of wood and were often elaborately carved. At one time, young men gave them to their sweethearts as love tokens.

CARVED WOODEN KNITTING SHEATHS

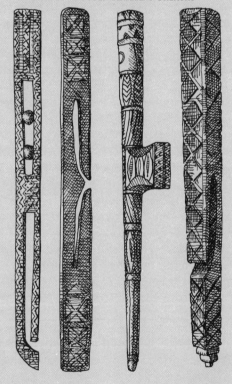

WORN ON THE BELT
The knitting sheath was so made that it could be hooked over a belt. This device allowed several knitting sheaths to be used at the same time without inconvenience to the knitter.

St Kilda, standing beside a perfectly enormous pile of knitted garments, which they were shipping to the mainland to pay the rent to some mainland landlord; surely, in all conscience, there should have been no rent to pay.

THE KNITTING GUILD

In the Middle Ages there was a guild of knitters in England. All the members were men: women were traditionally the spinners. In the late sixteenth century the guild members furiously turned away the inventor of the knitting machine and he had to flee to France. Possibly it was the invention of the stocking framing machine in 1589 that transformed hand knitting from a male-dominated activity into a female one and now, except for a few lightship crewmen and the odd man who might be considered slightly eccentric by his neighbours, knitting is the domain of women.

JERSEYS OR GANSEYS

Fishermen wear jerseys (which most of them call "ganseys") in Great Britain and, if you have ever tried hauling in any sort of a net at sea wearing a jacket with buttons on it, you will know *why* they wear jerseys! You spend all your time disengaging your net from your buttons and end up entirely bereft of the latter. Also, at sea, fishermen need the warmth and comfort of wool. So their wives and girlfriends knit jerseys for them.

Traditionally, fishermen's ganseys were knitted in the round—that is, as seamless tubes and not as shaped panels to be sewn together afterwards. Knitting in the round gives them a four-square look that is very becoming. Knitting shaped panels with two needles and sewing the panels together to form the jersey is a more modern and landlubberly practice altogether.

LOCAL KNITTING TRADITIONS

All around the coast of northern Europe there are local knitting traditions: cable knits, hearts and diamonds and herringbone patterns. Many of these patterns have stories attached to them and some have special meanings: one pattern represents true love, and another marital constancy. A Norwegian lady told me that if a young girl in her country is seen knitting a particularly elaborate and beautiful jersey, her parents wink and smile at each other knowingly, assuming that she has fallen in love. Wives and girlfriends used to knit special patterns into their men's ganseys in case they ever had to identify their bodies if they were drowned (as far too many were) at sea.

EXPLOITATION

When I first went to County Donegal in Ireland, perhaps twenty years ago, Father McDyer, whose parish was Glencolumcille, had just come back from New York, having fixed up a deal to supply several shops there with locally knitted so-called Aran sweaters. He had secured £5 per sweater for the ladies who knitted the sweaters. Hitherto, merchants had been paying them a tenth of this price and selling them for forty times as much. Working four hours a day, it might take two or three weeks to knit one of these absolutely magnificent garments. The craft is still practised all along the west coast of Ireland and the hand knitters compete successfully with the machines, for their products are of infinitely better quality.

THE PEGOTTY

The pegotty or "knitting Nancy" was a wooden gadget that had pegs protruding, either all round it, or from its corners. It was used for knitting long, tubular strips of wool.

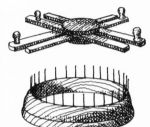

SHETLAND DRYING BOARD

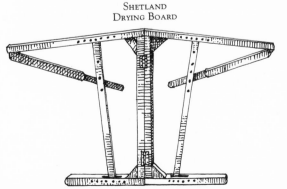

DRYING WOOL

When a Shetland sweater was finished, it was soaked thoroughly, rolled in a towel to remove the excess water and then left to dry on a drying board. As the wool shrank a little while it was drying, any unevenness in the knitting was unnoticeable once the sweater was dry.

MAKING & REPAIRING CLOTHES

PEWTER
THIMBLE

MID-VICTORIAN
THIMBLE

SILVER VIENNESE
THIMBLE

VICTORIAN SILVER
THIMBLE

NICKLE "FINGER NAIL"
THIMBLE

SILVER FINGER
PROTECTOR

CELLULOSE FINGER
SHIELD

HEN THE FIRST PALEOLITHIC LADY got a thorn and stuck it through a piece of hide and dragged a thread through the hole she probably didn't know what she was starting. There are people in Africa today who still wear only rawhide clothes and very nice they can look, too, although the material tends to be pretty stiff and inflexible.

Soft and flexible clothes came about with the invention of weaving. Indeed, it was the art of weaving that introduced the concept of straight lines and right angles, for a piece of woven cloth must start as a rectangle.

MAKING THE CLOTH

In the days before synthetic fibres the cloth that clothes were made of was woven from either animal fibres, such as wool or goat hair, or vegetable fibres.

In many temperate regions, beside making the best rope in the world, hemp made a tough and lasting cloth. It would again if people were allowed to grow it, but alas it is now grown only illegally and for quite other purposes. In the Middle Ages, nettles, a close relative of hemp, were cut and turned into a tough if rather coarse yarn for weaving into a strong cloth.

Flax, that marvellous gift of nature or God to humankind, besides giving us linseed oil, provided the fibres for the finest linen and the toughest sail cloth alike. As it requires hand labour to produce cloth made from flax, it has suffered a severe decline and is hardly produced at all these days.

Silk, originally brought from China in caravans of camels that wound their way along the Great Silk Road, was bound for the wealthy only until it began to be produced in France and prices fell. Its production there is happily now being revived.

Wool, that most noble of materials, clothed most of the population of Europe for most of its history. Cotton arrived in Europe from the East and the Americas in increasing quantities during the seventeenth and eighteenth centuries. Very cheap cotton, produced by slave labour in America, flooded into England, and other countries in Europe, and soon became the basis of the commonest fabric. It withstood block printing easily, and made gaily coloured cloth cheaply available for the first time.

THE COMING OF TROUSERS AND TUNICS

There can be little doubt that a Hindu gentleman of southern India would today feel more at home sartorially in the Athens of Pericles or the Rome of Vergil than he would in modern London. When men began to ride horses, trousers were invented. Herodotus described the Scythians, who lived on their horses (and so lacked cloth that they made handkerchiefs out of the scalps of their enemies), as wearing heavily embroidered trousers and padded jackets. The invention of the latter is, of course, hardly surprising in colder climates.

The simple tunic was a logical development to those who were physically active. For, it is extremely hampering trying to do hard work in a single rectangular garment. Sinhalese peasants today tuck their graceful sarongs up into their waistbands to enable

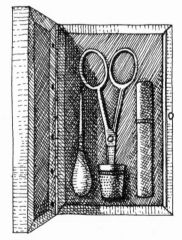

STORAGE AND CLAMPS
Basic sewing tools, such as scissors, needles and thimbles, were kept in special sewing cases or boxes, which were often highly decorated and given as presents. While sewing, it was useful to have a reel stand nearby which held reels of thread on short, wooden rods on a revolving base. Sewing clamps were used for holding pincushions, reels of thread and hemming birds, and could be clamped to the table.

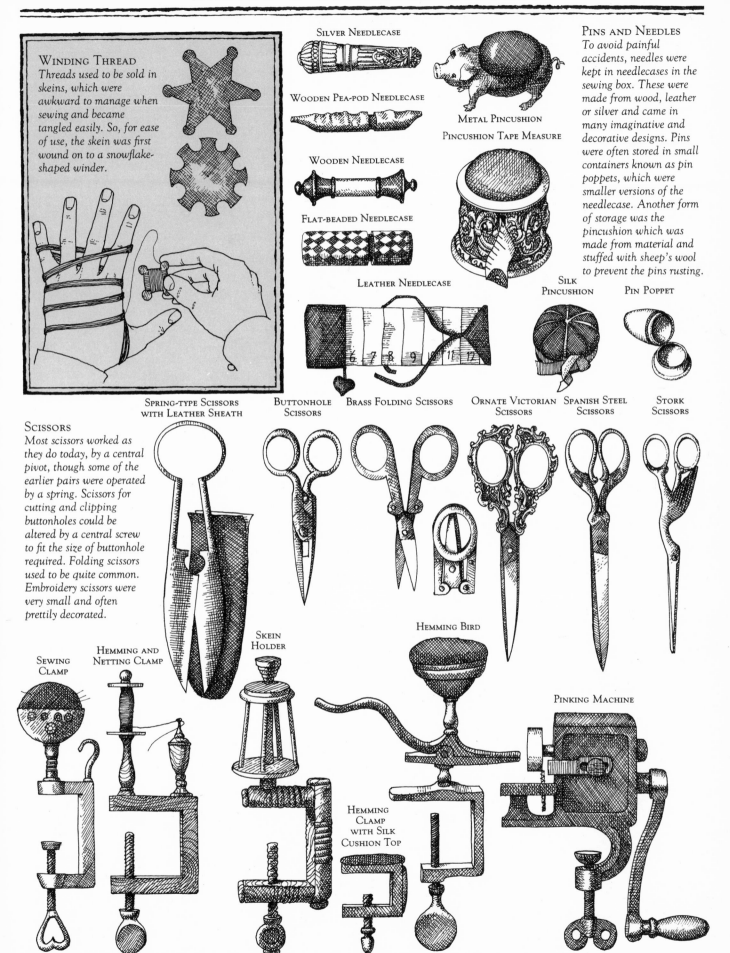

WINDING THREAD

Threads used to be sold in skeins, which were awkward to manage when sewing and became tangled easily. So, for ease of use, the skein was first wound on to a snowflake-shaped winder.

SILVER NEEDLECASE

WOODEN PEA-POD NEEDLECASE

WOODEN NEEDLECASE

FLAT-BEADED NEEDLECASE

LEATHER NEEDLECASE

METAL PINCUSHION

PINCUSHION TAPE MEASURE

PINS AND NEEDLES

To avoid painful accidents, needles were kept in needlecases in the sewing box. These were made from wood, leather or silver and came in many imaginative and decorative designs. Pins were often stored in small containers known as pin poppets, which were smaller versions of the needlecase. Another form of storage was the pincushion which was made from material and stuffed with sheep's wool to prevent the pins rusting.

SILK PINCUSHION

PIN POPPET

SPRING-TYPE SCISSORS WITH LEATHER SHEATH

BUTTONHOLE SCISSORS

BRASS FOLDING SCISSORS

ORNATE VICTORIAN SCISSORS

SPANISH STEEL SCISSORS

STORK SCISSORS

SCISSORS

Most scissors worked as they do today, by a central pivot, though some of the earlier pairs were operated by a spring. Scissors for cutting and clipping buttonholes could be altered by a central screw to fit the size of buttonhole required. Folding scissors used to be quite common. Embroidery scissors were very small and often prettily decorated.

SEWING CLAMP

HEMMING AND NETTING CLAMP

SKEIN HOLDER

HEMMING BIRD

HEMMING CLAMP WITH SILK CUSHION TOP

PINKING MACHINE

them to work better and Burmese men do the same with their lunghis. Such people understand better than Westerners the biblical injunction "gird up your loins"! They have to do it every time they enter a paddy field. The tunic is a practical working garment; it allows untrammelled freedom of the arms, just as trousers do of the legs. Tunics are made today, as they were made in Roman times, quite simply out of six pieces of rectangular cloth.

FASHION FOR RICH AND POOR

Breeches were almost universally worn by men up till the nineteenth century. They fastened just below the knee with buttons or buckles and were worn with stockings. Long trousers were worn only by sailors and poor shepherds until the Prince of Wales wore a pair of sailor's white trousers in 1807 while on holiday in Brighton. The trend was set: by the middle of the nineteenth century long trousers were the norm for all social classes. They were cut with a front flap, which was fastened at each side of the waist. While working trousers were made with front falls, fly fronts were fashionable for gentlemen. Until the end of the century, to accompany his long trousers, the average working man wore a wide-cut shirt and waistcoat with a neckerchief and, of course, a soft felt hat.

Working women, especially in rural areas, all wore the same basic costume up until the middle of the nineteenth century. It comprised a shift, an ankle-length petticoat, a low-necked overgown, a bibless apron and a large kerchief or shawl. From the 1820s it was no longer fashionable to wear a single, high-waisted garment and it was common for working women in rural areas to wear bodices and skirts at second, third or even fourth hand after they had gone out of fashion. They wore their skirts shorter than town or upper-class women, revealing sturdy boots or sensible shoes.

The practice of making clothes look beautiful with pattern and ornament was almost universal up to the first part of the nineteenth century. Then, although women's clothes continued to be ornamented, men's clothes became sombre and severe, and funereal black became the predominant colour. As G.K. Chesterton remarked, a Medieval prelate wore sackcloth next to his skin but cloth of gold on the outside, where it would be seen, whereas the Victorian rich man wore black where it could be seen and kept the gold next to his heart.

Women's clothes became more and more restrictive and less and less functional as the century wore on. This all changed with the First World War, when at last the female leg (or nether limb as the Victorians called it) became once again visible and the female waist was allowed to resume its normal proportions (although its position on the body tended to be unanatomical). However, in the 1920s a new fashion was universally adopted in the West by which the female mammary glands were made, by some alchemy, to disappear altogether.

FINE NEEDLEWORK

My own first experience of the needle and thread is limited to observation. I am old enough to remember the French lady's maid (yes, such beings did exist, although they are probably rarer in these days than French mermaids). It was generally allowed that they were consummately skilful with the needle. If you peer into old needlecraft books you will be surprised at the complexity the noble art of needlework attained.

DOMED BUTTONS
These were simple home-made buttons made from two circles of linen. Ravelling was placed in the centre of each circle, and the circle was then drawn up to form a "bag". The two bags were then sewn together to make the button.

DORSET CROSSWHEEL BUTTON
This type of button was made from a curtain ring and thread. First the ring was closely wrapped in thread. Then six threads were wound round the ring, making twelve spokes radiating from the centre. The wheel was then filled in by weaving thread in and out of the spokes to finish the button.

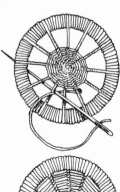

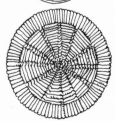

THE PAPER PATTERN
It was Ebenezer Butterick, a Massachusetts tailor, who first had the idea of cutting a paper pattern for his wife to follow, to make it easier for her to sew his shirts. Soon he was selling various shirt patterns locally and, in 1862, he made a pattern for the shirt worn by Garibaldi and his legion, which proved immensely popular. He started making paper tissue patterns for underwear, dresses and children's clothes along

DRESS PATTERN TRACER

with men's shirts and was so successful that in 1865 he was able to buy a New York fashion journal and sell patterns by mail all round the world. Queen Victoria bought several patterns from him. It did not take long for others to follow his example and, in England, Mrs Beeton's husband's magazine, *The Englishwoman's Domestic Magazine*, was the first to offer paper patterns to its readers. At last, housewives could sew fashionable garments easily and be sure that they would fit.

MEN'S CLOTHES
Virtually all nineteenth-century men wore collarless shirts and waistcoats. For working men, the shirt was generally wide-cut and often doubled as a nightshirt. Many farm labourers wore smocks.

CLOTH CAP

SLAT BONNET

FLANNEL SHIRT

SERGE WAISTCOAT

SERGE TROUSERS

WING COLLAR AND CRAVAT
American gentry began turning down the standing collar point over their rather bulky "mufflers", or cravats, in the 1840s. Gradually the muffler grew smaller until it was no more than a band.

WOMEN'S CLOTHES
Practical working women often made their own clothes, copying fashionable styles but toning down the extravagances that made them impractical, such as long trains and enormous bustles. They wore full, straight, hoopless skirts to allow maximum movement and lined bodices for extra warmth and strength. Anxious not to become suntanned they always wore a bonnet while out of doors.

COTTON DRESS

WOOLLEN CAPE

COTTON APRON

DETACHABLE POCKETS

COTTON OPEN DRAWERS

LACE-EDGED PETTICOAT

In France, the art of fine needlework did not die out as it did in England after the Edwardian era. The French have always been pre-eminent at this beautiful and most essential craft: by far the best book on the subject ever produced was written by Thérèse de Dillmont, a woman from the Alsace region of France.

THE HUSSIF

My next encounter with the needle and thread was in the Second World War via an object called the "hussif". We each carried a hussif, or little bag, in a little pocket sewn into our jungle battledresses, together with a first aid field dressing and a morphia syringe. The hussif contained a few needles, a thimble and some darning thread.

I was in the King's African Rifles and it was a stirring sight, back at base camp, during the period set aside for what was quaintly called internal economy, to see a thousand men, some of them self-confessed cannibals, squatting on the ground in parade formation all plying their needles and thread. Whether they were practising the French double seam, the antique or old German seam, the back stitch, the running stitch or just plain petit point I never found out. Certainly, we managed to keep our bottle-green battledresses hanging together until we went to Burma, where they rotted off our backs in the monsoon, thread and fabric alike; our boots went the same way. Replacement battledresses and boots were dropped to us from aeroplanes.

CLOTHES MADE TO LAST

In the nineteenth century every young girl, and many boys, of good households were taught the rudiments of sewing and mending. Over stitch, back stitch, running stitch, buttonhole stitch, chain stitch, cross stitch, whipping, darning, seaming and gathering were the basic stitches and sewing techniques taught. Despite this, it usually fell to the woman of the household to sew the clothing for all the family. This was an extremely time-consuming task, as she would probably have to manufacture the cloth first. Consequently, she made the family's clothes to last and patched and darned old clothes until they were truly beyond repair.

The clothes such women made generally bore little resemblance to the elegant silk gowns worn by the wealthy, who could afford to hire a dress maker or tailor to cut

DRESS MAKING
Most women could not afford to hire a professional seamstress and sewed all the family's clothes themselves. Their work was made much easier with the advent of the affordable domestic sewing machine and the paper pattern, which was often sold by, and sometimes even given away with, late Victorian women's magazines.

EXPANDING SKIRT STAND
This was an early form of the tailor's dummy and was a very useful sewing aid. It expanded and folded to cater for all sizes. To ensure the skirt was a perfect fit, it was tried on the stand and altered accordingly.

SEWING BY MACHINE

MACHINE SEWING HAS SEVERAL ADVANTAGES over hand sewing, the main one being the increased speed of stitching. In 1845, Elias Howe promoted his invention, the sewing machine, which sewed 250 stitches a minute, by challenging five of the fastest seamstresses who could be found to a sewing race. He maintained that he could finish five seams in the time it took for any one of them to finish one. He won, and what was more, his machine-stitched seams were judged to be the neatest and strongest: two more advantages of sewing by machine.

The first machines were designed primarily for use in tailors' shops and factories and were very expensive. The first family machine was not designed until 1856 by Isaac Singer. Called the "turtle back", it was smaller and lighter than the industrial models and came in a wooden cabinet, which doubled as a table for the machine to stand on. Sales were slow to begin with, as most men saw no reason to purchase what was still quite an expensive machine to do the work their wives and mothers had done, perfectly satisfactorily and at absolutely no cost to themselves, for years. And indeed, what would their wives do with the free time the machine afforded them? Newspapers printed letters, purportedly from women, who said they rued the day they finally persuaded their husbands to buy a machine, as they had tried and tried but found it impossible to operate successfully. But gradually the women and the sewing machine companies won the battle, with clever argument, hire-purchase schemes and decreasing cost, until the sewing machine became a standard item in virtually every household.

The basic lock-stitch sewing machine enabled the housewife to sew more complicated styles of dress than before, especially with the increasing availability of paper patterns (see p.164). The clothes she made were more sturdy, too, as the seams did not fall apart if a stitch was torn.

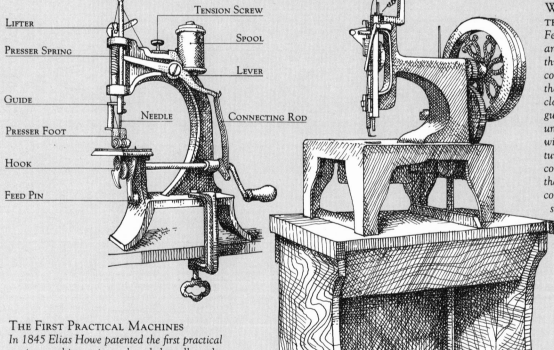

LIFTER
PRESSER SPRING
GUIDE
PRESSER FOOT
HOOK
FEED PIN
TENSION SCREW
SPOOL
LEVER
NEEDLE
CONNECTING ROD

THE FIRST PRACTICAL MACHINES
In 1845 Elias Howe patented the first practical sewing machine, using a threaded needle and a shuttle for a second thread, to make a lock stitch: seams stitched on Howe's machine did not fall apart. Singer's machine, patented in 1851, had one significant advantage over Howe's: you could sew a continuous straight or curving line, however long the length of the seam. The Singer machine had all the essential features required of a practical working sewing machine: an eye needle, a shuttle, the lock stitch, continuous thread from spools, continuous feed, tension controls, the ability to sew in straight or curved lines, a presser foot, a horizontal table and an overhanging arm.

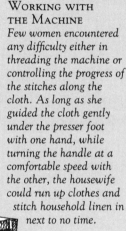

WORKING WITH THE MACHINE
Few women encountered any difficulty either in threading the machine or controlling the progress of the stitches along the cloth. As long as she guided the cloth gently under the presser foot with one hand, while turning the handle at a comfortable speed with the other, the housewife could run up clothes and stitch household linen in next to no time.

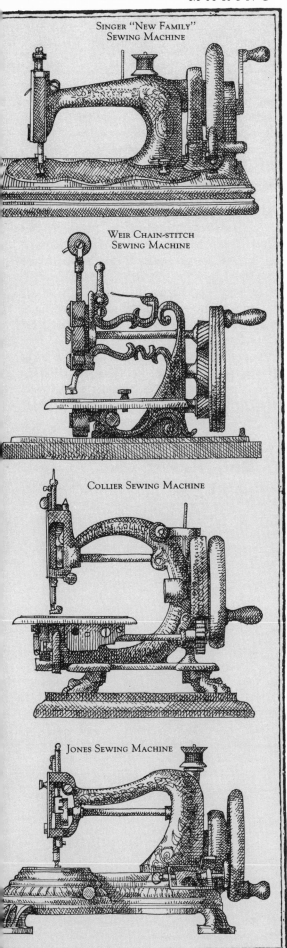

SINGER "NEW FAMILY" SEWING MACHINE

WEIR CHAIN-STITCH SEWING MACHINE

COLLIER SEWING MACHINE

JONES SEWING MACHINE

and sew their dresses and suits. However, they were neatly sewn, with wide seams so that they could be let out, if necessary! Even then, we are told, the mistress of the house could make eight shirts out of a piece of linen a yard wide, although we are not told how long it was.

Most women did not have the luxury of using patterns and simply cut the shirt or dress to the same size as the last shirt or dress made for that person, incorporating allowances for seams and changes in shape! Experienced sewers had no trouble cutting the fabric to the appropriate size, but novices were advised (if they could afford it) to go to a dress maker to get the person fitted for the item of clothing. Then, if it was a dress, to rip out one sleeve, half the waist, half the back and half the front and cut out paper patterns for each section. These were then used as a guide next time, when the sewer would not need to return to the dress maker but would be sure of a good fit.

SEWING EQUIPMENT
The mistress of the house always had a well-equipped work basket. In it would be needles of different sizes for wool and cotton, small and large darning needles, and a tin of pins. There would be fine scissors, common scissors and buttonhole scissors; tapes of all sizes and colours; spools of white and coloured thread; a bag for buttons and another for braid and cord. Two thimbles were generally kept in the basket in case one was lost, and if the basket was a large one a brick cushion might be found in it! This was simply a pincushion positioned on top of a covered brick for extra stability.

MENDING CLOTHES
Darning and patching were high arts until this age of factory-made, throw-away garments. Stockings worn thin at the heel were usually patched with hose before a hole appeared to save darning them. Trousers were often "reseated" when they became thin, and if the sleeves of a dress or shirt became worn or thin, they were ripped out and new ones sewn in their place. In every case, rather than discard a worn garment, it would be looked at carefully and if the worn area could be replaced, it would be, and often, you'd be hard put to see the join. Even if the garment was beyond repair the material was not thrown away, but thrown into the rag bag. Whole new garments were made from the contents of the rag bag.

EMERGENCY MENDING
The darning ball was dropped inside a sock or stocking to make a firm foundation for darning a hole. This gadget was later superseded by the darning mushroom which had a handle and was easier to hold. The darning stick served a similar function for the fingers of gloves that needed mending.

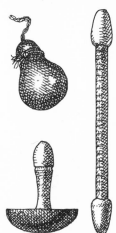

DARNING EQUIPMENT

QUILTING & PATCHWORK

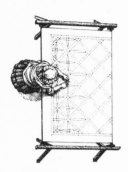

QUILTING FRAMES
Quilting frames were about four feet long and made from strips of wood. The quilt was stretched between the sides of the frame, and held in place with quick stitches. This stretching ensured that the quilt did not become out of shape and baggy while it was being made. As each width was finished, it was rolled up.

ADDED QUILTING WAS BORN OUT OF the practical need to provide warmth and is still made today. A layer of wadding is sandwiched between two layers of fabric and the top layer sewn with attractive stitch patterns or patchwork. Some clothing was made in this way, and today you can buy quilted waterproof coats, but the most commonly made quilted item was the bedcover, so much so, indeed, that it became known as the quilt.

STRETCHING THE FABRIC

For best quilting results, the layers of fabric and wadding are stretched on a frame. In this way, the layers are kept taut and together and the stitching appears in deeper relief when the finished quilt is removed from the frame, therefore emphasizing the pattern.

Women often gathered together to make a communal quilt, usually to give as a present. These gatherings were often known as quilting bees, especially in America, and the quilt was often given to a girl about to be married. Decorative cotton panels to commemorate special occasions, such as jubilees, were sewn into the centre of quilts and coverlets made as gifts. Such "friendship" quilts were very common around the middle of the nineteenth century.

DECORATIVE QUILTING

A later development from the practical wadded quilting was Italian, or cord, quilting. This was purely decorative and did not involve any wadding. Two layers of fabric are placed together and narrow lines of stitching are sewn to make mainly pictorial patterns. Cord is then threaded between the lines of stitching to raise the pattern.

Trapunto or padded quilting is purely decorative. Again, using only two layers of fabric, the pattern or motif is stitched through both layers and padding inserted from the back to raise the pattern.

Patterns for all varieties of quilting have been handed down from mother to daughter through the centuries.

MAKING NEW FROM OLD

Even today, wherever cloth is scarce and expensive, articles of clothing are conserved when partially worn out and the good parts cut out and used to make patchwork. Such thrift has always been practised in peasant societies. To begin with pieces of cloth of all sizes and very rough shapes were sewn together until the required size was reached, but gradually quite sophisticated designs were developed. Instead of simply sewing together large oblongs or squares of different sizes, identical diamond-, hexagon-, octagon- or square-shaped patches were cut out, using templates. This gave the patchworker much greater control over the look of the finished patchwork article.

Templates were usually made of wood, tin or card, but were sometimes made from more expensive material, such as pewter, copper, brass or even silver. The patchworker would place the template of the shape required on a piece of paper, draw round it and cut out the shape. She would cut out as many pieces as she needed for the patchwork and then pin them to the material and cut out the shapes in the cloth. Quite often the lining paper would be left on the inside of the quilt when it was finished.

HIGH ART

The early American colonists brought the art of patchwork to its highest expression. The American weaving industry was still in its infancy and most cloth had to be shipped from England. Consequently, all cloth was very expensive and none was wasted. My brother has a beautiful bed counterpane made from diamond shapes of two shades of blue. It was made by my great great grandmother before she got married, using scraps of material from the liveries of the household slaves of her husband and her own household, for she lived in the South before the days of emancipation.

Quilts were not the only articles decorated with patchwork: tea cosies, egg cosies and coffee pot cosies made of crazy patchwork were common. Pieces of brightly coloured cloth of all sorts of shapes, sizes and designs were arranged haphazardly and stitched along the edges to cover the raw edges of the fabric. People who amassed large drawers full of worn-out articles had a wide store of different fabrics and colours to draw from and were able to make beautiful patchwork counterpanes, chair covers and sometimes even curtains.

PATCHWORK AND QUILT DESIGNS

Traditional patchwork designs were made from templates arranged in an overall pattern, comprising a dominant centre with linked border and corner motifs. Early designs were usually symmetrical. A widely used motif was the tulip, as it was a popular flower and had the advantage of a simple outline.

Repeated block patterns, such as that used in the nine-patch design, produced a strong visual image. This design was made up of one-inch squares that formed a nine-patch block, hence its name. Mosaic patterns were created by repeating a geometric shape, such as a square, triangle or hexagon. The sunburst pattern was made entirely from diamond patches in shades of orange and brown. Diamond shapes were also used in the tumbling block pattern, the three-dimensional effect being created by the use of colours. The feathered star pattern was one of the classic patchwork designs—it was made from tiny triangles.

Some patterns were created with texture instead of colour. Wadding was placed between two pieces of fabric and then designs were sewn through the layers. Motifs included flowers, leaves and hearts. This was known as stuffed quilting and could be used in conjunction with other forms of quilting and patchwork.

ROSE OF SHARON   TREE OF LIFE   FRIENDSHIP

PRINCESS FEATHER   PENNSYLVANIA PINEAPPLE   TULIPS AND RIBBONS

STORM AT SEA   SUNBURST   TUMBLING BLOCK

FEATHERED STAR   MARINER'S COMPASS   NINE-PATCH

SMOCKING

N THE DAYS WHEN MEN AND WOMEN were contented with the station in life to which "they had been called" (as indeed they had to be), people could be identified as to the calling by their garments. Merchant sailormen really did wear bell-bottomed trousers and a coat of navy blue when ashore and coal miners were proud to wear the white silk neckerchief while out of the mine.

Countrymen such as farm workers used to wear smocked overalls. The smocking was usually overlaid with embroidered designs and made of tough linen. The patterns worked sometimes denoted the trade of the wearer. A design of shepherds' crooks and sheep hurdles meant that the wearer was a shepherd, while horse-shoes and sheaves of wheat indicated a ploughman.

Smocks for All Occasions
There were two kinds of smock: the working smock and the ceremonial smock. The smocking on the working smock was functional; it was a simple way of shaping what would otherwise have been a purely cylindrical garment. Smocking at the bottom of the sleeves constricted them at the wrists and kept the weather out. The ceremonial smock was highly decorated and worn for special occasions, such as harvest suppers. It was handed down from father to son and often served four to five generations.

In considering the smock it must be remembered that linen, which could be produced in any parish in England and Wales from home-grown flax, was an absolutely splendid material. Heavy, dyed flax cloth, such as was used to make country smocks, would keep its wearer warm and dry in all but the hardest rain, and because it was a wide-skirted garment it was a cool and well-ventilated garment to wear in summer.

The art of smocking is on the increase today but mostly for women's garments. It would be nice to think that women will some day again be proud to make fine and decorative working smocks for their menfolk and that men would be proud to wear them. I certainly would.

DRAWING UP THE GATHERS
First, several rows of even stitches are sewn over the area of the garment to be gathered. Then the threads are pulled gently by the loose ends to make evenly spaced gathers, and secured round a pin.

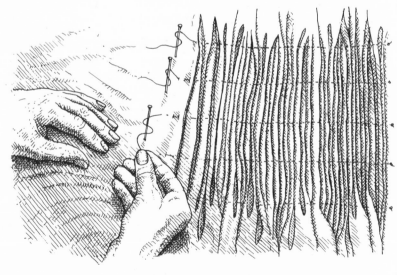

SECURING WITH STITCHES
The gathers are held in place with various ornamental stitches. Basic stitches are outline stem stitch (top) and surface honeycomb stitch (bottom). The gathering threads are then removed and the smocking is complete.

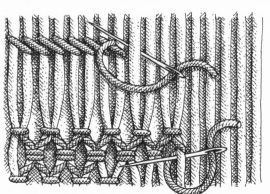

EMBROIDERY

MBROIDERY IS THE DELICATE ART OF drawing on cloth with stitches of thread. It is applied to cloth that is already woven and is quite distinct from tapestry. With tapestry, the designs are actually woven into the cloth as it is created on the loom. The warp threads of tapestry cloth are constant, but spaced fairly far apart so that they are not very prominent and the weft is dominant. Whenever the pattern calls for a different colour thread, the weft is interrupted during the weaving and the new colour woven in for the length required. In this way the picture is gradually built up within the weave and can be quite intricate if made by an accomplished weaver.

Embroidery is stitched on to already woven cloth. It is an embellishment of decorative stitches with thread of many colours. The Bayeux tapestry is not a tapestry at all but a piece of embroidery and a splendid piece, too, full of vigour and drama. Like all the best embroidery it is as good in its way as the best contemporary painting or drawing.

STRENGTHS AND LIMITATIONS

Good embroiderers understand the limitations of their medium and exploit them. They do not have the almost infinite range of colours that painters use at their disposal: their "palette" is much more limited. However, by using colours strongly and boldly this apparent defect can be turned into an advantage. Instead of trying to make natural-looking pictures, they create stylized or abstract designs.

Medieval embroidery, such little of it as remains in good condition—much has decayed and much was looted for its gold and silver thread—is magnificent and reveals a perfect understanding of the nature of the medium. *Opus Anglicanum*, Norman-English embroidery of the thirteenth and fourteenth centuries, was famous throughout Europe. Ecclesiastical garments and fabrics, horse-trappings (the cloth draped over horses when they went into battle), the jupons of their riders (garments worn over armour), ladies' gowns, bed-hangings and much more were all richly embroidered.

TAMBOUR WORK
This was so called because the frame resembled a tambourine. Crêpe or another fine cloth was stretched between two wooden hoops and looped stitches of gold thread were made in it, using a needle that looked similar to a crochet hook.

PATTERNS AND DESIGNS
Wooden stamps were used to print a pattern on to the material to provide guidelines for embroidering. Flowers and birds were common print designs. The designs were first worked out on a piece of paper. This paper pattern was glued on to the base of a flat wooden block and the design scored into the wood. Pewter or copper strips were then inserted into the scored lines. When the block was dipped in ink and stamped on the material, the image of the pattern was imprinted.

EMBROIDERY STAMPS

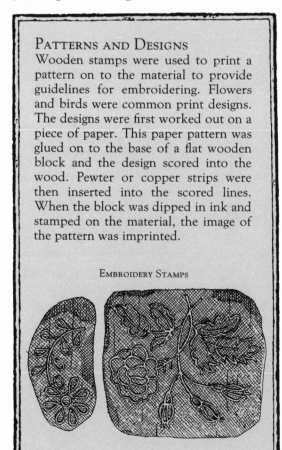

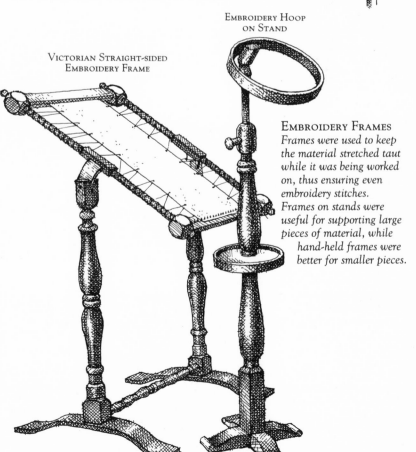

EMBROIDERY HOOP
ON STAND

VICTORIAN STRAIGHT-SIDED
EMBROIDERY FRAME

EMBROIDERY FRAMES
Frames were used to keep the material stretched taut while it was being worked on, thus ensuring even embroidery stitches. Frames on stands were useful for supporting large pieces of material, while hand-held frames were better for smaller pieces.

As time went on, more and more stitches were invented at home and imported from various parts of the world, and the art of embroidery became more and more sophisticated. It reached its peak in Tudor and early Stuart times but in the eighteenth century magnificent embroidery was still being stitched and was commonly found on clothing for both men and women, as readers of *The Tailor of Gloucester* will know.

It became seen as a duty that gentlewomen should learn fine embroidery. Many developed a lifelong interest in fine needlework and embroidered all the household articles it was practical to embroider: very little was missed even by the busiest of women.

Decline of the Art
In Victorian times the standard of embroidery fell as it was practised more widely. Every Victorian lady embroidered as though her life depended on it, and embroidered fabrics soon covered everything from tea cosies to crinolines. Books abounded on the subject of ladies' fancy work. Gentlewomen were urged to embroider initial letters on a corner of a gentleman's handkerchief, concealing the line of the letter with a drapery of stems, foliage and

fruit. As the nineteenth century wore on so taste declined (according to my taste at least) and embroidery reached perhaps its pit in Berlin wool-work, in which designs, generally of appalling sentimentality, were coarsely worked on canvas using garish wool.

On second thoughts, perhaps this was not the bottom of the pit, perhaps that has been reached today, when ready-to-embroider canvases are sold in the high street. Clumsy representations of the paintings of old masters are already painted on them and the coloured wool to create the picture is supplied with it. This is not what the high art of embroidery is all about.

A Fine Art
The fine art of embroidery can be found when wandering among the mountains of Crete. There you will find mothers embroidering household fabrics that they have woven beautifully themselves with strange and fanciful patterns, many of which have been handed down from mother to daughter since the Minoan civilization. These articles are then packed away in a bottom drawer, or a chest, and kept against the day when their daughter gets married, at which point they will form part of her dowry. She, in her turn, will hand it on to her daughter and so on.

There are signs of revival in the embroiderer's art in the rest of the world. The Embroiderers' Guild and the Royal School of Needlework in England are striving to improve standards. Perhaps a new school of *Opus Anglicanum*, or even *Opus Americanum*, is in the process of gestation. Let us hope that the skills developed over thousands of years will not be thrown away in a couple of generations.

EMBROIDERY SAMPLERS
Letters of the alphabet occurred frequently in embroidery samplers. Initial capital letters offered great scope for perfecting decorative and intricate stitchwork.

EMBROIDERY SAMPLER

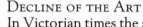

AN EXTRAVAGANT DISPLAY
There were endless opportunities for displaying embroidery skills in the home. The covering of this eighteenth-century sofa was rather extravagantly embroidered with a decorative floral design in shades of green, pink and cream.

18TH-CENTURY SOFA

DECORATIVE CRAFTS

Before the Industrial Revolution every object made by man or woman was decorated fittingly and beautifully. In fact, the pre-industrial scientist would have found it hateful to work with apparatus unembellished by the work of the artist. Can you imagine a modern-day chemist asking a glass engraver to cut beautiful designs upon his test tubes? Farm machinery was one of the last classes of object to surrender to pure utilitarianism. Up until the 1950s farm machinery, even that designed to be pulled by tractors, was painted in the factory with panels and scrolls. Carts and wagons had chamfering carved on all their timbers, often skilfully "lined-out" in paint by the wainwright, and beautiful "fiddle-heads" were carved on projecting timbers. Today, no tractor manufacturer would consider doing such a thing. Objects manufactured for domestic use have suffered similarly but the living tradition of the decorative arts has not died out entirely and there is a growing number of craftspeople who are trying to revive the art of true decoration.

PAINTING & PAPERING

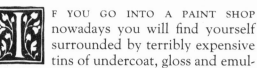

IF YOU GO INTO A PAINT SHOP nowadays you will find yourself surrounded by terribly expensive tins of undercoat, gloss and emulsion paint. The colours can be rather bright and garish, but the resulting painted walls are lacking somehow in character.

MIXING PAINTS

Up to the Second World War, when there was still a paint shop in every country town in England, you would find not tins of proprietary paints but sacks or wooden barrels filled with coloured powder. You bought the powder and mixed it yourself with water, linseed oil (obtainable from the same shop) or turpentine, depending on the sort of paint you required.

Going back even earlier, most country people made their own paints. They took coloured clays that they found in their locality, or bought from itinerant tradesmen just like the raddleman of Hardy's *Mayor of Casterbridge*, and mixed them with such unlikely substances as sour milk and lime. The acid sour milk and the alkaline lime (slaked lime) were mixed together in the correct proportions and neutralized one another.

Lime is mixed with water today to make limewash. In many Mediterranean countries there is almost a ritual whitewashing of houses where limewash is applied inside and out, once a year every spring. In Suffolk, England, red ochre is traditionally added to limewash to make that muted but attractive colour, "Suffolk pink".

In the middle of the nineteenth century an attractive paint finish became fashionable in living rooms of the middle and upper classes in America, where stencilled walls (see p.178) were much more popular than in England, where wallpaper was all the rage. Where a bookcase ran all around the room, which was often the case in grand houses, an Indian red wash was often applied to the wall area above the bookcase and a dull gold stencil pattern applied on top to create the effect of a frieze.

GRAINING

A folk art or craft that has practically died out these days is graining. It might seem strange that anybody should go to the trouble of covering up the natural grain of wood, which looks pretty nice in itself, then laboriously paint a depiction of wood grain on it, but where the wood was cheap deal, and the craftsman knew his job, the result could be very pleasing. The cabins and fo'c'sles of sailing barges, the "snug" bars of country ale houses, and many a cottage kitchen were once "grained out". There is very little graining left now, and sadly today you would be hard put to find anyone who knew how to do it.

SWELLING BRUSHES
Before use, in order that the brush would keep its shape, it was first suspended in water, handle-down, up to the bristles. This caused the brush to swell in its binding without making the bristles flabby.

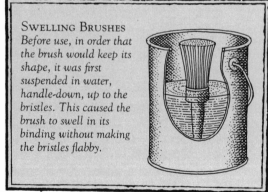

GRINDING PIGMENTS
Before the introduction of tinned paints, merchants sold paint in powdered form, consisting of ground pigments. Some machines enabled them to mix in the oil or water whilst grinding the pigment, but this was normally done at a later stage by the buyer.

COLOUR MILL

DECORATING BRUSHES
Painting and decorating brushes came in a wide variety of shapes, sizes and qualities, as they do today. Early brushes ranged from inexpensive oval painters' dusters to flat, white-bristled wall brushes bound in brass.

WHITEWASH BRUSH

FLAT AND OVAL PAINTING AND DECORATING BRUSHES

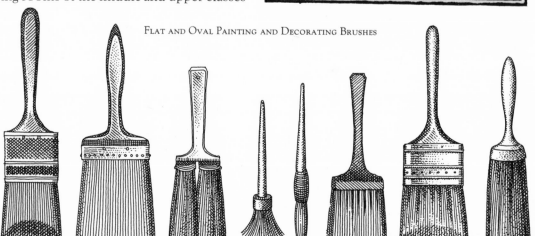

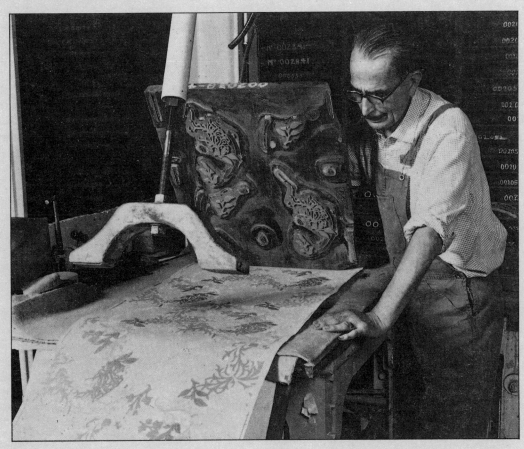

WALLPAPER
BLOCKING
The first wallpapers were printed by hand and were labour-intensive. Once the pattern had been designed, it was separated into its component colours and each one carefully engraved on to a large pearwood block. Excess wood was then removed so that the design stood out in relief to hold the ink for printing. In early print shops the pressure required to transfer the paint on the block to the wallpaper was applied by human weight! Boys were employed to sit on cantilevered beams, which were positioned over the blocks. As in the William Morris design being printed here, some patterns required eight or nine blockings.

DECORATIVE PLASTERWORK

In the elegant Georgian times there was a wonderful development of decorative plasterwork created in England largely by Italian craftsmen. Staircases featured panels of exquisite pargeting, and intricate mouldings were created around fireplaces and doorways. Their brothers were doing the same sort of work, with far greater luxuriance and elaboration, for the Moghul emperors.

WALLPAPERING

The earliest wallpapers were hand printed with wood blocks and came in some attractive patterns. In the Victorian era printed wallpaper was mass produced and the standard of design fell swiftly to abysmal depths. It was the deplorable taste of the Victorian mass producers of wallpaper that caused William Morris to start designing wallpaper of his own. He set up a factory and employed dedicated craftsmen to make his elaborate intertwining floral designs: the first "designer" wallpapers.

The Victorians had a passion for wallpaper and applied it with vigour to every available wall. When one covering of paper got tatty they simply stuck another layer over the top of it: they did not bother with soaping the original layer off first. When I bought my farmhouse in Pembrokeshire I stripped six layers of wallpaper off the walls, each one more hideous than the previous one. Linoleum, too, was a terrible Victorian vice. In that same house I shovelled out five or six layers of lino, each progressively more rotten and infested with woodlice.

Different styles of wallpaper were advocated for different rooms. Complex designs of fruit, flowers and foliage with threads of dull gold running through them were recommended for the drawing room. Deeper tones but similar designs were considered appropriate for the library and dining room, while lighter coloured, less stylized paper was allowed in the bedrooms.

The model for many a trendy domestic interior of the 1920s and 1930s seems to have been the operating theatre. Patterned wallpaper gave way to bare, colour-washed walls and decorative plasterwork became extinct, not only because it was not desired but because there were no longer any craftsmen skilled enough to do it.

GRAINING
Cheap wood was often camouflaged by painting a wood grain over the original. The paint was applied and a graining comb dragged over the wet surface to achieve the desired effect.

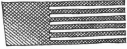

GRAINING COMB

STENCILLING

T O STENCIL YOU SIMPLY CUT THE basic design out of a piece of stiff material, fix it on the wall, piece of furniture, book or material to be stencilled and then daub on your paint with a paintbrush. Stencilling is ideal for creating a repetitive design over a large surface and was used extensively on the inner walls of churches in many parts of Europe from Medieval times.

STENCILLING IN CHURCHES
Many church wall stencils imitate fabric by repeating a simple design on the background. In East Anglia in the east of England, in particular, there are some splendid stencilled wooden rood screens richly patterned in gold, black, white, blue, green, yellow and red. Some screens have stencilled backgrounds with hand-painted pictures of the saints on top. The church in the tiny village of Ranworth near the Norfolk Broads contains a very fine example of this, although the faces of the saints shown in the painting were touched up by a Victorian artist to look like local worthies!

STENCILLING WALLS AND FLOORS
Towards the end of the eighteenth century, journeyman artists began going about the villages seeking patronage. Instead of taking rolls of expensive wallpaper, as before, they took a stencilling kit of brushes, a selection of stencils cut from thick paper, dry colours and measuring tools.

For borders to outline windows, doors and mantels, they used stencils of flowers, leaves and stems and stencils of geometric designs. Friezes of swags, scattered flowers and festoons were often made to edge the ceilings and single motifs were repeated on the broad wall spaces.

Separate motifs were usually made with one stencil, as only one colour would be needed. For more elaborate motifs, a combination of stencils was used, the number depending on the number of colours used. Two colours were usually used for the bold pattern on large friezes: the painter would first go round the top of all four walls with one colour and then, when the paint was dry, go round again with the second stencil and the second colour.

Similar motifs were often used on the floorboards, and stencilled floors were popular in the eighteenth century, especially in America. Bold designs were favoured and some stencilled floors resembled mosaic tiling or marquetry.

STENCILLING FURNITURE
The traditional way of stencilling wooden furniture is first to apply a thin coat of size made of varnish and turpentine to the area to be stencilled. This acts as a binder for the bronze powders, which you apply with small velvet pads through the thin paper stencil, just before the adhesive dries. Pure gold powder was used on only the best furniture because it was so expensive.

**WORKING UP
A PATTERN**
Borders of repeating patterns were usually achieved with a combination of several stencils. In this example, there were two stencils— one for the leaf motif, which was stencilled first, and one for the vein markings, which was added when the paint was dry from the first stencil.

AMERICAN STENCILS
In the nineteenth century stencilled decoration was very popular in America. Stencil designs often depicted flowers, leaves and circular sunbursts, or else they were simply decorative shapes. The stencils were used in a repeating pattern on walls and floors, sometimes to decorate the entire surface, and often to highlight a particular feature, such as the skirting or a door frame. The simpler the design, the more effective the overall pattern.

FURNITURE & FURNISHINGS

IN THE MIDDLE AGES EVEN A RICH man's house was little more than a large farmhouse. Draughts were no doubt very prevalent at a time when glass was so scarce and expensive that kings carried glass panes in their baggage trains as they travelled from castle to castle. Decoration generally expressed itself in rich hangings, which also served the practical purpose of preventing draughts from entering the room. Such hangings were usually of heavy woollen cloth, sometimes beautifully embroidered. It was but a short step from draught-excluding hangings to beautiful tapestries that hung on the bare stone walls and provided decoration only.

INCREASING COMFORT
Most Tudor mansions had long galleries, which someone once told me were made long in order that the ladies could exercise in rainy weather. There was always a great fire in the middle of such rooms, before which were placed wooden chairs. In the seventeenth century it became the practice to upholster the chairs to make them more comfortable to sit on. Strong flax canvas was the material generally used for upholstering such chairs as it was hardwearing. Once the chairs had been upholstered, the ladies would decorate them with needlepoint.

With the invention of window glass, it became possible to sit still for longer periods during the winter and screens to confine the heat of the fire became common. These screens would be decorated elaborately with many kinds of embellishment, from woven tapestry to stencilled paint. Later, in Victorian times, young ladies would decorate wooden fire screens by pasting on pictures that they had cut out of magazines to create a picture patchwork.

BED-HANGINGS AND CHINOISERIE
The four-poster bed was so popular not only because of the privacy it afforded but also because the bed-hangings kept out the ubiquitous draughts! Bed-hangings, too, were lavishly embroidered. Even portable folding camp or field beds were usually fitted with curtains, so that the occupant could be completely enclosed. When not in use the curtains were held up by cords looped over a button. A simple arrangement for an

STENCILLED TALL CLOCK

METAL DECORATION
Punched tinplate was sometimes used to decorate furniture and household boxes. Pieces of metal were first cut to the right shape. Then the metal was punched from the inside so that a protruding hole formed on the outside. Intricate interlacings of patterns could be achieved with punched tinplate.

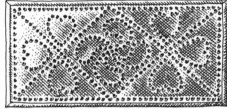
PUNCHED TINPLATE DECORATION

STENCILLED FURNITURE
Many items of furniture were elaborately ornamented with painted or stencilled designs. Wardrobes, chairs, clocks and pianos were all decorated, often with conventional designs of fruit or flowers. Some intricate and delicate designs contained a painstaking amount of detail, while other examples of folk art were whimsical in character, depicting homely village scenes, usually in bright reds, blues, greens, and yellows. Whatever the design, stencilled furniture was always cheerful.

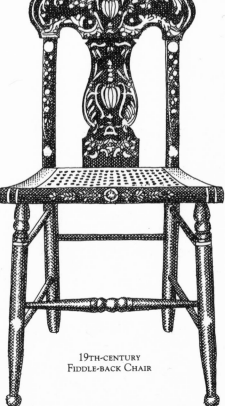
19TH-CENTURY
FIDDLE-BACK CHAIR

ordinary static bed was to drape a curtain over a bracket positioned at the centre of the bed. Whatever the type of bed and curtain arrangement, it was considered good taste to match the bed-hangings as exactly as possible to the window curtains in the room.

In Regency times chinoiserie became rampant, to culminate in that absurd extravaganza, the Brighton Pavilion. Chinoiserie had a recrudescence in the 1920s and 30s, when it competed with art deco and art nouveau. I well remember friends of my mother who would not move without the disgusting little snuffling peke dogs that went with it.

RAMPANT DECORATION
In Victorian times the furniture that crammed every room was heavy and ornate. Made mostly of mahogany and stained even

darker, the wood was concealed for the most part by a plentitude of tasselled fabrics. The upholsterer reigned supreme: everything that could be upholstered was upholstered. Any furniture made of a natural material was covered: nakedness, in things as well as people, was not allowed.

The work of keeping all this litter clean, let alone free from fleas, before the age of the vacuum cleaner was immense. But then that was done by the servants. When women of "the better sort" found that they could no longer afford to pay servants, all the clutter went out the door. It was the same with the huge tonnage of Victorian ornaments and knick-knacks: it took some time to get rid of them but they went.

Loose covers were being made in the seventeenth century. Chairs were often finished in coarse linen and covered with velvet

THE FIREPLACE
As the fireplace was the focal point of the room, it was often elegantly decorated. Gilt borders edged the fireplace itself, while ornamental tassels hung from the mantelpiece and heavy brocade drapes added the finishing touch.

GUARDS, SCREENS AND BOARDS
Fire guards were placed in front of the fire to prevent hot coals and sparks from flying out into the room. They were often made of brass or leaded glass and some had folding sides. Fire screens protected a person sitting too near the fire from fierce heat. They were elegantly decorated with embroidered needlework. Chimney boards served a practical as well as a decorative function. When the fire was not in use, the board was placed in front of the fireplace to hide the grate and block the draughts.

PINE CHIMNEY BOARD

EMBROIDERED POLE SCREEN

FOLDING LEADED FIRE GUARD

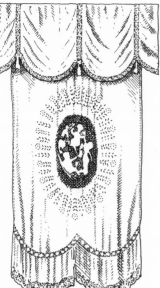

LAWN AND NET
INNER CURTAIN

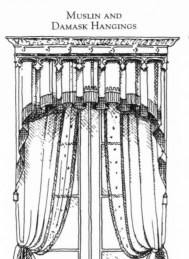

MUSLIN AND
DAMASK HANGINGS

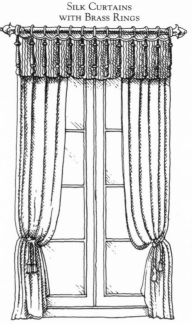

SILK CURTAINS
WITH BRASS RINGS

WINDOW CURTAINS
The quality of your curtain hangings was an indicator of your social standing. Handsome drapes of damask or silk lent an air of elegance to a room, and embellishments of tassels and valances added a touch of luxury.

LACED WINDOW BLINDS

BLINDS
Blinds were hung partly to protect curtains and furniture from strong sunlight, and partly to provide privacy from any passers-by. They were made out of stiff fabric and were often edged with crochet lace.

or damask slip covers of red and green. These handsome covers were removed for ordinary use. In the next century such costly materials were superseded by lighter, washable materials, which were left on all the time (apart from when they were being washed) and often concealed shabby, worn furniture. Red and green, and blue and white check patterns were exceedingly popular and window curtains were often made from the same material. Housewives often made up their own slip covers in the nineteenth century.

The anti-macassar was originally designed to prevent the upholstered backs of high chairs from being stained by the Macassar oil with which gentlemen plentifully anointed their hair. The anti-macassar became more and more elaborately decorated, usually with crochet work, and was always heavily betasselled. However, you could still remove it from the chair and launder it from time to time, as required.

Crocheted mantelpiece covers and cushion covers were common, as were lampshades, made in all sorts of ingenious ways—macramé and the rest. Lace curtains became beloved by the Victorians because they could hide behind them and peer through the window at the neighbours.

FOLK ART
Meanwhile, the labouring part of the population went on, in isolated pockets, creating their folk art. The cabins of narrow boats—those beautiful wooden craft that carried most of Britain's heavy freight traffic along

two thousand miles of canals—were magnificently painted with bold designs in bright primary colours. The pictures painted on the boats were of the same kind as those found on the famous watering cans and coal scuttles: roses and castles were the most popular. Of course, the fairy castles depicted standing beside lakes surrounded by mountains had never been seen by the canal boatmen, only imagined.

Vardos, or horse-drawn caravans, were similarly decorated, their interiors lined with brightly coloured curtain material, chamfering carved into all exposed timbers and fiddle-heads on their ends. Expensive Crown Derby china stood (and still stands) in the corner cupboard of the poorest vardo and there was brass everywhere.

RESTRAINED DECORATION
In Scandinavia, the Alps and any other region where wood was the chief building material, the art of wood carving was practised on all wooden furnishings. This beautiful but simple hand-carved furniture was the very antithesis of the dark, over-patterned furnishings so popular in England.

After the awful over-decoration of the Victorian period and the frightful aseptic sterility of the 1960s and 1970s, it is heartening to see people today decorating their houses with hand-woven cloth, good original paintings that really mean something, fine simple wooden furniture, either old or made by the new generation of craftsmen, hand-thrown pottery, and other articles of honest craftsmanship.

THE ANTI-MACASSAR
This was a piece of highly decorated crochet lace or cloth that hung over the back of a chair to prevent the upholstery being stained by men's hair oil, known as Macassar oil.

ORNAMENTING THE HOME

WEATHER VANES

As weather vanes had to be visible from a distance, their designs were fairly basic. Popular subjects were cockerels, archers, fish and angels. Early vanes were carved from wood and then painted in bright reds and yellows. The later metal vanes were usually left in an unpainted state but were sometimes gilded.

 ICTORIAN AND EDWARDIAN YOUNG ladies, and no doubt Regency and Georgian young ladies before them, having absolutely nothing to do, invented an amazing variety of ways of making ornamental objects. Harmless wooden articles were attacked with red-hot pokers, to burn patterns into them, and boxes were covered with sea shells, arranged in tasteful patterns.

Actually, this is not a lost art: I know an old sailor who lives on the cliffs of the south coast of County Wexford, who has covered every inch of his house and out buildings with sea shells. Even the chimney has been decorated. He has also made a scale model of the Tusker light house.

ORNAMENTAL FASHION

Victorian ladies also made amazing pictures and objects out of feathers, pressed flowers, dead butterflies, beads and rolled-up paper. They worked tirelessly at their embroidery frames and at their tatting, crocheting and macramé: they were indefatigable. One moment cutting out silhouettes was all the rage, the next it was making hideous paper beads out of scraps of paper. It almost seems as though genteel young ladies were prohibited from making anything useful.

USELESS OBJECTS

I am not old enough to remember the Victorian era itself but I am old enough to remember survivals from it. I remember the two Misses Weeley, who lived together in Weeley Hall in the village of Weeley in Essex, the nearest village to my own. Although desperately poor they were highly respected because they were gentry. Their house, in which I was always welcome and loved to go, was absolutely cluttered with useless objects. Every horizontal surface—and there were plenty—was crammed with china dogs, cats, cows, presents from seaside resorts and much much more. There is no way I could enumerate or describe the enormous variety of objects which these two dear old ladies considered absolutely essential to their well-being.

SHOP-BOUGHT ORNAMENTS

The Victorians loved to clutter every available horizontal surface with ornaments. If they had neither the patience nor the interest to make their own from shells and beads, there was always a great variety of china, wooden or bronze ornaments available to buy. Pottery and porcelain figures and animals were common, porcelain being the more favoured because of its translucent quality. There was also a fashion at one time for miniature china cottages and houses. Toby jugs were always popular, and these were made in numerous sizes and guises. In fact, many of these ornaments have since become collectors' items.

GOSS CHINA HOUSE

WOODEN ROOSTER

DRIED FLOWER ORNAMENT

POTTERY PARROT

BRONZE ELEPHANT

MINIATURE PORCELAIN TOBY JUG

HOME-MADE ORNAMENTS

Silhouette pictures provided popular ornamentation in the home. The silhouettes were usually of figures, either cut out of black paper or painted with black paint, and they were recognized by their shape. Fire papers, made from pieces of coloured tissue paper, were very simple to make. They were hung in the fireplace when the fire was not in use. Baskets of wax fruit, artistically arranged and trimmed with ribbon, were frequently displayed on the sideboard and in the fireplace during the summer months. Shells were used to decorate trinket boxes and pincushions, and even to cover up cracks on china bottles. They were also used to make borders for scenic paintings. Earthenware flower pots, considered too plain for general view, were often decorated with painted Egyptian figures, while brightly coloured motifs of birds, fruit and flowers were painted on tin kitchen boxes and pots.

PAPER SILHOUETTE PICTURE

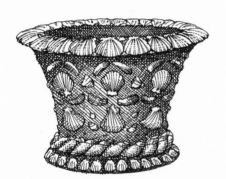

SHELL TOILETTE BOX

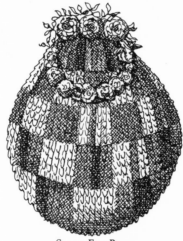

SIMPLE FIRE PAPER

HAND-PAINTED WOOD

Wooden articles were often decorated with painted designs. The wood had to be hard to stop the paint from running, and with a light grain—a heavy grain could spoil the design. First the outline was drawn on the wood in pencil. Then the design was painted in with water-colours or inks. Next, using a fine pen, the outline was inked over to give a crisp finish. Finally, when the paint and ink were dry, varnish was applied.

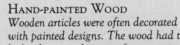

WOODEN SALAD SPOON AND FORK

PENNSYLVANIA COOKIE BOX

PAINTED COFFEE POT

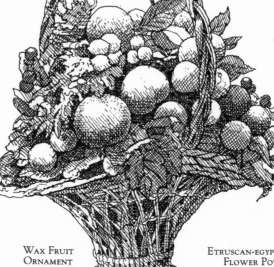

WAX FRUIT
ORNAMENT

ETRUSCAN-EGYPTIAN
FLOWER POT

FESTIVALS & DECORATIONS

 HEREVER IN THE WORLD THERE ARE such things as calendars there are special celebrations. Even before calendars were invented mankind went to great trouble to establish such fixed points of the year as mid-summer and mid-winter in order to celebrate them.

It is not surprising that a celebration just after the shortest day should be universal in more northerly latitudes and should assume such great importance. As man worked his way northwards to occupy the lands being liberated by the retreating Ice Age he must have found it daunting that the days became shorter and shorter as well as colder and colder. As growth of vegetation lessened, he must have feared that the world was indeed about to die. At this point, perhaps, one of the more observant among them would have

noticed that the days were lengthening again and that the sun was a fraction higher at midday. Naturally they would have greeted the change with great joy and celebrated!

CHRISTMAS

Christians are lucky in that the most splendid event in the calendar—Christmas—occurs just at the time when our spirits are cast down by darker and darker days and gloomy skies. Suddenly we are enjoined to make merry and rejoice, for the great universal principle of regeneration is vindicated.

The present-day orgy of rampant consumerism had not manifested itself by the time of my childhood. All I knew of the impending arrival of Christmas was that I was told to hang a stocking—a *large* stocking that was wont to adorn a much larger leg

THE CHRISTMAS CRACKER

The Christmas cracker was invented in 1860 by a man named Tom Smith, who, no doubt, wanted to make the most of the seasonal goodwill. His crackers proved to be immensely popular and, unlike their modern counterparts, generously contained all manner of goodies, from love messages, charms and toys to jokes, candies and trinkets.

THE CHRISTMAS TREE
The Christmas tree, bedecked with tinsel and baubles, is as much a part of Christmas today as roast turkey and plum pudding. Yet it was only in the last century that the Christmas tree became a part of the Yuletide festivities. There is a story that tells of Martin Luther originating the Christmas tree. While out walking one Christmas Eve, so the story goes, he was so moved by the night stars, glistening through the trees, that he rushed home to recreate the effect for his family, with candles and a small fir tree.

Traditional decorations for the tree consisted of fruit, nuts, gingerbread, candies, paper strips and lighted candles. An angel topped the tree, which was usually a spruce. Over the years, as commercialism took a firm hold, glass baubles replaced the fruit and nuts, multi-coloured electric bulbs replaced the candles, and the angel turned into a fairy!

than mine—at the foot of the bed. Then my mother would read a poem to my brother and me as we sat in front of the bright log fire. It began: "T'was the night before Christmas and all through the house not a creature was stirring, not even a mouse."

Then my brother and I would go to bed and fight to keep awake so that we should actually *see* that strange portly figure squeezing himself out of the small bedroom fireplace. We never did. We never thought of him as Father Christmas but always as Saint Nicholas; perhaps that was an Americanism.

Before daylight we would wake up to a new world. The whole house had been miraculously bedecked with holly bright with red berries (that was before most of the hedges had been bulldozed and there were tons of it), and a magnificent tree with *real* candles stood in the living room, tinsel-bedecked and beautiful with, and this was the most important part about it, a mound of intriguingly shaped parcels at the foot.

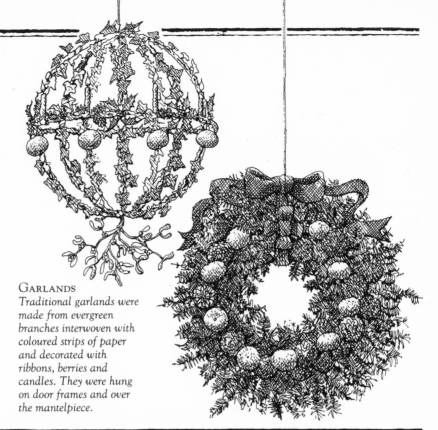

GARLANDS
Traditional garlands were made from evergreen branches interwoven with coloured strips of paper and decorated with ribbons, berries and candles. They were hung on door frames and over the mantelpiece.

BRINGING HOME THE TREE
Before the days of the reusable tinsel Christmas tree, spruce trees were chopped down from the local forest and taken home. Carrying a Christmas tree while riding a bicycle, with snow on the ground, cannot have been easy, but it was certainly no chore! After all, the arrival of the Christmas tree meant the festivities could start!

CORN DOLLIES

The celebration of harvest used to be the most important seasonal festival. It was thought that all forms of nature were controlled by the corn mother; if there was a good corn harvest, it meant that the corn mother was pleased and there would be enough food to last the winter. The custom arose of decorating a wagon of harvested sheaves with ribbons and flowers. The top sheaf—the last to be gathered—was shaped to look like the figure of the corn mother. It was believed that the corn spirit lived in this last sheaf and to preserve it, corn idols (or dollies) were made from it by plaiting the straw to produce bells, horseshoes, fans, crosses and figures. These were then hung in the kitchen to ward off evil spirits. Many believed that if they hung a corn dolly in the larder, especially the Arûseh doll, their families would never want for food.

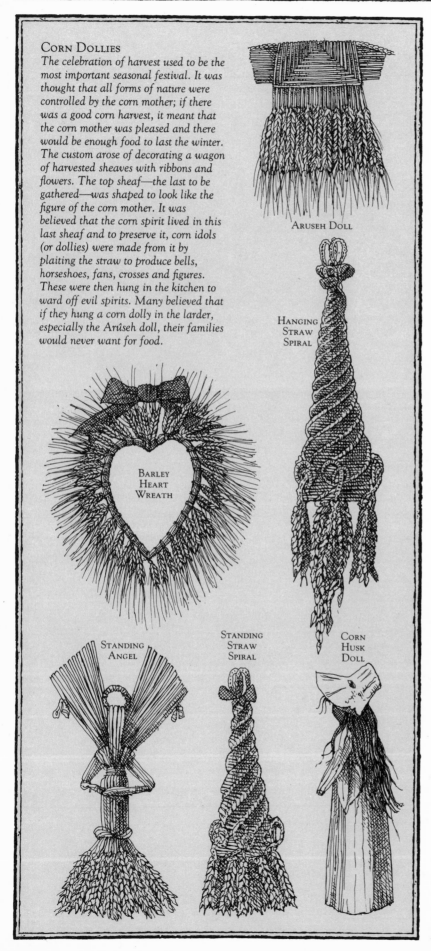

ARUSEH DOLL

HANGING STRAW SPIRAL

BARLEY HEART WREATH

STANDING ANGEL

STANDING STRAW SPIRAL

CORN HUSK DOLL

EPIPHANY

There are other ways of celebrating in wintertime. I stood once with my own children on the quay of a little Spanish fishing village and watched the customs launch, heavily disguised with coloured canvas and brilliant with whirling Catherine wheels, firing salvoes of rockets as she came steaming towards us to unload three gorgeously apparelled kings to be greeted by three equally gorgeously apparelled pages leading caparisoned horses. The kings mounted the horses, rather unsteadily as they were more accustomed to riding the waves, and were led to the town hall. There a huge pile of parcels awaited them, which the kings set about dispensing to every child in the village (mine, too) amid much rejoicing. This was not 25th December but epiphany.

I once celebrated epiphany with a couple of hundred Yugoslavs, refugees from their country, having fought on the wrong side during the war, who were living in a camp in England. Epiphany went on for three days and three nights: a large pig was roasted whole with an apple in its mouth, a small oak tree was dragged in decked with apples and toasted with a thousand glasses of slivovitz. We formed long human chains of dancing men, our arms around each others' necks, and were regaled with absolutely magnificent songs by three gorgeous Croatian folk singers, brought down from London specially for the occasion.

HARVEST TIME

On plough Sunday the instrument on which all civilized life depended was dragged in triumph around every English village, bedecked with ribands, and every householder was expected to contribute largesse. Largesse (in the form of money) was exacted too by the reapers in the harvest field. Corn reaping in the English countryside was accompanied by much badinage and ancient ceremony. The leader of the reapers was named "lord of the harvest" and his second-in-command, although equally a man, named his "lady". Any stranger who happened to pass by, who looked as though he might have some money, would be greeted by them with cries of "Largesse!" This meant one thing—he had to put his hand in his pocket. The cash collected would go towards providing beer for the thirsty reapers.

The subsequent harvest supper was a magnificent affair. The farmer's wife would provide a repast of great splendour, with

EASTER EGGS
The art of dyeing and decorating eggs at Easter was popular long before the advent of chocolate eggs. First the eggs were hard-boiled in water that contained a plant dye such as anemone or broom flowers. Then patterns were painted on the coloured shells.

huge barons of roast beef, roast legs of mutton and beer in lavish quantities. There would be much singing and playing of instruments during the evening and the telling of stories would go on far into the night.

EASTER

The celebration of the return of life after the winter, or Easter in Christian countries, was a great event. In Ireland, where I now live, it still is, for it ends the fast of Lent, which is still observed in this country. When I first came here thirty years ago I observed the melancholy fact that the front door of every pub was locked every day during Lent and the curtains drawn. It was some time before I discovered that the *back* doors were open, or would be opened in response to a discreet knock. Easter morning puts a glorious end to all these austerities, with the cry in church of "Christ has risen".

In Greece, Easter is the great event of the year. They have all-night vigils in the churches there, and there are no seats to sit down on. Young lambs, roasted whole, are eaten, washed down with wine and raki and the dancing which follows continues right the way through the night.

Besides Easter lambs, eggs and bunny rabbits are part of the Easter tradition. In Germany they paint pretty patterns on hard-boiled eggs, which they then hide all over the garden and the children have to hunt for them. This custom also prevails in America.

HALLOWE'EN

The Americans also make much of Hallowe'en, as do the Irish. The Welsh, Scots and English have rather forgotten this pagan survival in their celebration of the rather ghoulish Guy Fawkes' Day, during which the effigy of the man who was accused of trying to blow up the Protestant Houses of Parliament is burnt on a thousand bonfires. For fairly obvious reasons this event is not celebrated in Catholic Ireland and nor, of course, in North America.

FEAST DAYS

In Medieval times, the year was punctuated by numerous feast days in memory of various saints, and when people talk of the unremitting labour of the Medieval countryman they should remember that these "holy days" were indeed holidays—days of rest and jollification. It was not until the Industrial Revolution that the lives of working people became lives of unremitting toil. The idea that industrialism has relieved people of labour is an illusion. In those areas of the world in which there are still true peasants, excuses for spending the day in celebration are numerous. It does not, in fact, take many man or woman hours of labour a year for a family of subsistence peasants to make their living.

NEW YEAR'S EVE

The new calendar instituted by Pope Gregory in the sixteenth century has never been accepted in the Gwaun Valley of Pembrokeshire in west Wales, where I used to live. Although the people there have accepted the new date for Christmas, they still celebrate "Hen Nos Galan", or the Old New Year, on 13th January. On that day and night, "cwrw gatre", or home-brewed beer, is drunk in copious amounts and magnificent songs are sung in the Welsh language. In the same area, but more particularly in the southern half of Pembrokeshire (which is commonly known as "the English" because that language is spoken there), and in various parts of Ireland, too, a most peculiar ceremony is sometimes still performed. A wren is caught and put in a cage which is then hung on a pole. The caged wren is carried around the village on the pole by a gang of boys who sing particular songs outside each house, for which they are rewarded with cakes and home-brewed ale. In ancient times at the end of the evening the wren was brutally beaten to death. Fortunately that barbaric part of the ceremony is nowhere observed today.

HALLOWE'EN LANTERNS
Hallowe'en lanterns were made by hollowing out a pumpkin or turnip, cutting out a gruesome face from the remaining "shell" and then inserting a candle inside it. On a dark Hallowe'en night, these lanterns looked very menacing!

INDEX

Page numbers in *italic* refer to the
illustrations and captions

Aga cookers, 33
Aladdin lamps, 126
Alarm clocks, 112
Ale and beer making, 57-8, *57-9*
Ale mullers, *59*
Alexandra, Queen, 136
American fireplaces, *24*
American washers, *92*
Animals, 64-6, *65-6*
Anti-macassars, 181, *181*
Appert, Nicholas, 40-1
Applejack, 61
Apples, cider making, *60-1*, 61
Argand, Ami, 125
Auer, Dr Karl, 126, 128
Axes, *104*

Bags, 36
Bakehouses, *35*
Bakestones, 28, 35, *35*
Baking, 34-5, *34-5*
Baking irons, 35, *35*
Baluster measures, *20*
Banister brushes, *130*
Bannock spades, *35*
Bantams, 66
Barley, beer making, 57
Barrels: beer, 57, 58, *58*
  cider, *61*
Barrows, peat cutting, *105*
Bathrooms, 114-15
Baths, 114-15, *114*, *115*
Beating, food preparation, 22
Bed bugs, 134
Bed pans, *113*
Bed-wagons, *111*
Bedrooms, 111-12
Beds, 110-11, *110-11*, 179-80
Beds lace, 155
Bee stingers, 68
Beef suet, 18
Beer casks, *57*, 58
Beer making, 57-8, *57-9*
Beer measures, *59*
Beer tankards, *59*
Bees, 67-8, *67-8*
Beeswax: candles, 123-4
  polishes, 135
Beetles (washing implements), 90
Beeton, Mrs, 22, 135, 164
Bell glasses, *62*
Bellows, 98, 106, *107*
Bells, servants', 112
Besom brooms, 130, *131*
Betty lamps, *126*
Biscuit barrels, *37*
Bissell, Melville, 133, 136
Black lead, 48
Bleaching linen, 92-3

Blinds, *181*
"Blue" bag, 93
Bobbins, lace making, 154, 156-7,
  156, *157*
Bodley, George, 31
Boilers, wash, 50, 92, *95*
Boiling, 26
Boms, 105, *106*
Booth, Hubert, 136, *136*
Boswell, Gordon, 90, 96
Bottle washers, *50*
Bottles, 37, *41*
  marble stoppers, 37, *41*
Bottling food, 40-1, *40-1*
Box irons, 98, 100, *101*
Brahmah, Joseph, 116
Braunche, Robert, 119
Bread: baking, 28, 34-5
  shapes, *34*
  storage, 37
  trenchers, *51*, 119
Breakfast, 118-19, *121*
Breeches, *164*
Brewing beer, 57-8, *57*, *58*
Brick floors, 131
Brooms, 130, *130*, *131*
Brownstone, 134
Brushes: banister, *130*
  chamois leather, *135*
  chimney sweeping, *138*
  crumb, *50*
  decanter, *50*
  dusting, *131*
  flue, *46*
  furniture, *130*
  hearth, 47, *131*
  laundry, 92, *130*
  paint, *176*
  plate, *50*
  scrubbing, *47*
  sink, 47, 50, *130*
  slipper, *131*
  stove, 47, 48
  wardrobe, *130*
  whisk, 130, *131*
Brussels lace, 155
Buckets, 87
  coal, *107*
Bucks lace, *154*, 155
Butlers, 48
Butter, 74, 75-9, *75-9*
Butter hands, 75, *79*
Butter prints, 78, 79, *79*
Butterick, Ebenezer, 164
Buttermilk, 75-8
Buttons, 164

Caddies, tea, 54
Cake mixes, 22
Calendars, 184, 187
Calico bags, 36
Calvados, 61
Cambridge pudding, 21
Cambridge University, 119
Can openers, 40, *40*
Canal boats, 181
Candelabra, *124*

Candles, *122*, 123-5, *124*, *125*
Candlesticks, 124, *124*
Canning food, 40-1, *40-1*
Canteens, cutlery, *118*
Caravans, horse-drawn, 111, 181
Carbide lamps, 128
Carding, wool, 144-5, *144*, *145*
Carpet beaters, *133*
Carpet sweepers, 133, *134*, 136
Carrying water, 86-7, *86*
Carving, wood, 181
Catherine of Aragon, 43
Catherine de Medici, 84
Cats, 64, 142
Cauldrons, *24*, 26
Caustic soda, making soap with,
  88-9
Chairs, 179, *179*, 180-1
Chamber pots, 112, *112*
Chamois leather brushes, *135*
Charcoal irons, 98, 100, *101*
Charcoal stoves, 108
Chesterton, G.K., 164
Chickens, 64-6, *65*, 66
Chilling food, 44-5, *44-5*
Chimney cranes, 28
Chimneys, 25-6, 48
  smoking food in, 39, *39*
  sweeping, 32, 138-9, *138-9*
China: ornaments, *182*
  storage, 48
  washing up, 50, *51*
Chinoiserie, 180
Chocolate moulds, *43*
Choppers, 21, *21*, 22, 63
Christmas, 184-5, *184-5*
Christmas crackers, *184*
Christmas trees, 184, 185, *185*
Churches, stencilled decoration,
  178
Churns: butter, 75, 76, *77*
  milk, 70, *71*
Cider making, *60-1*, 61
Cider presses, *60*
Cistercians, 116
Cleaning, 130-6, *130-7*
  kitchens, 46-9, *48-9*
Clogs, *47*
Clothes: drying, 96-7, *96-7*
  making and repairing, 162-9,
    162-9
  pressing, 98-100, *98-101*
  washing, 90-5, *90-5*
  see also Textile crafts
Clothes maiden, *96*
Clothes pegs, 96-7, *96*
Clothes sprinklers, *98*
Clotted cream, 74
Clubs, tree felling, *104*
Coal: fires, 26, 30, 47, *107*, 134,
  138
  stoves, 108, *108*
Cobbett, William, 53, 64, 69, 121
Cockroaches, *142*
Coffee making, 55, *55-6*
Coffee mills, 55
Coffee pots, 56
Coffee roasters, 55
Colanders, *21*
Collars, *165*
College pudding, 21

Commodes, 115, *117*
Communal ovens, *35*
Compost heaps, 140
Confectionery, 42-3, *42-3*
Cookers: Agas, 33
  electric, 33
  gas, 32-3, *32*
  open-hearth, 24-8, *24-9*
  ranges, 30-2, *30-2*
Cooking: baking, 34-5, *34-5*
  preparing food, 18-23, *18-23*
Cooking pots, 26, 29, 30-1, *33*
  cleaning, 47
Copper bowls, 22
Coppers, washing, 92, *95*
Corers, fruit, *42*
Corkscrews, *61*
Corn dollies, *186*
Cotton, 162
  dyeing, 102
Cows, 64, 69, 70, 72, *72*
Crackers, Christmas, *184*
Cranes, chimney, 28
Crapper, 116
Cravats, *165*
Cream, 21, 73-4, *73-4*
Creamers, 74
Crimping, 99
Crochet, 158, *158*, 181, *181*
Crumb brushes, *50*
Crusies, *126*
Culm, *105*
Cummings, Alexander, 116
Cupboard beds, 111
Cups and saucers, 53
Curds, cheese making, 80, 81-2
Curtains, *181*
Cutlery, 118, *118*
  cleaning, 48

Dairy crafts, 69-84
  butter, 74, 75-9, *75-9*
  cheese making, 80-2, *80-2*
  cream, 73-4, *73-4*
  ice cream, 84, *84*
  milk and milk treatments, 70-2,
    70-2
Dangle-spits, *26*, 32
Darning, 169, *169*
Davy lamps, 128
De Gaulle, General, 82
Decanter brushes, *50*
Decorations, 184-7, *184-7*
Decorative crafts, 175-87
  crochet, 181, *181*
  festivals and decorations, 184-7,
    184-7
  furniture and furnishings, 179-81,
    179-81
  ornamenting the home, 182,
    182-3
  painting and papering, 176-7,
    176-7
  stencilling, 178, *178*, *179*
Desserts, 20-1, *43*, 84
Digesters, *29*
Dillmont, Thérèse de, 154-5, 166

— 188 —

Lace making, 154-7, *154-7*
Ladles, *25*
Lamps, oil, 125-6, *126-7*
Langstroth, 68
Lanterns, *125*
  Hallowe'en, *187*
Larders, 36, *37*, 46
Latch-hook rugs, *152*, 153
Laundry brushes, 92, *130*
Laundry crafts, 85-102
  drawing water, 86-7, *86-7*
  drying linen, 96-7, *96-7*
  dyeing, 102, *102*
  making lye and soap, 88-9, *88-9*
  pressing linen, 98-100, *98-101*
  washing linen, 10, 90-5, *90-5*
Lavatories, 115-17, *117*
Lavender, 99, *99*
Lazy-backs, *29*
Leblanc, Nicholas, 89
Lemon squeezers, 21, *21*
Lent, 187
Lice, 134
Lifts, for swilling, *47*
Light, Mrs, 48
Light fittings, *129*
Lighting, 122-9
  candles, *122*, 123-5, *124*, *125*
  electric, 128-9, *128*
  gas, 128-9, *128*
  oil lamps, 125-6, *126-7*
  rushlights, 123, *124*, 124
Limewash, 176
Linen: drying, 96-7, *96-7*
  dyeing, 102
  pressing, 98-100, *98-101*
  smocks, 172
  spinning yarn, 145, 148
  washing, 90-5, *90-5*
Linen presses, 98
Linoleum, 177
Linseed oil, 135
Livestock, 64-6, *65-6*
Looms, 149-51, *149-51*
Loose covers, 180-1
Louis XIV, King of France, 111, 123
Luther, Martin, *184*
Lye, 88, *88*
Lye droppers, 88, *88*

McDyer, Father, 161
Macramé, 159, *159*
Maintenance, kitchens, 46-9, *48-9*
Malting barley, 57
Mangles, 96, *96*
Mantles: gas lamps, *128*
  oil lamps, *126*
Marble stoppers, bottles, 37, *41*
Markets, 79
Marking irons, peat cutting, *105*
Marmalade, 43
Marmalade cutters, *42*
Mat and rug making, 152-3, *152-3*
Matches, 123, *123*
Mattresses, 111
Mayonnaise, 22
Measures, beer, *59*

Meat: cooking, 24
  drying and smoking, 39
  potting, 40
  roasting, *26*, 28
  salting and pickling, 38, *38*
  storing, 36, *36*
Meat hooks, 64
Meat safes, 36
Medicine, 113
Medicine bottles, *41*
Mending clothes, 169
Meringues, 21
Metal Box Company, 41
Metal decorations, furniture, *179*
Metal polish, 134
Mice, 142, *142*
Milk, 70-2, *70-2*
Moliquets, 22
Mops, 47, *50*
Mordaunts, dyes, 102
Morris, William, 177, *177*
Mortars, 21, *63*
Moulds: butter, 78
  candles, *122*
  cheese, 80, *82*
  confectionery, *43*
  ice cream, 84, *84*
Mullers, ale, *59*
Murdoch, William, 128
Mushroom irons, 99

Nailsea glass rolling pins, *23*
Napkins, *119*
Napoleon I, Emperor, 40
Narrow boats, *181*
Needlecases, *163*
Needlepoint lace, 154
Needles, *163*, 169
Needletuft rugs, 152
Nelson, Admiral, 54
New Year's Eve, 187
Night carts, 141, *141*
Night lights, *126*

Oatmeal, *35*
Oil-burning stoves, 108, *109*
Oil lamps, 125-6, *126-7*
Open-hearth cooking, 24-8, *24-9*
Ornaments, 182, *182-3*
Orwell, George, 17
Ovens, baking, 34-5, *34*, *35*
  ranges, 30, *31*
  see also Cookers
Oxford University, 119

Paint brushes, 176
Painting, 176, *176*, 177
  stencilling, 178, *178*
Pantries, 36
Paper patterns, dress making, *164*
Papin, Denis, 29,
Paring irons, peat cutting, *105*

Parlours, 46
Pasteur, Louis, 41
Pastry, 23
Patching clothes, 169
Patchwork, 171, *171*
Pattens, 47
Peat fires, 24, 26, 35, 105, *105*
Pectin, 43
Peels, iron, *35*
Pegotty, *161*
Pegs, clothes, 96-7, *96*
Pepper mills, *63*
Percolators, 56
Pestles and mortars, *63*
Pests, 142, *142*
Pewter plates, *51*
Pickle jars, 38
Pickling food, 38, *38*
Pigeons, 64
Pigments, paints, 176, *176*
Pigs, 64-6, *66*, 141
Pigsties, 64, 65, *65*
Pillows, lace making, *155*, 157
Pincushions, *163*, 169
Pins, *163*
Plasterwork, 177
Plate brushes, *50*
Plates, *51*
  warming, *29*, 119
Plumbing, 114-15
Poaching, 64
Point lace, 157, *157*
Polishes, 134-5
Polishing irons, 98
Pot chains, *50*
Pot hangers, *29*
Pot hooks, 26, *29*
Pot ovens, *34*
Potato mashers, *22*
Potting meat, 40
Preserves, 42-3, *42-3*
Presses: cheese, 82, *82*
  linen, 98
Pressing linen, 98-100, *98-101*
Pressure cookers, *29*
Primus stoves, 108-9
Prints, butter, *78*, 79, *79*
Privies, 117
Puddings: iced, *84*
  savoury, 18-20
Pumpkins, Hallowe'en lanterns, 187
Pumps, water, 87, *87*
Punch-hook rugs, *152*, 153, *153*

Quilting, 170-1, *170-1*
Quilting bees, 14, 170
Quilting frames, *170*

Rabbits, 64
Racks: drying, *96*
  storage, 48
Rag rugs, *152*, 153
Rain butts, 52
Raisin stoners, *42*
Ranges: cleaning, 46, *46*, 48
  cooking at, 30-2, *30-2*

Raplin ice-makers, *45*
Rats, 142, *142*
Real Ale Campaign, 58
Reckitt and Sons, 93
Reels, wool, 148
Refrigerators, 45
Rennet, 80, 81
Riddleboards, *35*
Ridge rollers, *35*
Roasting: coffee, *55*
  meat, *26*, 28
Roasting screens, 28
Robinson, Thomas, 30
Rolling pins, 23, *23*
Royal Navy, 41
Rubbish, 140-1, *140-1*
Rug making, 152-3, *152-3*
Rumford, Count, 56, 125
Rush mats, 152, *152*
Rushes, floor coverings, 131
Rushlights, 123, *124*, 124

Saints' days, 187
Salamanders, *35*
Salt, storage, *37*
Salting: butter, 78
  meat, 38, *38*
Salting troughs, 38
Samplers, embroidered, *174*
Sand man, 47, *133*
Saucepans, *33*
Savoury puddings, 18-20
Sawdust, floor coverings, 133
Saws, *104*
Scales, *20*, 76
Scissors, *163*, 169
Scoops: butter, *76*
  ice-cream, *84*
Scotch hands, 79
Scouring, 134
Screens, fire, *108*, 179, *180*
Scrubbing, 134
Scrubbing brushes, *47*
Sculleries, 46, 52
Scuttles, coal, *107*
Separators, cream, 74
Settle-beds, *110*
Sewage disposal, 115-17, *117*, 141, *141*
Sewing, 162-9, *162-9*
Sewing machines, 168, *168-9*
Shaw-Smith, David, 148
Shellac, 135
Shells, decorations, 182, *183*
Shirley, Thomas, 128
Shower rings, 115
Shuttles: tatting, 159, *159*
  weaving, 149, *149*, 151
Sideboards, 121
Silhouette pictures, 182, *183*
Silk, 162
Silver, cleaning, 48
Sinclair, Upton, 41
Singer, Isaac, 168
Sink baskets, *51*
Sink brushes, 47, *50*, *130*
Sinks, *50*, 51
Skeps, bee, 67-8, *67*
Skimmers, *25*, 74
Slanes, peat cutting, 105, *105*
Sledgehammers, *104*
Slices, cooking, *25*

National Trust Properties

All the properties listed below are owned by the National Trust and are open to the public between April and October. They feature buildings, rooms, collections and artefacts of particular interest to readers of *Forgotten Household Crafts* and, for easy reference, they have been grouped according to subject under the chapter headings used in the book.

KITCHEN CRAFTS

Apiaries
Attingham Park, Shropshire
– *bee houses*
Packwood House, Warwickshire
– *bee boles*

Breweries
Charlecote Park, Warwickshire
– *16th-century brewhouse*
Hailes Abbey, Gloucestershire
Lacock Abbey, Wiltshire
Springhill, Co. Londonderry

Herb Gardens
Acorn Bank, Cumbria
Bateman's, East Sussex
East Riddlesden Hall, Yorkshire
Gunby Hall, Lincolnshire
Hardwick Hall, Derbyshire
Little Moreton Hall, Cheshire
Melford Hall, Suffolk
Moseley Old Hall, Staffordshire
St Michael's Mount, Cornwall
Scotney Castle Garden, Kent
Westbury Court Garden,
  Gloucestershire

Home Farms
Ardress House, Co. Armagh
East Riddlesden Hall, Yorkshire
Tatton Park, Cheshire
Wimpole Home Farm,
  Cambridgeshire

Ice Houses
Blickling Hall, Norfolk
Hatchlands, Surrey
Killerton, Devon
Penrhyn Castle, Gwynedd
– *ice well*
Scotney Castle, Kent
Stourhead, Wiltshire
Wallington, Northumberland

Kitchens
Barrington Court, Somerset
– *Tudor*
Buckland Abbey, Devon
Castle Drogo, Devon
Charlecote Park, Warwickshire
– *Victorian*
Cragside, Northumbria
Dunham Massey, Cheshire
Erddig, Clwyd
Lanhydrock, Cornwall
Springhill, Co. Londonderry
– *cottage kitchen*
Townend, Cumbria

DAIRY CRAFTS

Dairies
Barrington Court, Somerset
Bradley Manor, Devon
Compton Castle, Devon
Lanhydrock, Cornwall
Plas Newydd, Gwynedd
Uppark, Sussex
Wimpole Hall, Cambridgeshire

LAUNDRY CRAFTS

Laundries
The Argory, Co. Tyrone
Beningbrough Hall, Yorkshire
Castle Drogo, Devon
Charlecote Park, Warwickshire
Dunham Massey, Cheshire
Erddig, Clwyd
Springhill, Co. Londonderry

Wells
Clevedon Court, Avon
Compton Castle, Devon
– *Medieval well*
Greys Court, Oxfordshire
– *Tudor donkey wheel*

AROUND THE HOME

Bathrooms
Antony House, Cornwall
– *bath pond house*
Calke Abbey, Derbyshire
Castle Drogo, Devon
– *Lutyens bathroom*
Erddig, Clwyd
Kedleston, Derbyshire
– *Adam bath house*
Packwood, Warwickshire
Wallington, Northumberland
Wimpole Hall, Cambridgeshire

Cleaning
Uppark, West Sussex
– *butler's pantry with cleaning
  materials, etc*

Power
The Argory, Co. Tyrone
– *acetylene gas plant*
Cragside, Northumbria
– *Victorian hydro-electric scheme*

TEXTILE CRAFTS

Costume Collections
Bath Assembly Rooms, Avon
Ham House, Surrey
Killerton, Devon
Shugborough, Staffordshire
Sizergh Castle, Cumbria
Springhill, Co. Londonderry

Needlework and Embroidery
Blickling Hall, Norfolk
– *tapestry workshop*
Buckland Abbey, Devon
– *craft exhibition, lace making*
Canons Ashby, Northants
– *needlework chairs*
Gawthorpe Hall, Lancashire
– *Kay-Shuttleworth collection of
  textiles, embroideries and lace*
Hardwick Hall, Derbyshire
– *tapestry and embroidery*
Standen, West Sussex
– *needlework chairs*

Patchwork Quilts
Hill Top, Cumbria

Spinning and Weaving
Snowshill Manor, Gloucestershire
– *tools*
Standen, West Sussex
– *woven curtains*
Styal, Cheshire
– *cotton mill*
Townend, Cumbria
– *local 18th-century woven fabrics*

DECORATIVE CRAFTS

Festivals
Cotehele, Cornwall
– *Cotehele Christmas*

Fine Decoration and Stencils
Castle Drogo, Devon
– *hand-painted walls in dining room*
Ightham Mote, Kent
– *hand-painted Chinese wallpaper*
Springhill, Co. Londonderry
– *hand-blocked wallpaper*
Standen, West Sussex
– *Morris wallpaper*

Acknowledgments

Dorling Kindersley would like to thank the following individuals and organizations for their invaluable advice, help and information: Brooke Bond Oxo Ltd; Crosse and Blackwell; Monica Ellis for her book *Ice and Icehouses through the Ages*; Greater London Record office and History Library; Mike Keeble, National Cattle Breeders' Association; Robert Lee (Bee Supplies) Ltd; Metal Box plc; David J. Parker; Rare Breeds Survival Trust; Agnes Robertson, Glenesk Folk Museum; Ian Ross, City of Westminster Cleansing Dept.; Springwood Books for their book *Patons: A Story of Handknitting*; Cecil Tonsley (editor), *British Bee Journal*; Eve Williams, Preston Library, Wembley, Middlesex.

Illustrators: Brian Delf, Robert Micklewright, Donald Myall, Richard Phipps, Eric Thomas, John Woodcock

Text and picture researchers: Valerie Janitch, Angela Murphy

Indexer: Hilary Bird

Special thanks to: Sandra Archer, Lynn Bresler, Arthur Brown, Fiona Macmillan, Fraser Newman, Tessa Richardson-Jones, Jane Rollason, Patrizio Semproni and Henrietta Winthrop for their help with the editing, design and production of this book.

Picture credits: 1 North of England Open Air Museum, Beamish, Durham; **8** Mrs J. Knock/Museum of English Rural Life, University of Reading, Berkshire; **14** Frank Meadow Sutcliffe/The Sutcliffe Gallery, Whitby, Yorkshire; **23** Pitstone Local History Society, Bedfordshire; **35** North of England Open Air Museum, Beamish, Durham; **39** Henry E. Huntington Library, San Marino, California; **46** Munby Collection, Trinity College, Cambridge; **54** Bruce Castle Museum, Tottenham, London N17; **63** Buckinghamshire County Museum, Aylesbury; **67–8** *British Bee Journal*; **70** The Beaford Centre, Devon; **75** Museum of English Rural Life, University of Reading, Berkshire; **76** North of England Open Air Museum, Beamish, Durham; **79** Cambridge and County Folk Museum, Cambridge; **81** North of England Open Air Museum, Beamish, Durham; **86** Birmingham City Reference Library; **90** Weybridge Museum, Surrey; **93** The Harry Ransom Research Center, University of Texas at Austin, USA; **99** North of England Open Air Museum, Beamish, Durham; **105** Frank Meadow Sutcliffe/The Sutcliffe Gallery, Whitby, Yorkshire; **109** Manor House Local History Department, Deptford; **122** Welsh Folk Museum, St Fagan's, Cardiff; **131** North of England Open Air Museum, Beamish, Durham; **134** Suffolk Record Office, Ipswich; **136** Mansell Collection, London; **138** Frank Meadow Sutcliffe/The Sutcliffe Gallery, Whitby, Yorkshire; **145, 150, 153** Doris Ullmann Foundation, Berea College, Kentucky, USA; **155** Buckinghamshire County Museum, Aylesbury; **158** North of England Open Air Museum, Beamish, Durham; **160** National Museums of Scotland; **161** Shetland Museum, Lerwick; **170** Minnesota Historical Society, USA; **172** Buckinghamshire County Museum, Aylesbury; **177** Arthur Sanderson & Co., London; **180** The Beaford Centre, Devon.